■ VIETNAM | JOURNEYS OF BODY, MIND, AND SPIRIT

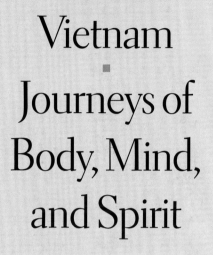

Vietnam

·

Journeys of
Body, Mind,
and Spirit

Nguyen Van Huy

and Laurel Kendall,

editors

UNIVERSITY OF CALIFORNIA PRESS   BERKELEY LOS ANGELES LONDON

IN ASSOCIATION WITH THE AMERICAN MUSEUM OF NATURAL HISTORY,

NEW YORK, AND THE VIETNAM MUSEUM OF ETHNOLOGY, HANOI

University of California Press
Berkeley and Los Angeles, California

University of California Press, Ltd.
London, England

Library of Congress Cataloging-in-Publication Data

Vietnam : journeys of body, mind, and spirit / Nguyen Van Huy and Laurel Kendall,
editors.
      p.   cm.
    Includes bibliographical references and index.
    ISBN 0-520-23871-0 (cloth : alk. paper) — ISBN 0-520-23872-9 (paper : alk. paper)
    1. Vietnam—Social life and customs.   I. Nguyễn, Văn Huy, 1945– .   II. Kendall,
Laurel.
DS556.42.V54 2003
394.269597—dc21   2002011199

Manufactured in Canada

12   11   10   09   08   07   06   05   04   03

10   9   8   7   6   5   4   3   2   1

The paper used in this publication meets the minimum requirements
of ANSI/NISO z39.48-1992 (R 1997) (*Permanence of Paper*). ∞

Photo on page ii: Pilgrimage to Chua Huong by Ellen Kaplowitz

THE PUBLISHER GRATEFULLY ACKNOWLEDGES
THE GENEROUS CONTRIBUTION TO THIS BOOK
PROVIDED BY THE GENERAL ENDOWMENT OF
THE UNIVERSITY OF CALIFORNIA PRESS ASSOCIATES.

CONTENTS

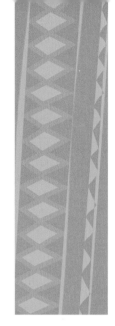

ACKNOWLEDGMENTS

I F A PROJECT IS ALSO A JOURNEY, this volume is the intersection of many different paths of experience, research, and scholarship—Vietnamese, American, and European. The editors would like to thank our colleagues for sharing the burden of hard work along the way. At the Vietnam Museum of Ethnology (VME), Luu Hung, Director of Research, helped to identify most of the authors and guided their work. Tran Trung Hieu translated most of the essays originally written in Vietnamese and interpreted during Kendall's sessions with individual authors. Hoang Thi Thu Hang assisted our seemingly endless research in VME's photographic archive. At the American Museum of Natural History (AMNH), Maron L. Waxman, Director of Special Publishing, and a project team that included Ann Fitzgerald, Elizabeth Murray, Nguyen Thi Thu Huong, Nguyen Thi Hien, and Jorge Guzman brought photographs and text together and prepared the manuscript for publication, aided by many loyal AMNH volunteers. Bridget Thomas, of the Anthropology Department, AMNH, designed the map.

We are grateful to the individual photographers and the several photographic archives whose work is credited in this volume for sharing their images with us and for providing us with additional information. Sheila Levine of University of California Press helped us to get this far.

We would like to offer special thanks to the Vietnam National Center for Social Sciences and Humanities for fostering the collaboration between VME and AMNH, and the Ford Foundation for financial support of our work together, including the preparation of this publication.

■ VIETNAM | JOURNEYS OF BODY, MIND, AND SPIRIT

Boats and rafts on the Red River, northern Vietnam, 1995.

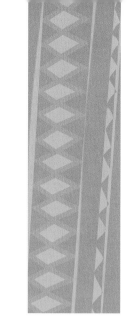

INTRODUCTION:

A JOURNEY BETWEEN

TWO MUSEUMS

Laurel Kendall and Nguyen Van Huy

A JOURNEY IS A BRIDGE BETWEEN TWO POINTS. In Vietnam, some journeys take place on roads, some on highways, some on railways, rivers, and footpaths as family members come home for the new year, hunters travel into the forest, and traders carry goods precariously balanced on bicycles or on their backs. Other journeys are metaphorical: life is a journey marked by significant rituals, and the year is a journey mapped by a calendar, with holidays as significant milestones along the way. Souls travel to the netherworld, while gods and ancestors return to the human world during celebrations in their honor. A shaman journeys to other realms to restore a patient's soul.

Vietnam: Journeys of Body, Mind, and Spirit also is a bridge between two points. This book, together with the exhibition on which it is based, is

A bicycle provides a convenient means of reaching rice fields located at a distance from the house. Without mechanization, rice cultivation is a labor-intensive activity, as glimpsed outside Ho Chi Minh City (formerly Saigon), 1995.

the first major collaboration between a Vietnamese museum and an American museum to present Vietnamese culture, a journey that moves both nations beyond our troubled wartime history to an understanding of how Vietnamese—Vietnamese of different ages, ethnicities, occupations, and circumstances—live at the start of the twenty-first century, more than a decade after Vietnam's opening to the global market and more than a quarter century after the cessation of hostility between our two governments. We believe that such a journey is a necessary part of the process of healing.

At this time, American curiosity about Vietnam is undeniable, but Vietnam reaches the public in highly mediated fragments. The American experience of the Vietnam War (alternatively known as the Second Indochina War or American War) remains a perennial topic, as sensitively demonstrated in recent documentary retrospectives by Barbara Sonneborn (*Regret to Inform*, 1998), John Haptas and Kristine Samuelson (*Riding the Tiger*, 1999), and Kim-Chi Tyler (*Chac*, 2000). Since the opening of Vietnam to global investment and international tourism, the images that have for so long dominated American consciousness of Vietnam—jungle warfare, napalm, body bags being loaded onto helicopters—have come to coexist with tourist images of spectacular landscapes, vintage architecture, and photogenic people in conical hats. Replaying older colonial images of "Indochina" as a sensuous and mysterious landscape, two high-profile films, *The Lover* (1992) and *Indochine* (1992), offer romanticized visions of the passions of expatriates in French colonial times. French Vietnamese director Tran Anh Hung's *The Scent of Green Papaya* (1993) replays nostalgia in a different key, portraying life in an upper-class Vietnamese household in the 1950s and '60s. His *Cyclo* (1995) was a surreal journey into the underworld of Ho Chi Minh City (formerly Saigon), and the more recent *Vertical Ray of the Sun* (2000) offered a gorgeous portrait of Hanoi as a city unmoored from time.

While these feature films were well received in American theaters, none of them captures the texture and substance of Vietnamese life in the present tense. Vietnam today is a society of both urban and rural people who are ethnically diverse and live in geographically varied and socially diverse circumstances. In presenting *Vietnam: Journeys*, our aim is to show how these different Vietnamese live, work, and celebrate critical passages of life and time. We invite you on a vicarious journey through Vietnam at the

A Yao ritual master in Yen Bai province, 1997. A Yao ritual master claims the power of the spirits. When he was an initiate, his soul traveled to the spirits' realms.

start of the twenty-first century, through different urban neighborhoods, from city to village, and to the upland communities of Vietnam's ethnic minorities.

This is not a tourist's journey with a predictable itinerary of scenic and historical spots, but rather an attempt to travel in different kinds of Vietnamese "shoes," both on the ground and in the imagination. The idea of a journey becomes a broad metaphor for different kinds of human experiences. Processions, as symbolic journeys, mark the village tutelary god's royal progress from the temple to the communal house and back again, a bride's passage to her husband's family, or the funereal passage of the dead from the living family and community to the grave. New Year (Tet) and the Mid-Autumn Festival mark a journey through the lunar year. Contrasts among the weddings, funerals, and other celebrations of the majority Kinh (Viet) population and the ethnic minorities illustrate diversity within Vietnam and indicate a range of possible personal and communal journeys, different ways of navigating life transitions.

Our use of the term *journey* borrows on the anthropologist's understanding of a "ritual passage," described by Arnold Van Gennep as the cultural means of marking transformations in status over the life course and more broadly applied by Victor Turner to the social and spiritual transitions implicit in such phenomena as healing rituals and pilgrimages.[1]

Several of the journeys that we describe are loosely characterized as "traditions," repetitive acts and events that nations and ethnic groups recognize as "what we do" or "what has meaning for us." Traditions evoke the past: this is what Kinh or Giarai people do because this is what Kinh or Giarai ancestors did. But the traditions we describe are also, quite significantly, enacted in and shaped by the contemporary moment.[2] Much of the ritual activity described in these pages was banned or severely curtailed during the period of national struggle and has only recently been revived, in some cases, after careful and cautious discussion (see Huy's essay in this volume). Even so, local enthusiasm for festivals and other revived practices testifies to the deep resonances these activities have in contemporary Vietnamese life.[3]

Many festivals include a dragon dance, as portrayed in this late-twentieth-century woodblock print on a traditional theme.

In 1986 the government of the Socialist Republic of Vietnam initiated Doi Moi (Renovation), heralding individual responsibility in agriculture and encouraging commerce. This fostering of a market economy brought new levels of consumption, including the consumption of tradition, but also accelerated disparities of income and environmental damage.[4] The Doi Moi era provides the horizons within which the exhibit's journeys unfold. For example, journeys of people and goods take place in new and fluid circumstances, be they the tourist trade in the Sapa market or the introduction of new consumer goods as gifts and status objects, signifying new desires and accomplishments available to both the living and—in the form of paper votive goods—the dead. New markets and goods have thus had an impact on various domains of contemporary social life across a broad spectrum of Vietnamese experience, from handicraft production to dealings with the spirit world. In Vietnam, no less than anywhere else, "culture" is a dynamic process that responds to changes in the local and global environment and incorporates new material. This is a measure of its vitality.

■ Between New York and Hanoi

THE AMERICAN MUSEUM OF NATURAL HISTORY (AMNH) in New York City, established in 1869, is one of the oldest museums in the Western Hemisphere, with a long history of documenting and exhibiting the peoples and cultures of the globe. This history is something of a double-edged sword, however. On the one hand, it gives the collections, some of which are more than a century old, considerable value as anthropological records, as time capsules of different human experiences. On the other, it can provide an entrée for those who criticize museums for representing non-Western peoples as outside modern experience and, consequently, as "exotic," "primitive," or "backward." In response, curators have made an effort in recent exhibits to include contemporary material and to show old objects as part of a history that extends into the present and future, inspiring ongoing utilitarian, artistic, and sacred activities. Western phenomena have also become the subjects of ethnographic displays.[5]

The Vietnam Museum of Ethnology (VME), in contrast, is one of the world's newest museums, opened to the public in 1997 with a commitment to presenting, preserving, and fostering respect for the diverse traditions of Vietnam's fifty-four ethnicities, both majority and minority, in a contemporary context. As such, the VME is not burdened by preconceptions of a museum as a place that displays only old, rare, and exotic objects. Indeed, most of the objects in its vitrines were collected just a few years before the opening of the museum, often from the very people who made or used them. On the museum grounds, ethnic minority people have had a hand in constructing full-scale replicas of their traditional houses, while inside the museum, dioramas with manikins are juxtaposed to video screens showing objects in use and rituals being performed. Visitors are impressed and surprised by the contemporary look of the people in the videos, some of whom wear familiar clothing such as tee shirts and athletic shoes. Any inclination

During the Tet holidays, boats of pilgrims travel along a shallow stream to the Perfume Pagoda (Chua Huong), several hours from Hanoi, where people hike up a mountain trail behind the temple to a cave grotto to pray for good fortune in the coming year.

to regard the subjects of these exhibits as primitive and timeless is thoroughly subverted.

Vietnam: Journeys of Body, Mind, and Spirit is similarly cast in the present tense and told, wherever possible, in the voices of its subjects. Most of the objects that were displayed in the exhibit date from the second half of the twentieth century. Some were commissioned and manufactured for the exhibit by Vietnamese artisans of handicrafts and ritual goods. Every presentation is based on fieldwork by VME teams who have photographed, videotaped, and recorded interviews with the subjects of all of the journeys we portray. We use this interview material to convey a sense of immediate encounters. Many of our subjects are aware of the exhibit and pleased to be participating in it.

Amid the traffic of Ho Chi Minh City (formerly Saigon) in the mid-1990s, two women in a cyclo carry home a huge cake box.

Our two museums have worked together in shaping the narrative of this book and exhibit and developing the individual journeys that we present. The project evolved as a series of international conversations, brain-storming sessions, methodological workshops, and critique meetings. While VME staff shared their scholarly knowledge of Vietnam's majority and minority cultures, AMNH staff worked with VME staff in Hanoi developing better conservation, exhibition, label-writing, and photographic techniques. In 2001, AMNH curatorial, exhibition, and media people worked together with VME staff in documenting the arrival of the year of the snake in Hanoi and Ho Chi Minh City (formerly Saigon) and a pilgrimage to the Perfume Pagoda as a prelude to designing this section of the exhibit. During this implementation phase of the project, VME staff joined the curatorial and conservation teams in New York to ensure accurate exhibition designs and label copy and helped to edit a wealth of moving media. All of our work together has been conducted in an atmosphere of mutually constructive criticism and learning, inspired by the common goal of presenting contemporary Vietnam to an international audience.

The preparation of this book was a part of this complex and enriching process. Once the two editors had determined its shape, Nguyen Van Huy identified and commissioned most of the authors. Chapters written in Vietnamese were translated, edited, and then back-translated to the authors. With Tran Trung Hieu of the International Relations Staff of VME acting as interpreter, Laurel Kendall worked with each author to verify nuances and clarify outstanding questions. These sessions often led to animated discussions over ethnographic fine points, resulting in far richer final versions of individual chapters.

This volume describes the many journeys that form the substance of our exhibit. The first two chapters sketch background and setting in bold strokes. In chapter 1, Oscar Salemink provides a broad overview of Vietnam's history, cultural geography, and the role of regionalism and describes how Doi Moi, by ushering in new economic opportunities and risks, has affected Vietnamese life. In chapter 2, Frank Proschan outlines the complex ethnographic map of Vietnam, a country that, with fifty-four officially recognized ethnicities, has the largest and most varied ethnic population in Southeast Asia.

Chapters 3 through 5 conceptualize the year as a journey through time, mapped by a calendar, with holidays as signposts along the way. In chapter 3, Nguyen Van Huy describes the lunar new year (Tet) as it is celebrated in Hanoi today, with activities oriented toward making an auspicious beginning. In anticipation of the holiday, houses are cleaned, and flowering trees and orange bushes are purchased and transported through the city in the trunks of cars, on cyclos and motorbikes, and the roofs of buses. People buy ritual goods and holiday foods and sweets. There are public displays of banners and lights and midnight fireworks. The celebration is a constellation of journeys: Fish are released to mark the Kitchen God's journey to report to heaven. People crowd onto buses with holiday gifts and pile flowering trees on the roof. The god of the new year is welcomed into the home, ancestors visit the household altar, and a special meal is shared. Families visit their relatives, go to temples in and around Hanoi to pray for luck in the coming year, and make pilgrimages to more distant sites. Huy's essay conveys all the color of a Tet celebration in the contemporary Doi Moi era, as well as memories of leaner times when anticipation of the holiday meant standing in long lines to secure the preparations for festive foods and bus or train tickets to travel home for the holiday.

The Mid-Autumn Festival is the focus of chapter 4, also by Nguyen Van Huy. This is a time of fulfillment, a pause in the year's journey marked by the full harvest moon. For the Kinh and Hoa (Chinese) who celebrate this festival, the full moon of the eighth lunar month—usually in September—signifies fertility. Originally a harvest festival when people prayed for a good crop and the abundance of all living things, it has become a popular children's festival with special toys and treats and lantern parades. Masks collected during the Mid-Autumn Festival in 2000 reflect the cosmopolitan worldview of an urban Vietnamese child, including characters from Mickey Mouse to the heroes and heroines of Chinese swordsmen movies and Japanese anime. Although in village settings traditional handcrafted toys and decorations can still be seen, in the cities they compete with flashy factory-made toys from China. The Mid-Autumn Festival is a nostalgic time as adults of various ages remember their own childhoods. A sense of the present and of memory is captured in this chapter through the juxtaposition of

Large glazed jars, like those in this early-twentieth-century Ede long-house in the vicinity of Buon Ma Thuot, Dak Lak province, have changed identity as they journeyed from lowland markets to highland longhouses. Made to transport wine, oil, and other commercial goods, originally they were purely utilitarian objects. When traded to highland peoples, they became precious heirlooms and were filled with wine for consumption during important ceremonies.

archival and contemporary photographs and the reminiscences of a variety of Hanoi residents, both young and old.

The timing of Tet and the Mid-Autumn Festival is set by the lunisolar calendar used by the Kinh majority population in common with Chinese, Japanese, Korean, and Mongolian people. But this widespread device for mapping the year is only one alternative to the Gregorian (solar) calendar that marks official time in Vietnam. Some ethnic minorities have their own systems for reckoning the passage of time. In chapter 5, "Four Ways to Map a Year's Journey," Chu Van Khanh outlines the basic principles of the lunar calendar used by the Kinh majority as well as the very different calendar system that members of the Muong minority use, engraving it on bamboo strips. The calendar of the Hmong is described by A Bao, and Cam Trong describes the Thai system of reckoning the passage of days, weeks, and months.

The Hmong in the northern mountains of Vietnam use horses to transport both people and goods between village and market. Here a Hmong woman leads a pony along a mountain trail.

In a more literal sort of journey, material goods can be seen to map global encounters. Vietnamese ceramics appear in a Paris boutique. Backpack travelers wear caps fashioned by Hmong traders from embroidered collar bands. Chapters 6 and 7 present two journeys of people and goods that are a direct consequence of Vietnam's opening to the global marketplace in the late 1980s. The positive and negative consequences of these encounters may be debated, but it cannot be denied that they have transformed all who have participated in them.

On the streets of Hanoi, bicycles balancing stacked ceramics from the kilns at Bat Trang navigate roads that are increasingly clogged with vehicular traffic. Several centuries ago, ceramics from the Red River Delta traveled by river and sea into a larger Southeast Asian market, and some wares reached the eastern Mediterranean. Today Bat Trang wares travel by boat and truck, across Vietnam and into a global marketplace. Nguyen Anh Ngoc, in "Bat Trang Pottery Village Today" (chapter 6), describes this booming enterprise through encounters with a master artisan, a successful woman factory owner, and a young couple who commute by bicycle from a neighboring village to work in a Bat Trang ceramics factory.

In chapter 7, Claire Burkert offers a vivid first-hand description of a weekend in Sapa, a market town near Vietnam's northern border. Frequented by

The "mouse's wedding" is a popular motif in Kinh (Viet) graphic art, as in this late-twentieth-century wood-block print. The cat is an official who exacts a toll before the procession may proceed. According to some experts, the figure in the chair is actually a scholar of dynastic times who is being carried home in state after successfully passing the civil service exam that entitles him to a career in high office.

Yao, Hmong, and other ethnic traders, Sapa has become a mecca for tourism. As in other such encounters, this new market has been a mixed blessing for local people. Vendors sell heirlooms and made-for-tourist handicrafts to tourists, but those positioned to make the greatest profit are the shop owners, who are from the majority population. Burkert draws on a deep knowledge of Sapa traders gained through her work on a collaborative project between VME and Craft Link, a nongovernmental development agency committed to working with local ethnic artisans to revive and sustain traditional handicraft and to return the profits directly to these artisans.

"Passage rites" are rituals marking changes in the life cycle. Coming-of-age ceremonies, weddings, and funerals mark journeys from one life state to another. The symbolism of such journeying, an explicit theme in the life transitions of many of the peoples living in Vietnam, is described in chapters 8 through 10.

Among the Yao in the north of Vietnam, an elaborate sequence of rites marks a young man's transition to the status of a mature ritual specialist. Ly Hanh Son describes this process in "The Yao Initiation Ceremony in the New Market Economy" (chapter 8). While this elaborate ritual is conducted with great enthusiasm, enabled by improved economic conditions, young Yao men in the community Son describes no longer succeed in mastering

The elaborate funeral procession of a rich man moves through the streets of Hanoi in the early twentieth century.

the complex ideographs of the Yao sacred texts that must be chanted as part of the ritual. Son leaves it as an open question whether rote memorization will be sufficient to perpetuate this tradition. Some more elaborate rituals, marking further stages of competency in Yao ritual lore, have already been lost in this region.

Marking transitions from one life status to another, the weddings and funerals of the majority Kinh population include processions that usher the bride to her husband's family home and that escort the dead out of the community of the living. A wedding may be preceded by other ceremonious journeys for matchmaking and for the formal delivery of betrothal gifts carefully arranged on rented red lacquer trays and boxes. Funerals provide social support for cathartic expressions of deep grief and perform the necessary emotional work of sending the dead to the netherworld. For Kinh people, the journey of the dead is enacted through an elaborate funeral procession, with the children of the deceased, dressed in special mourners' garb, supporting themselves on mourners' staves. In chapter 9, Shaun Malarney describes the importance of weddings and funerals in the ritual and social life of the majority population. He also describes how notions of proper weddings and funerals have shifted over the course of twentieth-century

Vietnamese history in accord with changing social ideals both under social-ism and as the new economy has ushered in a revival of old forms and an appetite for new fashions.

The notion that death rites are a progress toward ancestorship is also elaborated in the funerals of some of Vietnam's minority peoples. In chapter 10, "Other Journeys of the Dead," ethnologists Luu Hung, Nguyen Trung Dung, Tran Thi Thu Thuy, Vi Van An, and Vo Thi Thuong describe how five very different ethnic groups—the Khmer, the Hmong, the Muong, the Giarai, and the Thai—confront mortality. Like the Kinh, Thais mark this transition with a procession to the tomb. There, simulated "trees" are erected to mark the ascent of the soul. In the north of Vietnam, Hmong souls are "shown the way" to the land of the ancestors by a shaman who guides them through the dangerous journey. At Muong funerals the chants of the *mo*, the ritual master, send the soul to bid farewell to a familiar land-scape. The Giarai, who live in the Central Highlands, send the dead to the land of the ancestors with an elaborate grave-leaving ceremony. This cere-mony may be held ten or more years after death when the families of the departed feel emotionally ready to send them away and when there are enough pigs, oxen, buffaloes, chickens, alcohol, and rice for the ceremony, which includes feasting, drumming, and dancing in front of an elaborate mortuary house. For the Khmer, death is one brief passage in a chain of rein-carnation, and as a consequence, funeral rites are relatively simple.

Not only living (and dead) people embark on journeys, but gods, spirits, and souls do as well—as we explore in chapters 11 through 13. At village fes-tivals, the local tutelary god is invited from his temple to the village com-munal house, or from the communal house around the community, in an elaborate procession that mimics the regalia and pomp of a dynastic man-darin or king's progress. In the Red River Delta in the north, these festivals are held in the spring for an auspicious beginning to the agricultural cycle. In fishing villages along the central coast, whale bones are wrapped and carried in state in the manner of tutelary gods, and the festival is a prayer for the safety and prosperity of fishermen at the start of the fishing season.

Visiting gods are sometimes feted with a musical or theatrical perform-ance. On the central coast, special songs are sung to appease the spirits of drowned fishermen. In the Red River Delta, performances by water puppets are popular. In the festival of Thay Pagoda, the puppeteers of Binh Phu commune celebrate the founder of their art, Tu Dao Hanh, by having the puppets carry his image in a miniature festival palanquin.

Chapter 11, "The Village God's Journey," gives background on some of these colorful traditions. Nguyen Van Huy describes the festival honoring the tutelary god Ly Phuc Man in Yen So village, comparing this celebration to the one described by his father, Nguyen Van Huyen, in this same village in the 1930s. Nguyen Anh Ngoc describes the festival of Man Thai ward, Danang City, on the central coast, where whale bones are carried in state. Nguyen Huy Hong, and Nguyen Trung Dung present the water puppet performances as festival entertainment.

In many shamanic traditions, the entranced shaman travels to other realms to do battle with ominous forces to win back the patient's soul. In chapter 12, La Cong Y describes how this is accomplished among Vietnam's Tay people. Here, the shaman and her attendants, representing a spirit army, chant and enact an elaborate journey over mountains, across oceans, into the courts of various mandarins, and onto the turf of monsters that must be defeated in battle.

Among the Kinh majority, shamanic practices take a different form: spirits travel to the Len Dong ritual in a Mother Goddess temple, where they manifest themselves through an appropriately costumed ritual specialist and are entertained with appropriate songs. In chapter 13, Ngo Duc Thinh describes a ceremony held for a market woman in Hanoi, in which a sequence of suitably garbed and beautifully coifed spirits greet the delighted spectators with dance and mime. Attractively arranged offerings of fruit,

At the cremation of a prominent religious figure in the Cham community in Phan Rang district, Ninh Thuan province, in 1974, relatives prostrate themselves in single file as the corpse, on a richly decorated bier, is carried over them.

This richly embroidered cotton vest was worn by a White Thai shaman in Hoa Binh province during rituals when he guided the souls of the deceased to other realms. Late twentieth century.

This late-twentieth-century wood-block print by Nguyen Dang Che of Dong Ho village evokes the story of the legendary Thanh Giong on his iron horse with his magic Dang Nga bamboo as a weapon. One of four immortals in Vietnamese folk belief, Thanh Giong helped the sixth Hung King to repulse invaders.

beer, soft drinks, candy, and packaged noodles are given to the spirits and then shared among the spectators as a showering of the spirit's blessings.

The theme of "journeying" provides us with a wide-ranging metaphor, broad enough to carry us through Vietnam at the start of the twenty-first century, through different urban neighborhoods, from city to village, and to the upland communities of Vietnam's ethnic minorities. To repeat, this is not a tourist's journey, but rather an attempt to travel in different kinds of Vietnamese "shoes," along different roads, highways, railways, rivers, and footpaths, but also to travel in state with tutelary gods or to fly with souls to other realms described in songs and stories. A recounting of this sampling of journeys assumes that there are many more left to be imagined and undertaken.

National Highway 1, stretching the length of Vietnam from the Chinese border in the north to the Mekong Delta in the south, allows the transport of people and goods along the country's 3,260 kilometers of coastline. Shown here is Hai Van Pass (Pass of the Ocean of Clouds), a steep and sometimes perilous mountain pass between Hue and Danang in central Vietnam.

ONE COUNTRY,

MANY JOURNEYS

Oscar Salemink

1

M ANY PEOPLE ARE SURPRISED TO LEARN that Vietnam has the second largest population in Southeast Asia after Indonesia. At almost 80 million (over 76 million according to the 1999 census), it is larger than France, England, or Italy. Vietnam's population is also immensely diverse, with over fifty officially recognized ethnic groups speaking more than fifty languages (some linguists claim more than one hundred) belonging to three language families subdivided into eight language groups. In addition, most of the world's major religions are represented in Vietnam—Buddhism, Confucianism, Taoism, Islam, Hinduism, Christianity (Catholic and Protestant)—besides myriad other religious beliefs and practices, often described as animism, shamanism, spirit worship, or ancestor worship.

In Hue a Vietnamese tourist dons the imperial robes of the Nguyen dynasty, traveling back imaginatively to a moment in the past for a souvenir photograph.

This diverse reality may clash with some images that Westerners have of Vietnam. For decades American and European interest in Vietnam was largely provoked by wars and related events during the Cold War. Westerners were caught by the image of Vietnam either as an enemy of the free world or as David defeating a series of imperialist Goliaths. Both of these images are far from an accurate picture of the country and its history.

In numerous books, reports, and films about Vietnam, the people with the conical hats are portrayed as living in rural village communities that have changed little over time, their lives steeped in tradition. The irony is that such notions and their attendant visual images emerged when Vietnamese society was undergoing a sea change, when much of the countryside was ravaged and villages were being resettled, when much of its population had left the villages to fight a war whose horizons lay far beyond the village boundaries, when migration, both domestic and international, was increasing, when Vietnam's global integration was accelerated by virtue of its being one arena in which the international Cold War was fought. The irony is, too, that a great deal of Vietnam's history and culture is about movement, migration, travel, and change, as revealed by much of its popular art and literature. Rather than discuss various images of Vietnam (accurate or inaccurate), therefore, this overview will pay attention to changes—the journeys of the Vietnamese people over time, in space, and spiritually—without, however, denying *significant* continuities in Vietnam's culture and history.

■ River Deltas, Coasts, and Mountains

VIETNAM IS A TROPICAL COUNTRY in mainland Southeast Asia, located between the Tropic of Cancer and the eighth parallel in the Northern Hemisphere. To the south and east we find the South China Sea (East Sea) and, farther on, the islands of Hainan and Taiwan, the archipelago of the Philippines, and the island of Borneo. To the north Vietnam shares a border with China, and to the west lie Laos and Cambodia, which until 1954 were, with Vietnam, part of French Indochina. The shape of present-day Vietnam is like an S, with the major deltas of the Red River and the Mekong connected by a narrow coastal strip and a mountain range known as the Annam Cordillera (Truong Son in Vietnamese). The northern delta, where the capital, Hanoi, is located, has four seasons, with surprisingly cold winters brought by wet winds coming down from the northern Chinese mainland. The monsoon climate in the southern half of the country results in a rainy season from April to November and a dry season from December through March.

Historically, much of Southeast Asia's present population is the result of myriad waves of migration. Whereas it is assumed that insular Southeast Asia and Polynesia were settled by speakers of proto-Austronesian languages coming from the coasts of Vietnam and southern China, the population structure of mainland Southeast Asia is the result of successive migrations from China southward, of such groups as Thai, Burmese, Lao, and Hmong. According to tradition, the Vietnamese themselves had their origin in the Red River Delta, about two thousand years ago. The legend of Au Co and Lac Long Quan tells the story of the birth of Vietnam, the result of a marriage between the elements of water and land. This legend, graphically depicted in a four-hundred-year-old bas-relief

ONE DAY THE dragon god Lac Long Quan, who ruled the Kingdom of Lac Viet, eloped with the fairy Au Co, who came from

■ THE STORY OF ONE HUNDRED EGGS

the north (China). He lived in an underwater palace while she lived in a palace on top of a mountain. Out of their union she laid one hundred eggs from which one hundred human children hatched and grew. When Au Co went on a journey to visit her home country in the north, she was stopped at the border by Hoang De, the emperor of heaven, who threatened to invade Lac Viet. Lac Long

Quan then decided that he and Au Co belonged to different worlds. Because he was a dragon and she a fairy, they had to live apart—he in the water, and she on the land. Half the children would live with her on the land, and half would follow him under the water. They would live apart but help one another in times of need. Thus it happened, and the fifty children of Au Co became the rulers of Lac Viet, known as the Hung kings, the remote ancestors of the present-day Vietnamese.

[Adapted from *Vietnamese Legends and Folk Tales.* Hanoi 2001: The Gioi.]

In 248 C.E. Trieu Thi Trinh (Lady Trieu), at the age of nineteen, led a courageous insurrection against the Chinese. Legend has it that this woman general rode an elephant into battle, wearing golden armor, a golden scarf, and ivory clogs. Today she is a popular symbol of national unity and independence, as evoked in this woodblock print by Nguyen Dang Che of Dong Ho village.

in Binh Da village near Hanoi, is now taken to mean that all ethnic groups stem from the same source, thus signifying the essential national unity of the country. The revival of the celebration of the Hung King Festival in Phu Tho province has recently been taken up as symbol of the birth of an indigenous Vietnam before the Chinese became players in its history.

The French scholar George Coedès has stated that Indochina was not just a geographic space between India and China but also a site of cultural cross-fertilization by Indian and Chinese influences.[1] While Coedès described the Khmer and Lao civilizations as "Hinduized," Vietnam was "Sinicized," thoroughly influenced by Chinese civilization. From 211 B.C.E. to 938 C.E. the northern part of what is now Vietnam was occupied by a succession of Chinese dynasties. During this millennium, Chinese technology,

吳王權

In 938 Ngo Quyen vanquished the Chinese invaders and in 939 proclaimed himself king, setting up the first independent Vietnamese state, after nearly a thousand years under Chinese occupation. This woodblock print by Nguyen Dang Che depicts Ngo Quyen's successful battle in the Bach Dang Estuary, where retreating Chinese ships sank, impaled on the spikes his troops had submerged so they would not be visible to the invaders when they sailed in at high tide.

culture, and political and religious concepts exerted a deep influence over Vietnam. After breaking loose from China, Vietnam—as one of the states paying tribute to the Middle Kingdom—continued to model itself on China in many ways,[2] although part of the Vietnamese national narrative is the story of the struggle against China for independence. In recent years, however, Vietnamese archaeologists and historians have begun to stress that the roots of the Vietnamese nation preceded cultural influences from China and, to a lesser extent, India. These roots, found in the Dong Son culture with its famous bronze drums, are often portrayed as alien to Chinese civilization and resembling the material culture of some indigenous ethnic groups of the Annam Cordillera and Central Highlands. Even though such bronze drums have been found all over mainland and insular Southeast Asia, from Yunnan in China to Timor, Vietnamese historical narratives now appropriate the Dong Son culture as quintessentially proto-Vietnamese.

Another major part of the Vietnamese national narrative is the so-called Nam Tien, or March to the South, of the Kinh (Viet). When Vietnam finally became independent from China, the successive dynasties of Ly (1009–1225), Tran (1225–1400), and Le (1428–1786) attempted to pacify their border with China by recognizing China's suzerainty over Vietnam in the form of political and moral overlordship marked by regular tributes to the

Chinese emperor. That saved economic and military resources for expansion south through the gradual absorption of Champa, a seafaring Hinduized polity in what is now central Vietnam. The Austronesian-speaking Cham had developed a civilization bearing similarities to the Khmer civilization and the premodern states of Srivijaya and Mataram in what is now Indonesia. Beginning in the seventeenth century, the Kinh absorbed the declining Champa Kingdom. Kinh culture, actively promoted by the southern Nguyen lords, did not saturate the entire Mekong Delta until the twentieth century. During the seventeenth and eighteenth centuries, north and south remained politically separate. In the northern part of the country the Le dynasty was kept alive by the Trinh lords, whereas in the south the Nguyen lords had carved out a separate domain while formally recognizing the Le emperors. This led to a state of perennial hostility and a constant search for economic and military resources. The Nguyen lords in particular attempted to increase their domain through southward expansion, gradually absorbing areas where Cham and Khmer populations lived.

After the country's reunification by the Tay Son rebellion (1786) and the subsequent "reconquest" by the Nguyen dynasty, which from 1802 on asserted hegemony throughout Vietnam, the attention of Vietnam's rulers turned west. During parts of the nineteenth century, a stronger Vietnamese state controlled parts of what is now Cambodia and Laos and clashed with Siam (Thailand), which was expanding eastward.[3] This process was stopped by the imposition of French colonial rule and the marking of borders between French Indochina and Siam. Still now, at the dawn of the twenty-first century, Vietnam has privileged relationships with Cambodia and especially Laos. In the second half of the nineteenth century, the French first annexed the southern part of Vietnam, Cochin China, as a colony and imposed a protectorate over Annam and Tonkin, the central and northern parts of the country, formally leaving the Nguyen dynasty and its mandarinate intact. Vietnam's western borders with Laos and Cambodia became fixed under French colonial rule, creating the political space for a westward movement of the majority Kinh people into the highlands. The creation of a modern nation-state with fixed borders also meant that a variety of upland populations became ethnic minorities in Vietnam.

A key element of French colonial rule was the attempt to link people—both individuals and local/ethnic groups—to particular places, either

One of Vietnam's important national heroes, Le Loi led a successful ten-year (1418–1428) uprising against the Chinese. According to legend, Le Loi returned the sword that gave him victory to Hoan Kiem Lake (now the center of Hanoi), where it was retrieved by a giant turtle. Here, his story is portrayed by water puppets.

inhibiting movement or, where necessary, promoting tightly supervised migration. One example of such supervised migration was the exploitation of "coolies" from northern Vietnam on the rubber plantations in eastern Cochin China and the various plantations in the Central Highlands and Tonkin.[4] In terms of village rule, the French attempted to shore up their control of village administration by undermining traditional village autonomy.[5] Administrative measures imposed by the French made the movement and migration of peasants more difficult. According to Jan Breman and John Kleinen, such colonial interventions in village administration had the effect of creating more tightly knit communities, which were subsequently regarded as the traditional model of the village.[6]

Colonial rule introduced sweeping changes in Vietnam, propelling it into the modern world in sometimes unexpected ways. The modern nationalism of the twentieth century was largely fed by contacts with overseas intellectuals and often led by members of a diaspora of Vietnamese living in other Asian countries. The influential Dong Du movement (meaning "study in the east," i.e. in Japan) and the Vietnamese Communist Party leadership based in China until World War II are two examples of how travel and migration—the movement of people, goods, and ideas—

Labeled "The Automobile, the Bicycle, and the Hunt [courtship?]," these ironic woodblock prints from the mid-1920s by Vietnamese artists show the peculiar clothing, strange vehicles, and ambiguous courtship maneuvers of the French, who were a colonial presence from 1858 to 1954. The prints refer to these behaviors, perhaps sarcastically, as "new mores" and "the progress of civilization." The figures engage in obscure colloquial conversation, saying in the left-hand frame, "I couldn't give a damn," and in the right-hand one, "You watch it!"

were at the root of Vietnam's most successful nationalist movement. When the struggle for independence in Vietnam eventually resulted in an all-out guerrilla war against the French under the Communist Viet Minh movement, villagers from all over the country were mobilized. The temporary separation of the country in 1954 along the seventeenth parallel, after the Viet Minh victory over the French at Dien Bien Phu and the Geneva Agreements, undid the previous three-part division of Vietnam and almost restored the division between the Trinh and Nguyen lords that had existed before the Tay Son rebellion of 1786. This division was accompanied by a massive movement of Viet Minh cadres to the north and of anti-Communist Vietnamese, mostly Catholics, to the south.

Enormous upheavals and population movements resulted when the Second Indochina War (known as the Vietnam War or American War) broke out between North and South in 1960, aggravated by the deployment of U.S. troops in 1965. The famous Ho Chi Minh trail, the supply route for

HUẤN LUYỆN BÌNH DÂN HỌC VỤ

This woodblock print, originally made by Nguyen Dang Tuy in 1945 and reproduced here by his son Nguyen Dang Che, shows a literacy class for the common people. Mass literacy was a top priority for the revolutionary nationalist leadership fighting for Vietnam's independence from the French. Although Vietnam historically had a long educational tradition based on the Confucian canon and elite mastery of Chinese and Sino-Vietnamese (Han *nom*) ideographs, illiteracy prevailed during the colonial period. Vietnam's literacy rate is estimated at 85 percent.

troops and resources from north to south during that conflict, can be seen as a recapitulation of the Nam Tien in another form and historical context. Successive southern regimes resettled villages and populations on a massive scale in an attempt to gain control over these populations and separate them from the guerrillas. Many villagers from predominantly rural Vietnam fled the war in the countryside and settled in rapidly expanding cities, especially Saigon (now Ho Chi Minh City) and Danang.

After 1975, the now reunified Socialist Republic of Vietnam also resorted to resettlement as an instrument of political control and economic management. Many southern city-dwellers were moved to New Economic Zones in the Mekong Delta and the Central Highlands, many farmers from the densely populated northern deltas came to the south in search of land, and cadres from the north came south to establish social and ideological institutions that would serve as the foundation for the new regime. This movement can be seen in part as another instance of the Nam Tien, with

"Bravo for Vietnamese women! Heroes in production as well as in battle!" Celebrated as leaders in the family, as workers in the economy, and as soldiers in the wars for national independence, Vietnamese women are shown planting rice and ready to defend their country in this contemporary reproduction of a woodblock print from the 1960s.

the additional westward movement into the Central Highlands near the western border constituting something of a Tay Tien, or March to the West.

Vietnam remains a largely rural society, with over 75 percent of the population living in the countryside. For many villagers, service in the army constituted not only exposure to the horrors of war but also an escape from geographic and social immobility. After the war, countless demobilized soldiers or cadres settled in new places or returned to their home communities as agents of change. These population movements evoked feelings of bereavement and loss and an intense nostalgia for the home village (que huong) that was inextricably mixed with memories of childhood (tuoi tho), before adult worries and sorrows took away the innocence of youth. This feeling of nostalgia is the stuff of poetry and novels, music and films, both in Vietnam and in the Vietnamese diaspora. In contemporary literature, one of the most poignant evocations of nostalgia and loss of innocence is Bao Ninh's novel *The Sorrow of War*; in cinema, Tran Anh Hung's *The Scent of Green Papaya*.

If literature and biography can by any measure be taken as a mirror of society, then it is worthwhile to look at representative works from the literary canon in Vietnam. Vietnam's most famous novel is Nguyen Du's *Truyen Kieu* (The Tale of Kieu), written in 1813 and comprising 3,250 verses in *nom*, Vietnam's own character script. It tells the story, in beautiful verse, of a young girl's spiritual and geographic journey through medieval China. The girl, Kieu, rescues her family from ruin by sacrificing herself, giving up her true love. After a life's journey with a succession of husbands, lovers, and pimps, during which her spirit remains pure, she finds her family and her first love again. This novel, though set in China, has been embraced by generations of Vietnamese as representing profoundly Vietnam's cultural identity. Millions of Vietnamese can recite verses from the novel. But why? Perhaps because the novel tells a story of separation and alienation, of appropriation by strangers while preserving one's own spirit. However, when Kieu is finally reunited with her family and her first love, they cannot simply pick up where they left off; as in *The Sorrow of War*, the past cannot be redeemed, save in memory and nostalgia.[7]

Vietnam's most famous and influential biography is that of Ho Chi Minh, whose importance lies more in his exemplary life *(tam guong)* than in his writings, which together constitute what Vietnamese call "Ho Chi Minh thought" *(tu tuong* Ho Chi Minh). All Vietnamese are familiar with the main narrative of his official biography, especially his travels to the United States, France, the Soviet Union, and China. Moreover, he adopted many different identities, literally traveling from one identity to another, before finally becoming Ho Chi Minh—or Bac Ho (Uncle Ho), as he is affectionately called. The image of Ho Chi Minh as unmarried and childless, without family interests, makes it possible for everyone to see him as Bac Ho, Uncle Ho, the uncle of all of Vietnam's children. His portrait adorns many offices and homes, and in temples and pagodas Uncle Ho is not only revered but already worshipped as one of the legendary heroes who have become mediators with the spirit world or even as a *bodhisattva*.[8] Ho's journey, then, has many dimensions: geographic, temporal, political, ritual, and aesthetic.

This very sketchy history tells us that Vietnam's tortuous and eventful history of struggle is as much a saga of travel as it is of continuity and stability.

These scenes illustrate episodes from the most famous work of Vietnamese literature, The Tale of Kieu, by Nguyen Du (1765–1820). His work marked an important stage in the development of the Vietnamese language, and his portrait of his heroine's courageous struggle against feudalism and the strictures of Confucian society achieved great popularity.

Praying at the Cao Dai Temple in Tay Ninh. Caodaism was founded in 1926, and its followers are concentrated in the southeast. It is an eclectic mixture of Taoism, Buddhism, Confucianism, and indigenous beliefs, with some elements of Catholicism. Under "the supreme saint," the pantheon includes figures from world religions and also some historical figures such as Victor Hugo.

■ Culture, Religion, Politics

AS EMBODIED IN THE NAME INDOCHINA, Vietnam was influenced by both the Indian and Chinese civilizations, but because of the long Chinese occupation and China's proximity, Vietnam adopted most of its major cultural and political concepts from China. The word *nam* means "south," which situates Vietnam in relation to the cultural and political center, China, the Middle Kingdom. Three major religious traditions found their way to Vietnam from China: Buddhism, Confucianism, and Taoism.

Buddhism's Four Truths teach that adherence to eight moral precepts of perfection brings a gradual detachment from earthly suffering in successive reincarnations. A decentralized religion, Buddhism is visible in Vietnam's hundreds—perhaps thousands—of pagodas, important centers of learning inhabited and maintained by monks or nuns, who often meditate and study. Lay people regularly visit pagodas to pray and acquire wisdom. Buddhism was introduced to Vietnam from India in the third century C.E.; Zen (Thien) Buddhism arrived from China around 580. When Vietnam won independence in 938, Mahayana Buddhism, which offers broad possibilities for salvation through the merciful intercession of *bodhisattvas*, became the dominant religion and its temples the most important centers of learning. Elsewhere in Southeast Asia, Theravada Buddhism, which emphasizes a rigorous and solitary path to enlightenment, predominates.

Taoism is a philosophy and particular understanding of the world and the cosmos rather than a religion per se. Lao Tzu, the founder, seems to have lived in China in the sixth century B.C.E., but his teachings, known as the Tao Te Ching, were written down about three centuries later. The Tao (the Way, Dao in Vietnamese) deals with balance within the cosmos, between nature and man, between mind and body, and especially between the various forces or principles shaping the world. The complementary yin and yang principles (in Vietnamese *am* and *duong*) have to be in balance in order to find or create harmony. This harmony leads to spiritual and physical health and well-being and affirms one's place in the cosmos. Such concepts are also important in traditional Asian medicine and acupuncture, geomancy (widely known as *feng shui*, or *phong thuy* in Vietnamese), astrology and fortune-telling, and martial arts.

These two boys are being raised in a Buddhist temple in Hue. When they are older, they will choose between a monk's calling or lay life. Buddhism is the predominant religion in Vietnam, and its traditional festivals have been revived.

A moral and political doctrine superimposed on ancient Chinese religious and social concepts about the relation between the celestial order and the affairs of the world, Confucianism was established by Confucius, who lived around 600 B.C.E. As a moral doctrine, Confucianism focused on proper relationships in family, society, and the cosmos. Within families, authority rested with male elders, and women had to subject themselves to the authority of their fathers, brothers, husbands, and, in old age, sons. Filial piety and respect were also key Confucian values. As a political doctrine, Confucianism established the relationship between rulers and subjects by emphasizing authority and respect, regulated and punctuated by correct behavior and rituals. At the same time, Confucius emphasized learning and wisdom as a condition for enlightened rule. Hanoi's Temple of Literature (Van Mieu), where the scholars and future mandarins of Vietnam have taken their exams since the eleventh century, is dedicated to Confucius.

During the Chinese occupation, Taoism and Confucianism were introduced into Vietnam and existed alongside Buddhism. In this era, Thien (Zen) Buddhism absorbed the mysticism of the Tao, emphasizing the individual search for Buddha within oneself through meditation, withdrawal from the world, and finally bliss. During the first centuries of Vietnam's independence from China, Buddhism was the dominant state doctrine and developed in opposition to Confucianism, which as a moral and political doctrine emphasized this-worldly virtues. With the development of the Vietnamese state, the ruling elite gradually turned to Confucianism as the moral and organizational basis for its regime, especially from the brief Chinese occupation in the early fifteenth century until the French conquest in the nineteenth century. Although Buddhism gradually lost its influence over the ruling classes and even lost the favor of the kings, it retained strong appeal for the largely rural population, who had little to expect in this life from Confucian doctrine.

Despite the several religious traditions practiced in Vietnam, for the large majority of the population distinctions between the various religions and cults are not overly important. In theory, Buddha is venerated in the temple *(chua)*; Confucius and Confucian saints in *van chi* or *mieu*; kings and national heroes in the temple *(den)*; the tutelary spirits of the village in the communal house *(dinh)*; and the ancestors at an altar in the home. In practice all these religions blend into one national brand characterized by syncretism. This combination of religious traditions makes Vietnam very different from the neighboring nations of Cambodia, Laos, Thailand, and Burma, which all follow Theravada Buddhism from India. In Vietnam we can easily imagine a state official who in the morning places offerings on his ancestors' altar at home, who attempts to uphold Confucian values of respect and hierarchy in dealing with both his family and his office staff, who seeks out a diviner to determine the propitious date for a new venture

Catholicism, introduced by Portuguese and Spanish missionaries in the seventeenth century, has about five million followers in Vietnam. Here, a woman with a rosary takes part in an Easter procession in a small village on the Nam Dinh coast, April 2000.

or a *feng shui* specialist for the location of a building, and visits the local pagoda on evenings of the fifteenth day of the lunar month. In the same vein, the portrait or bust of Ho Chi Minh will not only be in all government offices and in many homes, but also in many temples and pagodas.

While Vietnam's religious traditions were introduced by travelers, their development has been predicated on continued contacts with other countries and communities where these religions are practiced. During the past several centuries, a number of new and alien concepts were brought to Vietnam, some of which blended less well with the syncretistic mix in place.

In the seventeenth century Christianity was introduced to Vietnam by Portuguese, Spanish, and French missionaries, who met with mixed success. It seemed to temporarily gain a foothold when Pierre Pigneau de Béhaine, Catholic bishop of Adran, supported the pretender to the throne, Nguyen Anh, who became Emperor Gia Long, founder of the Nguyen dynasty. Gia Long tolerated the fairly successful Catholic missionaries, but his son and successor, Minh Mang, who reigned from 1820 to 1841, was less indulgent toward the Catholic community, which he saw (correctly, as it turned out) as a fifth column for French colonial designs on Southeast Asia. During the piecemeal French conquest of Vietnam under his successors, the French indeed used the need to protect the Catholic minority as an important pretext for incursion into Vietnam. This Catholic community has continued to stand apart in Vietnamese society. The Diem regime, allied with the United States in the early 1960s, was largely rooted in this Catholic community, which constituted only 10 percent of the population, a situation that resulted in significant Buddhist protests.[9]

Communism is another alien doctrine introduced into Vietnam. Although an atheist doctrine that rejects religion as an ideology of oppression, Communism shares a number of important aspects with religion: the expectation of liberation from suffering, organizational machinery, and devotion, including martyrdom. In actuality, the Vietnamese Communist Party has learned to tolerate religious beliefs and practices, even among its members, and has lately embraced a wide variety of religious practices as a way to chart a road toward modernization via the market economy. Besides, many Vietnamese point to similarities in Confucian and Marxist practice: the reliance on doctrinal texts, the emphasis on literacy and education, the bureaucratic nature of its governance, the idea of the perfectibility of people ("New Socialist Man").

Twice during its rule, the Communist Party attempted radical reform: with the land reforms in the North from 1953 to 1955 and with the massive collectivization of the economy after the reunification of the country in 1975. During these same years Marxist and like-minded scholars had a lively debate about the nature of Vietnam's society and its mode of production and socioeconomic formation. Participants in this debate shared a common belief in a unified national history—the idea that there was and is one Vietnam, emanating from a center (Hanoi and, briefly, Hue). Keith Taylor, however, convincingly debunked that notion by pointing out the regionalism in Vietnam's history, a regionalism that has been glossed over by the unifying narrative.[10] Taylor pointed to a number of decisive episodes in Vietnam's history that can be interpreted as a struggle for hegemony between various regions in what is now Vietnam. In some cases, national heroes like Le Loi, who liberated Vietnam from Chinese occupation in the fifteenth century, or the Tay Son brothers, three peasant rebels who overthrew the warring dynasties in the south and north and unified the country in the late eighteenth century, came from very marginal places in the mountains, not the typical Vietnamese heartland. Indeed, when Vietnamese travel about the country, they are constantly asked where they come

A calligrapher creates special requests and messages to the spirits that people will purchase and send up by burning them at temples during holidays such as Tet.

from by people hoping to find a bond based on common regional roots. If two people establish the existence of such shared roots, they bond in a way that is otherwise somewhat uncommon among Vietnamese. If Taylor's thesis is correct, then regionalism, and hence the journeys that bind regions, are a permanent factor in Vietnamese society.

■ Doi Moi: Renovation, Reform, and Growth

ONE REASON THE RADICAL CENTRALIZING REFORMS after 1953 and 1975 failed is that they did not take sufficient account of the heterogeneity of Vietnam's population, though there are many other factors. After reunification in 1975 collectivization resulted in a loss of productivity and a breakdown in the distribution system in a country that was almost 80 percent rural, bringing hunger to a large part of the population and demoralizing the most important resource for development: people. The swollen cities in the south had lived off the war economy and were largely unproductive, while the economic policies of the new government initially did very little to stimulate investment. On the contrary, the so-called bourgeois class—including many ethnic Chinese in Saigon—was distrusted. Many people deemed redundant and unproductive were sent to New Economic Zones, where they faced a life of hardship. Many people who had been affiliated with the former Saigon regime were sent to reeducation camps for months or years, often reappearing with broken spirits. In many cases, their potential to contribute productively and positively to Vietnam's development was overlooked and largely wasted. Moreover, a conflict with Democratic Cambodia under the Khmer Rouge degenerated into war by late 1978. In 1979 conflict with China not only brought further death and destruction but also forced an impoverished Vietnam to maintain one of the largest standing armies in Asia, absorbing millions of healthy young men and enormous resources in the process.

General poverty and extreme hardship, the lack of opportunity to overcome hardship with one's own resources in the collectivized economy, and disaffection among many who were affiliated with the former regime caused hundreds of thousands of people to take the desperate step of leaving the country by boat. Leaving behind everything and everybody, people spent significant sums to get into small, rickety boats, risking storms, starvation, and pirates, in the hope—fanned by radio stations outside Vietnam—of being picked up and accepted by a Western country. Many perished in the flight. In the 1980s such escape was replaced by the Orderly Departure Program, which provided eligible people with the opportunity to emigrate, supervised by international organizations and with the consent of the Vietnamese state. The result is a diaspora of millions of Vietnamese in such countries as the United States, Canada, Australia, France, and other countries in Western Europe. For Vietnam these events initially meant an enormous brain drain and destruction of human capital, but in the 1990s the economic significance of the overseas Vietnamese community came to be seen in a positive light. First, the remittances to family members and relatives in Vietnam amount to many billions of dollars each year, much more than foreign investment and international aid. Second, overseas Vietnamese spearhead foreign investment, perhaps not so much in monetary terms, but in providing the connections and know-how to do business in Vietnam.

In the early 1980s, when some regional leaders realized that continued collectivization would ruin the country, they started to experiment with systems allowing for a degree of private farming. After some successful experiments in the early 1980s, the champion of these local reforms, southern leader Nguyen Van Linh, became the secretary-general of the Communist Party. This paved the way to expansion, beginning in 1986, of local reforms, effectively stopping the centralizing forces by giving individual households the right to enjoy the fruits of their crops and labor and to use and manage their land on a long-term basis. A new, more liberal foreign investment law in 1987 opened the door to foreign investment and, consequently, to a wide range of contacts with the region and the world. As a result, Vietnam saw the slow introduction of economic reforms and the liberalization of the industrial and service sectors. This process of comprehensive market and other reforms is called Doi Moi, or Renovation, a term retaining some revolutionary rhetoric. The collapse of the Eastern European Communist bloc in 1989 and of the Soviet Union in the early 1990s had the dual effect of leaving Vietnam as one of the few remaining Communist countries and of abruptly ending the Cold War, facilitating the entry of Vietnam into regional and international bodies. An important benchmark of regional

In the mid 1990s billboards advertising international companies line the urban landscape of crowded Ho Chi Minh City (formerly Saigon), the main center of finance, industry, and tourism in the south.

integration was Vietnam's admission in 1995 to ASEAN (the Association of Southeast Asian Nations), which was originally set up in 1967 as an anti-Communist alliance. An important benchmark of international integration and cooperation was the signing of a comprehensive trade agreement with the United States, thus completing the normalization of U.S.–Vietnam relations begun in 1993 under President Clinton's leadership and paving the way for Vietnamese access to the World Trade Organization. To the outside world, Vietnam is no longer simply the site of a war but a "normal" country with a market economy and a society facing the opportunities and challenges of globalization.

Economic and social changes do not mean that Vietnam has completely given up on its socialist ambitions. Certainly at a rhetorical level, those ambitions remain. Slogans used in everyday life and posted everywhere

A cooperative pig farm in Dien Ban district, Quang Nam province, 1983. The economic era of collectivization and centralized planning changed in 1986 with the advent of Doi Moi (Renovation), the introduction of a limited free market and the corporatization of many state industries.

indicate that Vietnam is not implementing liberal capitalist reforms but is creating a "socialist market economy." The regime justifies its departure from orthodox socialism by promising that a socialist Vietnam will be fully industrialized and modernized by the year 2020. By then, Vietnam will be, as the slogans say, a "rich country, have a just and equal society, and its citizens will be civilized people." Most significantly, Vietnam strives to build "an advanced culture imbued with national identity." This rhetoric is important because in the eyes of many, industrialization and modernization essentially mean Westernization. Official support for expressions of national culture and conservation of heritage are seen to reinforce Vietnam's sovereignty as a counterweight to the seductions of the West.

■ The State of Vietnam's Population

VIETNAM IS A DENSELY POPULATED COUNTRY, with over 76 million people living on 330,000 square kilometers, an area about the size of the state of New Mexico. The population density is around 230 per square kilometer (similar to that of the United Kingdom), which is high for a country with a largely rural population and agrarian economy. The population is

An early-twentieth-century view of the backbreaking work of transplanting rice in water in southern Vietnam. Rice, which is still planted in this way, remains the most important crop in the country.

diverse, with fifty-three officially recognized ethnic minorities speaking perhaps more than a hundred languages, and among the majority Kinh (ethnic Viet) population many regional differences obtain.[11] Traditionally the Kinh—85 percent of the population—practice lowland wet-rice cultivation, which requires the construction and maintenance of elaborate irrigation works. Since the 1950s, however, many Kinh have migrated and settled in the midlands and uplands of Vietnam, the traditional abode of most ethnic minority groups. These highlands, almost three-quarters of Vietnam's land area, currently contain about one-third of the population—around 25 million—of whom almost 10 million can be classified as members of an ethnic minority. The modes of subsistence of these minority groups are extremely diverse but often entail some combination of wet-rice cultivation, permanent rain-fed cultivation, rotational or itinerant shifting cultivation, fruit orchards and cash crops, livestock, hunting, fishing, and harvesting of timber and other forest products.

Some 50 million people, then, are living in the lowlands of the Red River Delta, Mekong Delta, and the smaller delta pockets along the eastern seaboard. Despite the rapid growth of the cities in recent years and the

Coffee is one of the cash crops of the country, with farms concentrated in the Central Highlands. Members of the Ede minority, like this woman, are involved in coffee production.

massive influx of migrants, over 70 percent of Vietnam's population still lives in the rural areas—a high proportion compared with other countries in the region and developing nations elsewhere. Overall, more than half of Vietnam's entire population is engaged in agriculture, often as smallholders. The average size of Vietnam's smallholder farms in the lowlands is less than one hectare, and agriculture is very intensive. Despite its limited agricultural land, during the Doi Moi era Vietnam has become a major player in the world markets for rice (second global rice exporter in 2000) and coffee (second global coffee exporter in 2000), thereby subjecting itself to the vagaries of the global market.

With the continued reforms in the 1990s, farmers were allowed to buy and sell land (officially, they were granted long-term land use rights), and as a result social and economic differentiation is becoming increasingly manifest. Poor households, often lacking labor or knowledge and skills, become indebted because of a medical or natural calamity or lack of labor and must sell off their land, a challenge plaguing the many female-headed households in Vietnam. Many ethnic minority farmers in the Mekong Delta and the Central Highlands lack the skills to compete in the market and consequently lose their land, often because of indebtedness to loan sharks. The emphasis on cash crops creates economic opportunities but can make farmers more vulnerable. Coffee cultivation attracted hundreds of thousands of migrants from northern Vietnam to the Central Highlands, who cleared hundreds of thousands of hectares of forest to establish coffee gardens. But the drop in the price of coffee in the world market in the 1990s, especially the lower *robusta* quality grown in Vietnam, bankrupted thousands of smallholding coffee farmers, leading the government to develop a plan to convert one-third of the total coffee acreage in Vietnam.

Apart from large-scale and smallholder agriculture, other important economic activities in the rural areas are animal husbandry, fisheries, forestry, and handicrafts. Many farmers (i.e., the women) are raising pigs, cows, and poultry, for a variety of purposes but mostly to earn money in the local market. For farming households fish, especially sweetwater fish caught in rice fields, ponds, streams, and rivers, is a more important source of protein than meat. With the development of more powerful fishing boats and modern cooling and distribution systems, many marine fisheries have grown to commercial levels, catering to urban and international markets. Shrimp farming is a lucrative sideline to this trade.

Forestry is especially strong in the highlands, where most of the remaining forests are located. The forestry sector was slower to decentralize than the agricultural sector, partly because timber harvesting was—and is— more lucrative and partly because of the growing concern about the rapid rate of deforestation and concomitant degradation of land and other resources. These two considerations combined to slow down the allocation

Fishing is one of Vietnam's primary industries, and fish have traditionally provided a major source of protein in the Vietnamese diet. Fishing with beach seines, as seen here in May 2000 at Nam Dinh, dominated in the 1960s and 1970s but by 2000 was regarded as a side activity for farmers on the coast, while fishing from small boats has become more common.

of forest land to individual households or groups of households, as was done with agricultural land. In the context of the many foreign-funded forest protection and reforestation schemes, allocating the right to protect forest land for a fee and for certain limited harvesting rights is as far as the government wishes to go.

Handicrafts are an important source of income for many households, especially during slack seasons or through employment of otherwise unproductive labor, like the elderly. Handicrafts tend to be concentrated in craft villages that specialize in particular goods, like pottery (Bat Trang pottery village near Hanoi is famous; see chapter 6), basketry, carpentry, rattan and bamboo products, lacquer products, silk production and weaving, bronze casting, and paper and printing. In the 1990s, the export and general turnover in the handicraft sector has grown considerably, attracting more attention as a viable income-earner.

In the cities the industry and service sectors are quickly gaining ground, with annual two-digit growth rates. Vietnam's industrial exports have grown immensely since the 1980s, despite the Asian financial crisis of 1997. With its low GDP—somewhat more than $400 per capita, up from $200 in the 1980s—and consequent low wages, Vietnam is an attractive manufacturing base, especially for such capital-extensive and labor-intensive industries as the garment sector, which employs tens of thousands of young women and men from the countryside in factories in Ho Chi Minh City (formerly

The accelerated harvesting of wood has led to the denuding and shrinking of the country's forests, especially in the Central Highlands. These workers are in an Ede area in Dak Lak province, 2000.

Saigon), Hanoi, Bien Hoa, Can Tho, Vung Tau, Da Nang, and Hai Phong. The alleged abuses in the factories that produce for brand names like Nike have led to increased international scrutiny of the subcontracting system through which multinationals operate their production systems. Foreign and domestic investors tend to concentrate on the bigger cities that meet the logistical requirements of export production, and as a result the standard of living in these cities has risen dramatically since 1985. With the rising standard of living, these cities have diversified their economies, starting with their industrial base and their service sector, followed by their infrastructure and educational and health facilities. A new class of *nouveaux riches* and a new middle class display substantial wealth, considering it must have been accumulated in a relatively short period of time. The cities abound in cars and motorbikes, fancy houses and furnishings, fashionable clothes and personal gadgets like cell phones, and entertainment. More recently, people have been sending their children overseas to study.

In sharp contrast to this emerging upper and middle class stand the many people who are part of the so-called informal sector, the people who often bridge countryside and city. Every morning starting at two o'clock, women on bicycles bring flowers into Hanoi shops and markets from the surrounding villages, quietly chatting as they pedal along. And later in the morning other women in the open-air markets sell their flowers to middle-men who take the flowers to the shops. The informal sector can include almost anything—peddling food, newspapers, souvenirs, clothes, or cigarettes on the sidewalks or streets; selling fresh produce like vegetables, fruit, and flowers; picking up garbage and seeking out what can be profitably recycled; providing services ranging from transport on motorbikes and bicycle repairs to casual labor and sex. Informal work is not always low paid or badly regarded; for instance, many teachers and university professors conduct classes after hours for extra money. The distinctive feature of this sector is that it is not formally organized and that it escapes formal and official regulation. It can be very visible out on the street—as any visitor from a Western country can see—but it is not very visible to an administrative gaze. For many people, especially women, the informal sector provides a relatively secure, convenient, and solid income while allowing them to preserve their autonomy. Research into the informal sector has revealed that women often value the fact that they control their own time and thus can combine informal work with child care more easily than formal employment would allow.

Children are another ubiquitous sight in Vietnam's streets, a sure sign that the population is growing fast. Their presence outside is also a sign that the education system is overloaded, as many schools operate in shifts to accommodate all the students. Although many in the West think of Vietnam as a country tainted by war, most Vietnamese were born after 1975. They know about the French and American wars only from hearsay, from

A woman on her way to market in the Mekong Delta, one of the richest agricultural regions of the country for such crops as rice, coconuts, fruit, and sugarcane.

stories told by adults, or as history that they learn from books and films. Much like young people in North America and Europe in the 1960s who were not much interested in looking back at World War II, Vietnam's young people pursue interests that differ sharply from those of their parents. In a country that values formal education and prides itself on a high literacy rate (though the official figures of 85 percent may be a bit inflated), young people's first priority is to succeed at school. Students study hard and take extra classes in order to pass the entrance exams for the universities of their choice. For them and their parents, admission to a good university is a tangible sign of social success and a passport to a future career. Given the amount of time and money it takes to succeed in the ever more commercialized educational sector, with paid extra classes, fees, and private schools, the number of dropouts is considerable,[12] and there is a sharp social differentiation, with well-to-do urban citizens having a marked advantage. The second priority for contemporary Vietnamese youth is having fun, and young people complain about the lack of entertainment, though this is slowly changing in the big cities. Teenagers can be seen hanging out on the streets, like their Euro-American counterparts, experimenting and taking risks. Many experiment with sex, a situation that has led to one of the world's highest abortion rates for unmarried women,[13] and according to regular reports in the Vietnamese press, some experiment with drugs, a growing problem in high schools, colleges, and universities.

To limit population growth and be able to provide higher-quality services to fewer people, Vietnam implemented a rigorous birth control program in the 1990s, putting pressure on parents through a system of positive stimuli and fines to limit their number of children to two. Although this program has been praised by the United Nations Population Fund as effective in curtailing the population growth on a national scale, it has not been as effective in enhancing the reproductive rights of individual women. Partly as a consequence of postwar demographics, women are still a majority in Vietnam, rendering their position more precarious. Despite the influence of patriarchal Confucian morals, however, many observers state that gender relations in Vietnam resemble those of Southeast Asia rather than China; women are not as overtly subservient as in China and play a pivotal role in the household and in the household economy, being the ones who hold the purse strings. In general, women have comparatively good educational opportunities and are not formally barred from particular professions; in addition, the overall economic improvement during Doi Moi has created better work conditions and more opportunities for employment for many women, though the proportion of women in leadership positions is still very low.[14]

Despite progressive legislation and the activities of organizations like the Vietnam Women's Union and the National Commission for the Advancement of Women, several issues surfaced in the late 1990s that seem to indicate a downward trend for women, though perhaps they have only become more visible. I will mention two. Since the late 1990s it has become apparent that domestic violence persists. The incidence of wife beating remains high and is one of the major causes of divorce.[15] Another issue is ongoing trafficking in girls and women, often across borders. Girls and women, tricked by promises of employment or marriage, tend to end up as sex workers in brothels in Cambodia or Thailand or find themselves married to older men in Taiwan or China and reduced to the status of domestic servants, almost like slaves.[16] Measures are being taken by the Vietnamese authorities and nongovernmental organizations to counter these practices.

■ Conclusion

VIETNAM, A COUNTRY THAT STRUGGLES with many of the same challenges that face other countries today, including drugs, generation gaps, and fears of globalization, has been shaped by myriad movements in both space and time, ones involving the body, the mind, and the spirit. At the end of the twentieth century, the international image of Vietnam was colored by just a few of these journeys: the journey of American soldiers to Vietnam to fight against perceived Communist threats to freedom emanating from China and the Soviet Union, the hasty departure of these American soldiers, and the exodus of the refugees known as boat people. Although this dominant image is shaped by important contemporary events, it is far from hegemonic; indeed, when judged against the thousands of years of Vietnamese history, against the relations and movements that have been occurring for millennia, these events are but a tiny mark on Vietnam's journey through time.

A Hmong village in the far north of Vietnam, surrounded by terraced fields, 1990s. A labor-intensive enterprise in any circumstances, wet-rice agriculture on high mountain land is particularly challenging.

VIETNAM'S

ETHNIC MOSAIC

Frank Proschan

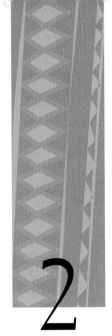

AT FIRST GLANCE, Vietnam's ethnic composition seems relatively simple: ethnic minorities make up only a small part of the nation's population, 13 percent (unlike its neighbor Laos, where minorities represent more than half of the population), and they inhabit primarily the remote mountainous regions of the country. However, the relatively small proportion of minorities in the overall national population belies what is in fact a very complicated ethnoscape. The highlands, where most minority groups dwell, are typically far from urban and industrial centers, population density is lower, communications and transportation are less developed, and standards of living are lower than in the densely populated plains and deltas inhabited by the Kinh (Viet) majority. Highland minorities also share in certain cultural traditions that differ from those of their lowland compatriots: most groups reside in stilt houses rather than earthen houses, they often consume as a staple glutinous rice or maize grown on dry hillside swiddens rather than ordinary rice grown in irrigated paddies, and they share patterns of kinship and marriage that distinguish them from the Kinh. Yet among the highland minorities there is also substantial cultural diversity, and environmental and economic conditions differ dramatically from place to place, even within a single locale. While generalizations are useful when seeking to understand Vietnam's ethnic mosaic, we must not lose sight of particularities.

For official and administrative purposes, Vietnamese ethnologists have classified the minorities into fifty-three groups (plus the majority Kinh), distinguished along cultural and linguistic lines.[1] Some of these minority groups, such as the Tay, Thai, Muong, and Khmer, number a million or more, while the smallest groups, such as the Brau, Rmam, and Odu, number between three and four hundred (1999 census). Among the ethnicities, some—for instance, the Muong and Tay—are relatively acculturated to the dominant culture of the Kinh, and their levels of education and literacy, standard of living, and access to government services are comparable to those of rural Kinh. Other ethnicities, especially the Tibeto-Burman and Hmong-Yao groups living in the highest mountains of the north, share much less in the national culture and are distinguished from the majority more sharply in terms of every socioeconomic and cultural indicator, including nutrition, education, literacy, health care, knowledge of the national language, and life expectancy.

Unlike ethnic minorities in some other parts of the world, those within Vietnam do not live in mutually exclusive, monoethnic territories. Rather, villages of different ethnic and linguistic groups are interspersed in most of the highlands, and it is not unusual to find a single commune with villages of two, three, or four different ethnic groups. Similarly, virtually none of the mountainous districts is home to a single ethnic group, and several provinces have more than a dozen distinct ethnicities within their borders. A particularly important aspect of Vietnam's ethnoscape, both historically and politically, is that more than half of its ethnicities—including all of the largest groups—also have members living in the neighboring countries of Cambodia, Laos, and China and as far afield as Thailand and Burma. For some ethnicities, the communities within Vietnam were established in recent

A young Red Yao woman in the north of Vietnam strikes an insouciant pose for a portrait photograph, early or mid–twentieth century.

centuries, leaving sister communities behind in the homeland; other ethnicities have lived for millennia where they currently reside. National boundaries have emerged with regard to geophysical features rather than ethnographic or linguistic characteristics.

Three lowland ethnicities merit special consideration because of their distinctive histories: the Hoa, Khmer, and Cham. The Hoa, or Sino-Vietnamese, are primarily urbanites, the descendants of immigrants who came to Vietnam as early as the fifteenth century; a large migration occurred in the nineteenth and early twentieth centuries from various regions of

A Khmer actor in My Tu district, Soc Trang province, in the Mekong Delta prepares for a *du ke* performance to celebrate the Khmer New Year in April 2001. The local troupe enacts the story of Prince Rama's epic war on the demon king, a tale well known and much performed throughout Southeast Asia.

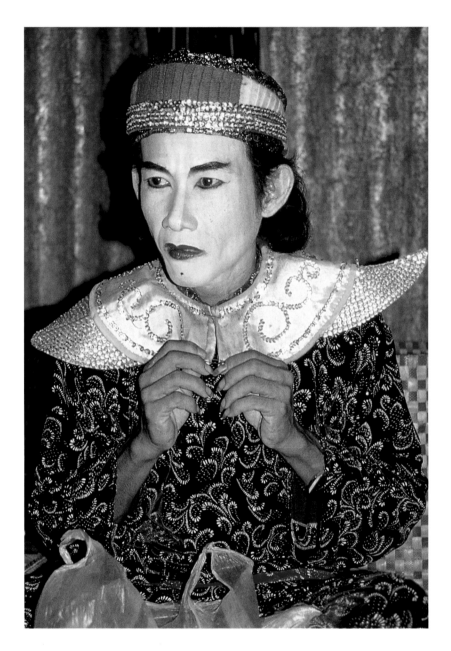

southern China. Today most reside in and around Ho Chi Minh City (formerly Saigon), but they are found in every large city and there are also some rural centers of Hoa population. The Khmer in the Mekong Delta share a language and culture with their neighbors in Cambodia. International political events, especially in the first decades following reunification in 1975, have greatly affected the status and conditions of both the

A woman of the Cham ethnicity, wearing a characteristic long smock, carries rice stalks home from the field in the vicinity of Phan Rang, Ninh Thuan province, 1974.

Khmer and the Hoa. The Cham are heirs of an ancient civilization that once extended throughout central and southern Vietnam; their language is in the Austronesian family, linking them to their neighbors throughout Indonesia, Malaysia, and the Philippines.

Underlying all considerations of ethnicity in Vietnam is the fundamental vision of the nation as multiethnic. First enunciated in policies of the Indochinese Communist Party in the 1930s, the principle was embodied in the 1946 Constitution of the Democratic Republic of Vietnam, which declared, "Vietnam is a Democratic Republic. All power in the country belongs to the people of Vietnam [nhan dan Viet Nam] without distinction of race [giong noi], sex, wealth, class, or religion." This has been restated in successive constitutions and laws, most recently in the 1992 Constitution: "The Socialist Republic of Vietnam state is a unified state of the ethnicities [cac dan toc] who live on Vietnamese territory. It implements the policy of equality, solidarity, and mutual assistance among all ethnicities and strictly forbids all discriminatory and divisive behavior among ethnicities."[2] However, although the principle of equality among ethnicities is firmly established in law, some socioeconomic inequities persist. Indeed, the situation became acute in the early renovation period after 1986, when ethnic

A Yao ritual master (right) ties a surrogate corpse of rice straw and banana leaves to two bamboo poles, simulating a funeral bier. The Yao hold two funerals, one to inter the body and another, some time later, to send the soul to the ancestors.

minorities often found themselves less able than the majority Kinh to take advantage of new economic opportunities and when some government services were restructured to reflect the nation's new economic direction.

▪ Historical Contacts and Exchanges

THE SITUATION OF ETHNIC MINORITIES in Vietnam today reflects long-standing historical relations between highlanders and lowlanders, minorities and the majority, the peripheries and the center. Events of the French colonial period and revolutionary era, along with decades of war, have certainly had their own influences, but in many ways attitudes toward ethnic minorities and relations forged centuries ago have remained remarkably persistent until the present day, even among many Kinh who are politically, intellectually, and ethically committed to multiethnic equality and cultural diversity. In its more benign forms, this can be a kind of paternalism that motivates efforts to assist those perceived as less fortunate or less sophisticated. In part this attitude reflects older Confucian conceptions. In the Confucian view, the state was a well-ordered kingdom, with the Son of Heaven at its center, his civilized subjects around

The Mon-Khmer populations of the Central Highlands have evolved distinctive architectural styles. Communal houses of the Bahnar, like this example from Lang Kon Ktu, Kon Tum township, in 2001, have tall, imposing roofs.

him, and the uncivilized "barbarians" on the margins of the kingdom. The perception that the Kinh are more advanced culturally, intellectually, economically, and politically than their minority neighbors was also reinforced by colonial and postcolonial theories of social evolution. Even more recently, many international development efforts that presuppose a unidirectional model of socioeconomic "progress" further reinforce such attitudes.

Cultural contact and interethnic exchange have marked Vietnam's cultural history since its earliest days. Regular ritual exchanges between highlanders and lowlanders existed in the premodern period. Ancient chronicles describe court ceremonies in which highland "tribes" periodically brought forest products such as honey and beeswax, eaglewood and benjamin, rhinoceros horns and elephant tusks, tiger skins and bear gall bladders, to the lowland courts and ritually exchanged them for goods such as textiles, housewares, other necessities, and luxury items. In 1434, for instance, the Thai Phouan of what is now Xiang Khouang, Laos, "sent a delegation [to the Le dynasty court at Thang Long-Hanoi] to offer local products. The King gave them in exchange two gowns embroidered with gold thread and some pieces of silk." The next year, the Thai Phouan again "offered elephant tusks, rhinoceros horns, silver, and fabric. . . . The King greeted them, giving their chief a coat embroidered in gold thread and compensating their envoys with silks, according to their rank."[3] Such ceremonies also took place in the nineteenth century at the Nguyen dynasty capital of Hue with the Thai, Austroasiatic, and Hmong-Yao minorities of the northwest and Truong Son (the Annam Cordillera) and especially with two shaman-chiefs of the Giarai of the Central Highlands, Thuy Xa (the King of Water) and Hoa Xa (the King of Fire). In these rituals, the highland minorities offered tribute and acknowledged the suzerainty of the Viet emperors and their superior temporal authority. In turn, the lowland court acknowledged the historical precedence of the highland minorities and their greater spiritual authority vis-à-vis the guardian spirits of the land. Anthropologist Nghiem Tham, describing the Giarai chiefs' tribute to the Hue court, points out, "Although the value of the gifts of the Giarai chiefs is inconsequential . . . these meager gifts have a special importance. All of the two chiefs' possessions had supernatural power, consequently these gifts were considered to have the special power of the spirits of the jungle and the mountains."[4] Within the symbolic sphere, these rituals represented the trade relations that constituted the primary interactions between majority and minority groups (when they were not engaged in the not-infrequent warfare, "banditry," or rebellion that otherwise held sway).

These tribute rituals, whether with the highland minorities or with neighboring kingdoms of the Thai, Cham, or Khmer peoples, also allowed the Vietnamese emperors to enhance their own prestige through the accumulation of vassal neighbors, replicating on a smaller scale the tributary relations between the Vietnamese and the Chinese. These rituals expressed the Vietnamese conception of a civilizing mission toward their neighbors on the peripheries of the Confucian state. As Emperor Minh Mang decreed in 1834, the Giarai chief of Thuy Xa and his people "are inquisitive and there is no reason they cannot be transformed. According to the gods we need to bring civilization to the barbarians, and we should teach them our rites and customs; even the savage can be taught to wear clothes. Thus their nation can submit tribute and understand the proper relations of the king and his subjects."[5]

In the premodern Vietnamese states, highland minorities generally lived outside the close purview of state power. Generally responsible for managing their own affairs, they might host a mandarin delegated by the Kinh

A silk ikat *mi* skirt, like this one from Quy Chau district, Nghe An province, is the most important and precious gift that a Thai bride receives from her parents-in-law. According to Thai custom, skirts are passed from mother-in-law to daughter-in-law and should not be sold. *Mi* skirts are worn during festivals and at the funerals of parents-in-law; daughters-in-law wear their *mi* skirts as an expression of gratitude for past kindness.

suzerain as their nominal administrator. Although they were sometimes subject to taxation and in some cases could be conscripted into armies, they were generally not considered full subjects and were not bound by the systematic legal codes of the Le and Nguyen dynasties.[6]

As noted above, trade has constituted the most common and frequent form of interethnic contact. Kinh traders with an entrepreneurial spirit

Flower Hmong women in the Bac Ha market in Lao Cai province do a brisk trade in batik-patterned skirts. Scraps of trade cloth and ribbon trim are combined with strips of batik to make infinitely varied combinations of pattern.

would travel to the remote areas bringing such staples as salt and such commercial goods as textiles and housewares. In return highland minorities provided natural resources extracted from the forests or precious metals and gems taken from the streams and rivers. Among the minorities themselves, there was also trade in goods, with some ethnicities specializing in bamboo and rattan crafts, while others produced metalware or textiles, each group trading its goods for those of their neighbors. In the northwest, for instance, the Thai were renowned for textiles, their Hmong neighbors for jewelry and silverwork, and the Khmu for bamboo baskets and rattan-ware. Few of the produced goods of the highland ethnicities were traded out of the mountains, but raw materials were. These long-standing patterns of interethnic trading continue today, although mass-produced goods such as plastic baskets have replaced those woven of bamboo and rattan, and commercially milled cloth with chemical dyes supplants handwoven fabric colored with natural dyes. The arrival of industrially produced goods also threatens to disrupt traditional patterns of interethnic commerce, since it is often lowland Kinh traders who have greater access to capital and can more easily establish a shop or stall than the highland consumers.

Exchanges of material culture and other traditions at the local level always reflected larger patterns of cultural contact, migration histories, and socioeconomic interactions. In some regions, diverse groups lived side by side for centuries, developing long-term relations of cultural interdepend-

Once hunted, elephants have been domesticated and are set to various tasks, such as hauling lumber for this man of the Mnong (Nong) ethnicity in Dak Lak province, 1997.

ence. For the Tay in the northeast, for instance, who have resided in the area since ancient times, bilingualism in their own language and in Vietnamese has long been the case, and elements of material culture have been exchanged over the centuries. Other groups that have arrived more recently within Vietnamese territory have had less extensive cultural contact with the Kinh majority. There were few if any Hmong settlements within Vietnam prior to 1800, and those Hmong who immigrated since have settled in the highest mountains, remote from Kinh settlements. Few Hmong men and even fewer women have had access to education, and literacy in the national language is low, limiting the opportunities for cultural interchange and for civic participation.

Interethnic exchanges, whether commercial or cultural, have depended on a high degree of multilingualism in areas where minorities are numerous. In the northwest, for instance, members of smaller groups such as the Khmu or Khang will speak their mother language at home and in the field, switching to Thai as a market language when they venture out of the village for trade, and using the national language, Vietnamese, for schooling and governmental affairs. In the Central Highlands, it is Ede rather than Thai that serves as the lingua franca or market language for smaller groups. It is not unusual for highland ethnicities to speak three, four, or even a half dozen languages, and some of the Kinh who have taken up residence in minority areas have also taken up the local languages.

Ede men from Buon Ky, Buon Ma Thuot township, Dak Lak province, construct the roof of a traditional longhouse on the grounds of the Vietnam Museum of Ethnology in 2000.

■ Shared Cultural Traits

THE HIGHLAND ETHNIC MINORITIES of Vietnam are heirs to ancient cultural traditions, many of which are shared across ethnic and linguistic boundaries. Whether derived from a common source or developed over centuries of cultural exchange, these shared cultural traits are often markedly different from those of the majority Kinh. Others are shared by both highlanders and lowlanders, both ancient populations and recent immigrants, both large groups and small. A visitor to a highland village would immediately recognize that the architecture, use of space, clothing, and material culture may be strikingly different from those in a Kinh village. Kinh families usually build houses directly on the ground, typically with wooden, earthen, or brick walls and tile or metal roofs. Although some ethnic minorities, including the Cham, Hoa, Hmong, and the smaller Tibeto-Burman groups, also build houses on the ground, for most ethnic minorities stilt houses are the rule, raised from the ground on columns. Such houses are ideally suited to the slopes of hills and mountains where villages are situated; with columns of different heights, following the contours of the land, the bamboo or plank floor that they support can be level. Stilt houses are also typical among the Kinh and Khmer in the

Ede men seated on the porch of a longhouse in Ma Wal village, Dak Lak province, sometime between 1925 and 1934. The longhouse is 492 feet long.

Mekong Delta, where frequent floods make it advantageous to live above the ground. For stilt houses, walls may be plaited from bamboo and roofs made from elephant grass, although many groups favor wooden walls and tile roofs. Where houses in a Kinh village will often be arranged in a rectilinear grid, those in a highland minority village will usually be situated according to the geographic setting—either perched along a mountain ridge or arrayed along the foot of a mountain or alongside a stream.

For many ethnicities, the prevalent mode of agriculture is not irrigated paddy fields but hillside swiddens. Some groups, such as the Khmer, Cham, Thai, and Tay, do practice wet-rice cultivation, either rain-fed or irrigated with complex systems of canals and waterworks, and some groups such as the Yao in certain localities have constructed elaborate terraced fields. But for most highlanders, the system of swiddening or shifting agriculture (also known as slash-and-burn agriculture) is most common. In rotational swidden systems such as those of the Mon-Khmer groups, villagers cultivate a number of fields near the home village, using one field for a year or two and then allowing it to have an extended fallow period while another field is cultivated. Over a period of twelve or fifteen years, the forest regrows and nutrients are stored in the biomass. When the time comes to reuse the field, the overgrowth is cut and burned, freeing the nutrients in the biomass so they can fertilize the crops. Such a system is environmentally sustainable unless population pressures constrain the amount of land available and villagers are compelled either to reuse the same field for too many years in succession or to return to a field too quickly, before the forest has regenerated. Another system of swiddening, typical of the Hmong and some other northern groups, is called pioneering swiddening. Here, land is cleared and the biomass burned, but the same field is used for as long as ten or more years, until all the nutrients are depleted. In contrast to the system of extended-fallow or long rotation, where villages may remain in place for decades, in the pioneering systems it is often necessary for an entire village to relocate when the fields have been depleted; with increasing population there is of course less and less land available for such cultivation.

The foodways of highlanders typically center on the staple of glutinous rice (sticky rice); for the Hmong and some others, maize is the staple food. Ethnobotanists are coming to believe that rice may have first been cultivated in dry swidden fields, and it is along the Vietnamese-Chinese borderland that they find the greatest genetic variation among rice plants, suggesting that this may have been the locale in which rice was first domesticated. Some highland villagers will grow as many as ten varieties of rice, each suited to certain environmental conditions, so that if the weather is bad or the crops are infested with pests, the likelihood is higher that at least some varieties will thrive. Vegetables and herbs are cultivated in house gardens or in the swidden fields alongside rice; these include a huge assortment of leafy greens such as water spinach, sweet potato vines, and the young leaves and flowers of pumpkins and gourds. Also very popular are garlic and shallots, herbs of many sorts, and spices such as capsicum peppers. Perhaps the oldest foods in the diet of highland minorities are root crops including yams and taro, as well as various kinds of cucurbits (pumpkins, gourds, and melons); these have a place in the daily diet and an even more important place in ritual life.

A Vietnamese Muslim engagement ceremony in the Al Rahim Mosque of Ho Chi Minh City (formerly Saigon), mid-1990s. These third-generation Vietnamese Muslims prepare for a wedding by carrying covered engagement boxes in the same manner in which (symbolic) gifts are presented at a Kinh engagement.

■ Cultural Challenges

AT THE BEGINNING OF THE TWENTY-FIRST CENTURY, Vietnam's ethnicities—whether minority or majority—increasingly face challenges to time-tested traditional modes of understanding and living. With populations continuing to grow in size, agricultural practices that were sustainable for centuries are now no longer viable, and villagers are faced with the challenge of finding alternatives that can provide for their needs in coming decades. In some locales this means the cultivation of cash crops such as tobacco and coffee and medicinal and industrial trees, but in others significant transportation and economic barriers hinder the development of market crops. Natural resources such as rattan that might allow the development of local handicraft industries are in increasingly short supply, even threatening the rich material-culture traditions of many ethnic groups. Mass-produced goods from plasticware to cloth are supplanting handcrafted goods, and the knowledge of how to produce them risks disappearance. Similarly, the unending influx of popular culture—whether domestic or foreign—over the radio waves and now through television threatens to overwhelm the ancient cultural traditions that give meaning to people's lives.

Red Yao children huddle under a store-bought umbrella. The little boy on the right clasps a plastic fountain pen, possibly a gift from a tourist. Sapa, Lao Cai province, 2001.

Vietnamese cultural policy is guided by the vision of building "an advanced Vietnamese culture deeply imbued with national identity," a culture that draws strength and vitality from the diversity of its ethnic and regional traditions. The shared goal of cultural institutions and offices is "to make full use of and bring into play the characteristic features and values of the cultures and arts of all ethnic groups in the country; and to forge unity in the diversity and abundance of Vietnamese culture."[7] The question that urgently confronts Vietnam's diverse communities today, therefore, is whether the inevitable processes of dynamic cultural change will be guided by the aspirations and wishes of culture-bearers themselves or whether they will be determined by outside forces. When we speak of these impending cultural changes—whether we are talking about minority languages, regional dialects of the national language, local cuisines and foodways, ethnic minority musics, religious beliefs and practices, or countless other cultural traditions that belong to one or another subgroup within Vietnam—the question becomes, "Who will determine the directions that cultural changes take in the coming years?" The challenge is to discover means by which communities can be effectively empowered to support and sustain their own traditions and to bring them to larger audiences throughout the nation and throughout the world. The continued vitality of those traditions depends on collaboration between local people and outsiders, but cultural mastery must remain with the culture-bearers who are their stewards and protectors if Vietnam's diverse local communities and ethnicities are to maintain their unique cultures in the face of globalization and international cultural influences.

These brightly glazed figurines represent Di Lac, a manifestation of the Buddha, whose happy smile is seen as bestowing good fortune. In preparation for the new year, people purchase new fittings and decorations for their family ancestral altars. These statues were part of the display spilling from shops to pavement along Hang Quat Street in Hanoi before Tet 2001.

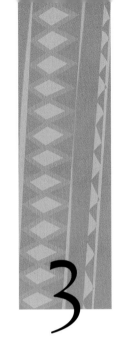

TET HOLIDAYS:

ANCESTRAL VISITS AND

SPRING JOURNEYS

Nguyen Van Huy

THE KINH (VIET) MAJORITY POPULATION in Vietnam have two new year celebrations, one based on the solar calendar and one on the lunar. The official calendar issued by the government includes both solar and lunar dates. The formal organization of time that regulates daily activities and the operation of government agencies, schools, and major enterprises has long been organized in accord with the solar calendar. However, activities associated with deep cultural traditions, such as festivals and the death anniversaries of ancestors, follow the lunar calendar. Thus, the Kinh welcome the solar new year with people all over the globe. In Vietnam, this is an official holiday and all government offices are closed. But the lunar new year, or Tet, is even more important as the emotionally significant end of the old year and beginning of the new. Each person, each family, and Vietnamese society as a whole approach the new year as a time of fresh aspiration and hope. During the Tet holidays people have four days off from work, from the thirtieth day of the twelfth lunar month through the third day of the new year. Although these four days constitute the official holiday, everybody begins to prepare for Tet a full month beforehand and continues to celebrate the new year for half a month after Tet. To that extent, Tet has deep cultural and spiritual significance in the life of the people of Vietnam.

■ Shopping

IF THE SOLAR NEW YEAR CAN BE CONSIDERED the government's Tet, the lunar new year is considered the family's Tet, the occasion for family members and relatives, the lineage and the community, to gather. Each family prepares offerings to worship ancestors and gifts for grandparents and parents as well as for respected members of the husband's and wife's families. Offerings on the ancestral altar usually include wine, tea, cigarettes, *mut tet*—candied fruits and nuts—and other sweets, flowers, and a plate of five kinds of fruits. Gifts for old people include such things as wine, tea, cigarettes, sweets, and fruits. In order to *di Tet*, to visit relatives and offer gifts, people busily shop for gifts. According to tradition, visits are made and gifts distributed during the week before Tet; on the first day of the new year itself, people simply say, "Happy New Year, [wishing you] longevity and happiness," but they do not give presents.

About ten to fifteen days before Tet many shops begin to feature Tet products. Vendors set their wares on the pavement under red banners declaring "Tet Shop," "Selling Tet Products," or "Happy New Year." In some commercial districts, the entire surface of the street is covered with displays of Tet goods and decorated with red banners. Square or hexagonal cardboard candy boxes bearing the legend "Happy New Year" are everywhere. Nearly every family will have at least one of these on its ancestral altar, filled with sweets as a wish for good luck. In Hanoi, Hang Dieu Street is famous for traditional sweets such as candied lotus seeds, coconut, and ginger. The stalls along Hang Buom and Hang Ngang Streets are fairly bursting with packaged cookies and candies, some of them imported. Some transactions are

Sweets signify an auspicious start for the new year and are a popular gift item, usually placed first on the ancestral altar. The shops on Hang Dieu Street in Hanoi are renowned for traditional candied fruits and seeds *(mut Tet)*, while the stalls along Hang Buom Street feature commercially packaged cookies, candy, and chocolates, some of them imported.

completed from the backs of motorbikes as busy city people accomplish their holiday errands on the way to and from work.

Hang ma—votive products—go on sale very early so that families will be prepared to send off the Kitchen God on the twenty-third day of the last month of the old year. Hang Ma Street, where the votives are sold, is famous in Hanoi. A few years ago some *hang ma* was also manufactured on that street, but now nearly all votive goods are transported from craft villages around Hanoi such as Dong Ho, Thuong Tin, and Phu Xuyen. Shops in Hang Ma Street are the busy hub of this industry where the artisans bring their finished products and buy supplies. Small-scale traders come to Hang Ma Street and carry goods back to their villages in the baskets of their bicycles or motorbikes. Large-scale traders buy goods on Hang Ma Street and distribute them to local traders throughout the north.

In anticipation of the new year, people come to Hang Ma Street to buy specially prepared paper hats, gowns, and boots and gold paper carp to burn as offerings for the Kitchen God and a red robe, hat, and boots for the god of the new year to burn at midnight on New Year's Eve. On these occasions they will also burn votive paper money. On Hang Ma Street people also buy decorations for their homes and ancestral altars. Small gold and silver trees and branches made of shiny foil are for the ancestral altar or are placed on the offering tray taken to a Mother Goddess temple (see chapter 13). Lanterns shaped like melons and strings of gold plastic coins and ingots

Along Hanoi's Hang Ma Street, shoppers contemplate the purchase of holiday decorations (mostly made in China) for their homes before Tet 2001. The coins and gold ingots are wishes for prosperity. The man holds two packets of red envelopes for dispensing New Year gifts of cash.

are hung in the house as a wish for prosperity and good fortune. Vendors also sell small red and gold envelopes that hold cash for children when they bring new year greetings to their elders. During the Tet holidays Hang Ma Street is full of people. In other parts of the city, one sees women vendors carrying votive goods in baskets suspended from their carry poles.

During the Tet season, some shops specialize in calendars. These are sold in a great variety of styles, and they are avidly purchased in anticipation of Tet even if the solar new year has already passed. Calendars are hung in the house not only to mark time but as ornaments that reflect the taste and style of family members. In the 1990s calendars with pictures of young girls sold well, but by 2000 people preferred calendars picturing landscapes, trees, or beautiful architecture. Although many people choose calendars with six or twelve pages, showing an entire month, others still like calendar blocks with a page for each passing day. The red backing on the calendar blocks contributes to happiness, warmth, and hope for the family on the first day of the new year.

The custom of hanging a new calendar during Tet has almost completely replaced the older custom of hanging paired couplets in Chinese

This old woman is a vendor of new year calendars, most in the auspicious color red. Calendars are displayed not only to mark time but also for their decorative value.

calligraphy and seems to have totally eclipsed the custom of putting up fresh woodblock prints depicting auspicious themes such as leaping carp or five-colored fruit. Woodblock prints by master artisans in Dong Ho village or in the Hang Trong tradition of Hanoi, where the artisan fills in the black outline with watercolors, are now valued as a specialized handicraft and folk art form rather than a new year decoration.

Fifty years ago, couplets painted in Chinese calligraphy on red paper would have been hung in nearly every house. Some Hanoi residents, especially the old people, still enjoy seeing, buying, and hanging couplets in their homes. In the last week of the old year, therefore, groups of calligraphers gather at the corner of Ba Trieu and Tran Hung Dao Streets and prepare inscriptions in Chinese or Vietnamese. As in the past, couplets are written on red paper with black ink, and the purchasers choose sentiments that reflect their hopes and aspirations.

This woodblock print is a playful representation of the character *phuc*, signifying happiness and good fortune. The print, made in 2000, is in the Hang Trong style, the black outline supplied by woodblock and the colors on the dragon and unicorn skillfully applied with a paintbrush.

Food shops specializing in *chung* cake appear as Tet draws near. It is described in an ancient couplet as an essential element of the new year:

Rich meats, salty onions, red couplets
Neu *tree, firecracker, and* chung *cake.*

Chung cake has always been essential to Tet, something that every family places on its ancestral altar. Square *chung* cake wrapped in large *dong* leaves is one popular form, both in Hanoi and throughout the country. In some places, however, people make cylindrical cakes called Tet cakes.

Until the mid-1980s, and especially before the reopening of the market, making *chung* cake was a long and arduous household task. It was necessary to accumulate and prepare a great quantity of sticky rice, green bean, meat, *dong* leaves, and string to make *chung* cakes for the ancestral altar and for the entire family, and so family members took turns lining up patiently to buy rationed goods. The family then gathered from the twenty-seventh or twenty-eighth day of the old year to make the cakes, so they would have enough to put on the altar on Tet Eve and to eat during the first days of the new year. If the family was small, they asked friends, relatives, or neighbors to help them make *chung* cakes or to share the cooker with them. People boiled the cakes for ten to twelve hours over fires fueled by charcoal or firewood and later in electric pressure cookers from Russia. Children liked to play around the hearth as they looked after the boiling cakes. Although wrapping and boiling the cakes was a joy for small children, it was a difficult and tedious task for their parents and older brothers and sisters, who had to do everything from scratch. By the 1990s, however, economic development had brought an improvement in the general standard of living, and many families in Hanoi gave up the habit of making their own *chung* cakes. Today they buy cakes at shops or order them in advance, liberating women in particular, who did most of this hard work. So although there are *chung* cakes on the altars of city families, they are not the product of family effort, and chil-

This streetside calligrapher writes matched couplets of auspicious sayings to be hung in the home as a good wish for the new year. Although it is now more common for people to buy commercially printed calendars than to hang hand-painted couplets, several calligraphers were hard at work on Hanoi sidewalks before Tet in 2001.

Banh chung, boiled, filled rice cakes, are an essential element of a Tet meal. Wrapped in broad leaves to make a square green package, the *banh chung* symbolizes earth. While the production of *banh chung* was once a time-consuming household task, most families now buy their holiday supply from stalls like these.

dren no longer know the joy, much less the traditional technique, of wrapping and boiling *chung* cakes.

The tasks of shopping and preparing for Tet are performed primarily by mothers and wives, who buy goods little by little when they have free time, on the weekends or after work. They do not have to wait in line as before. Today, goods, foods, and candies are abundant. In these much-changed times, stories of waiting in line before Tet and buying controlled goods have become the stuff of family legends. By the afternoon of the thirtieth day, everything is ready for the last ritual of the year and the meal to bid farewell to the old year.

■ Going to the Flower Market

NO ONE KNOWS WHEN HANOI PEOPLE began to bring flowering branches and small trees into their homes during the Tet holidays. Historical documents tell us that villages near Thang Long (the old name for Hanoi) have planted flowers specifically for Tet since the fourteenth and fifteenth centuries. Each village specialized in a particular kind of flower or plant. For example, Nhat Tan, Nghi Tam, and Quang Ba villages were famous for their peach flowers. Village gardeners are highly skilled and

A prospective buyer examines flowering peach trees in a new year flower market in February 1929. Peach blossoms have long been a popular new year decoration in the north of Vietnam; yellow plum flowers are favored in the south.

know how to make the peach flowers blossom on time, no matter what the weather. Recently, many other villages around Hanoi have begun to specialize in flowering plants. Nghi Tam village plants mandarin orange bushes. Peach blossoms, mandarin orange trees, and white plum blossoms are all symbols of spring in Hanoi, while in Ho Chi Minh City (formerly Saigon) spring is symbolized by yellow plum blossoms.

Although Hanoi residents are fond of flowers, not all families have fresh flowers in their homes on ordinary days. During Tet, however, flowers can be found on the altar and in the living room of every house. The favorites are peach branches and small potted mandarin trees. People flock to the flower market—especially men, for the master of the house likes to show his taste to visitors through his careful choice of plants. People go to the market not only to buy flowers but also to enjoy flowers and see flower buyers. In the past, the flower market was concentrated in Hang Luoc Street, and during the days before Tet both the sidewalk and the street itself became a flower forest as nearly everyone in Hanoi came here to buy and sell flowers. This created a traffic problem, so the government has recently opened several new areas for buying and selling flowers, including Phan Dinh Phung, Phan Chu Trinh, Tran Hung Dao, and

Mandarin orange trees are on sale in a new year flower market in the old quarter of Hanoi on the day before Tet 2001. According to one vendor, a good orange tree must have a full round shape and the leaves must be green; there should be many flowers, fruits, and buds and three branches at the base.

Giang Vo Streets. Giang Vo Street specializes in mandarin orange trees, Cau Moi market has every kind of flower, while Nhat Tan, Nghi Tam, Quang Ba, Buoi, and Quoc Tu Giam are filled with flowering peach and mandarin orange trees.

Not all of these vendors are gardeners or professional vendors. Most are people from around Hanoi and neighboring provinces who buy flowers in their home villages and bring them to Hanoi to sell in the streets in order to earn extra money for their families in their spare time. They try to sell all their stock on the last afternoon of the year so they can take the train or bus home for Tet Eve.

Professional gardeners typically sell flowers from their own nurseries. Hanoi people like to go to these garden villages to buy flowering peach trees, mandarin orange trees, and flowers. Young people consider this an occasion to share with each other their pleasure in seeing the beauty of flowers and the constant parade of other buyers. They compare observations regarding the beauty of the flowers this year and in years gone by. By going to the villages, city dwellers can buy fresh flowers inexpensively; they can also talk to the planters about caring for the flowers at home so that they will blossom on time. More demanding people may make a long-term arrangement with the planter so that after Tet they can bring their expensive, well-decorated trees back to the garden and have the gardener take

Flowering peach trees are brought into Hanoi from farms just outside the city and from more distant places. After Tet some of these trees will be returned to the tree farm to be tended until they are reclaimed before next year's celebration.

care of them until the next year, when they will come to the village and retrieve the trees.

The buyers carry flowers home by every means imaginable—bicycle, cyclo, car, motorbike, and small truck. The constant parade of vehicles loaded high with flowering peach trees or mandarin orange bushes is a joyful sight, and the buyers are happy with the spring gifts they have bought. This beautiful scene takes place one week before Tet.

▪ Journeys to Home Villages

THERE WAS A TIME WHEN THOUGHTS of Tet made people anxious about travel. Because people all over Vietnam expect to go to their home villages for Tet laden with gifts for the ancestral altars and their relatives, trains, buses, and boats were jammed with people. Buying a ticket to get home in time for the new year was not easy, and people had to wait in long lines, sometimes for the entire day. Temporary stalls were set up outside the train stations to try to control the crowding and to discourage black marketeers. Today transportation to home villages for Tet is more available, and no one misses a train or bus.

Hanoi residents hail from all over, but especially from surrounding villages. Although many do not know how long ago their ancestors moved to

Hanoi, they still maintain relations with their ancestral villages. As a rule, people working in certain professions and residing in particular parts of Hanoi come from the same ancestral village. For example, business people in Ha Trung Street are originally from Ninh Hiep village; embroidery workers in Hang Khay are originally from Thuong Tin district, Ha Tay province; bronze-making families in Ngu Xa Street are originally from Dai Bai village, Bac Ninh province; carpenter families came from Nhi Khe, Ha Tay province; photographers came from Lai Xa village, Ha Tay province. Before and after Tet, people go to their home villages to burn incense on the ancestral altars, visit ancestors' graves, and visit relatives. These are journeys of sentiment and obligation. People's sentiment toward lineage and home villages endures because of these journeys.

■ Sending the Kitchen God to Heaven

ACCORDING TO TRADITION, Tet starts on the twenty-third day of the twelfth month, traditionally called 23 Tet or Tet Ong Tao. This is the day when people worship the Kitchen Gods, the three Ong Tao who inhabit every home. The Ong Tao protect and support the family during the year, and on the twenty-third day of the twelfth month they journey on carps to the Heaven to report to the Heavenly King about their family's activities. The family holds a ritual to bid farewell to the Ong Tao. The offerings always include *hang ma*, three paper hats, three paper robes, and three pairs of paper shoes for the three gods to wear on this most important journey of the year. Also offered are a bowl with three small carp to be ridden by the gods on their journey to see the Heavenly King, votive paper money, and a meal for the gods consisting of sticky rice, chicken, wine, and fruits. People communicate with these and other spirits by burning incense. After the ritual, *hang ma* are burned, and the carp are set free in the nearest lake. In the 1990s it became common to see parents and children bringing their carp to lakes throughout Hanoi in the afternoon or evening of the twenty-third day of the twelfth month. The belief in the journey of the Kitchen God has been passed on through generations of Kinh families. This belief is the basis of a popular television program called the *Ong Cong, Ong Tao Show* in which, like the gods making their report, people praise, criticize, and make fun of the good points and shortcomings of their families and the society at large during the preceding year.

In the past, every family put a bamboo tree in the front door or drew a bow and arrow with white lime in the yard to chase away evil spirits. This custom was abandoned a long time ago in the cities, but in some rural areas the stalks of bamboo can still be seen, sometimes transformed into decorative trees. In some places in Thanh Hoa province, people still inscribe a bow and arrow in the front courtyard for protection.

▪ Journey of the Ancestors to Welcome the New Year with Their Descendants

WELCOMING A NEW YEAR is welcoming a new spring, welcoming new hope and luck for each person and each family. This sentiment is expressed in many ways, from the report of Ong Tao that will cause the Heavenly King to smile on the family to the decorating of the home with flowering branches. Visits to Buddhist temples and to the ancestors' graves during the new year season are occasions when prayers express hopes and aspirations for the future. The most important of all new year rituals, however, is the act of requesting the ancestors' protection at the family home altar.

To welcome the new year, the family cleans and tidies the altar for the ancestors' visit. Altars—the size of which depends on the family's circumstances—are made following traditional forms with varying degrees of elaboration. Household altars may be as simple as an ordinary table covered with offerings. A poor family or one living in a small house may use a wooden shelf 27–31 inches long and 11–15 inches wide attached to the wall—large enough for an incense burner, portraits, water cups, one or two plates of fruit, and a flower vase. In contrast, old, established families,

The men of the family enjoy the first festive meal of the new year in front of the ancestral altar in a Hanoi home in the early 1950s.

An ancestral altar at Tet in a Hanoi home, 2001. The household has placed traditional *chung* cakes, candied fruits, seeds, and a tray of fruit on the altar.

such as ones that have lived in the old quarter of Hanoi for many generations, often have exquisitely carved traditional altars holding portraits of three generations of ancestors. Contemporary household altars usually hold one or three incense burners, one brass pot, two candle holders, two water cups, and two flower vases. Portraits of deceased parents hang on the wall behind the altar, replacing the wood and lacquer tablets that were used in the past.

In addition to the offerings of *chung* cakes and red boxes of "Happy New Year" sweets and cakes, there should be a heaping plate—traditionally called the five-fruit tray but always holding more than five—piled with such fruits as *phat thu* (Buddha hand fruit), yellow pomelo, oranges, green bananas, mandarin oranges, and red peppers; mangoes and dragon fruit from the south and imported fruits such as grapes, apples, and pears may be included as well. Offerings of food depend on the family's economic circumstances and family traditions, but typically include a boiled chicken, a plate of sticky rice, a bowl of soup, a plate of fried meat, a plate of fried vegetables, and three cups of wine. A family might also honor an ancestor's particular tastes, providing a cup of coffee for an ancestor who is remembered to have been fond of coffee or cigarettes for an ancestor who liked to smoke.

In the late afternoon of the last day of the old year (or the first day of the new year), families hold a ceremony to honor the ancestors and invite them to enjoy Tet with the living family. The ancestors then descend onto the clean altars and enjoy their favorite offerings. With the bond between living and dead thus renewed, the ancestors will protect the family throughout the year. The Tet holidays are an occasion for all of the family members, living and dead, to gather. People who work or study in other parts of the country try to come home to participate in this ceremonial meal. No one wants to be away from home on these days.

As a "new custom," begun in 1947 during the French War, neighborhood or district committees end the old year by sending a delegation to pay homage to soldiers who died for the country by visiting their families on the twenty-ninth or thirtieth day of the last lunar month. This custom signifies that their sacrifice and contribution to the country are remembered and honored.

▪ Welcoming Tet Eve

TET EVE MARKS THE TRANSITION from the old year to the new year. Although everyone considers this a sacred, special time, different people mark it in different ways. Many Hanoi people, for example, welcome the new year at Hoan Kiem Lake—a custom whose origins are unknown. They may come in family groups or groups of friends in twos, threes, or more. During Tet 2001, a couple with their small child came to this place with a very simple reason: "Tet Eve is the moment of transition from the old year to the new year. We want to have a beautiful memory of this occasion because we now have a baby after ten years of marriage. Even though our child is still small, we want him to witness this important moment of transition between the two millenniums." In recent years, young boys and girls have taken to meeting in cafeterias and bars before going on to the lake in

Young women light sparklers as part of the celebration at Hoan Kiem Lake in Hanoi on the eve of Tet 2001. The lakeside is a popular gathering place for young residents of Hanoi, who enjoy staged performances and fireworks at midnight.

the evening. The lakeshore, paths, and surrounding streets are full of people. The trees are hung with lights. There are bands and other performances, and people can have their picture taken in photography concessions that feature whimsical props such as the year's horoscope animal. A visit to the lake is a splendid journey. At midnight the noisy crowds fall silent, sharing their anticipation of a new spring and a new year.

What marks this transitional moment? In the past, the cheerful atmosphere around Hoan Kiem Lake included the constant sound of firecrackers, large and small, but relentless all through the hours leading up to midnight, when there were even more and louder volleys. In 1996, however, the government issued a decree that forbade the burning of firecrackers, both to prevent accidents and as an economic measure. In 2000 firecrackers were replaced by spectacular public displays of fireworks. In addition, television or loudspeakers transmit the president's remarks, replicating the custom of past years when President Ho Chi Minh would read his new year greeting to the people.

People returning home from the lake like to bring back a branch of green leaves to symbolize bringing good luck for the new year into the family. In the past, they would simply pluck a branch from one of the trees around the lake or along the street; recently, though, people have been

At midnight fireworks explode over the The Huc bridge on Hoan Kiem Lake at the center of Hanoi to welcome the new year. This public display replaces the firecrackers that were banned in the early 1990s.

asked to give up this bad habit to protect the environment, and now lucky branches, brought by peasants from outside Hanoi, are sold around the lake. The branches, which are full of fruit and young leaves, are brought home and hung at the door or put on the altar with wishes for success in the new year. Recently, enterprising vendors have begun selling sugarcane with roots and leaves—a plant long considered lucky because it grows so rapidly—at Hoan Kiem Lake on Tet Eve as well. It is joyful to see groups of people carrying sugarcane home on their shoulders to start the new year. During the Tet holidays, sugarcane can be seen in front of many houses or next to ancestral altars.

At midnight, people burn incense on the altars to invite the ancestors to join in the new year ceremony and ask them to bestow happiness on the family. To worship Heaven and Earth and to welcome the Ong Cong of the new year, the god who presides over the family's land, families prepare a tray of offerings—sticky rice, fruit, alcohol, and a whole young rooster positioned attractively with its wings furled and a rose in its mouth—in the yard, on the balcony, on the veranda, or at the front door. Today the rooster is plucked, cleaned, and tied into position in the market, but in the past this was done at home. The new Ong Cong, who arrives with each new year, is represented by a paper hat and robe. The precise moment of transition occurs when Heaven meets Earth and yin and yang are in perfect balance.

Once the incense has been burned and the ancestors and Heaven and Earth have been invoked, it is time for the "first guest" (xong dat) to enter the house. This custom has ancient roots. People believe that the family's luck for the coming year will be largely determined by the horoscope of the first person who enters the house in the new year. Perhaps that is the reason people began to spend Tet Eve outside, to permit the person who is designated as xong dat to enter the house first, whereupon he or she is welcomed with great hospitality. The first person should be someone whose year horoscope is an auspicious match with the properties of the year. In practice, many families follow their own customs, usually having fathers or eldest sons enter first, since they are the pillars that support the family. According to one man, a firstborn son who is his own family's xong dat every year, "People choose those who have good morals and good character and are honest and successful in life" as the first guest. The mother and daughters place cookies, sugared fruit and nuts, candy, and cigarettes on trays and boxes to treat guests, and tea is often served; the whole family then eats and talks joyfully. In Confucian families, old people get paper and pens, recalling the custom whereby they would receive brushes to write auspicious sentiments for the new year. Children imitate the old people by writing a poem or inscribing their favorite literary passage on paper, thus expressing their hope and aspiration to study well and write beautifully in the new year.

▪ Spring Journeys

On the first day, stay in the father's house.
The second day is for going to the mother's family.
The third day is at the teacher's house.

This traditional verse summarizes the philosophy of new year journeys. On the first morning, the master of the house, whether father, mother, or oldest family member, burns incense to honor the ancestors, wish them a happy new year, and thank them for helping bring the family peace, success, and happiness in the past year. Parents tell children to pray for the granting of their greatest wish. In this atmosphere the ancestors seem to be present, listening to every one of the children's words. Members of the family wish happiness and success to each other and give small gifts of money to children. This significant meeting between the living and the dead is the first encounter in the new spring.

The first journey of the family is usually to the ancestral shrine of the father's or mother's lineage or to the home of the elders of the lineage. This is a pious journey, demonstrating respect for the elders. Journeys to one's own past or present teachers or to one's children's teachers are among the most important journeys made during the Tet holidays, as a sign of esteem for those who serve a guiding role for the family. In the first days of the new year, whenever people meet, they say "Happy New Year" and wish others happiness, prosperity, and success. Some standard traditional greetings are both sincere and literary, such as "May you be as happy as the Eastern Sea and have the longevity of the South Mountain" *(Phuc nhu Dong hai, tho ti Nam son)*.

Both old and young people like to go to Buddhist pagodas in the early hours of the new year, a custom that has grown in popularity in recent

Sons offer New Year greetings and wish longevity and good health to their father on the morning of Tet in Ha Dong province (now Ha Tay province) in the early twentieth century.

years. Crowds of people visit temples in Hanoi such as Quan Su, Dien Huu, Hai Ba Trung, and Ha to burn incense and ask for help with their ambitions and desires. Tay Ho Temple, where people worship the Mother Goddess, is considered by Hanoi residents to be one of the most auspicious for these prayers. The Perfume Pagoda, the most spectacular cave grotto in Vietnam, about forty miles from Hanoi, draws thousands of people in the first days of spring, who travel by boat along Yen Stream and then climb hundreds of steps to the cave grotto above the temple.

The number of pilgrims going to the temples is one measure of how Tet celebrations have changed in recent years. In the past, the holiday meant eating: in a time of scarcity, people exerted great effort to prepare festival foods. Now that the material conditions of life have improved, Tet is more a time for socializing and for spring journeys.

In the past, a *neu* tree, a long bamboo pole with a pineapple at the top, decorated with a bell, lantern, and flags, would be raised outside the house and the village communal house once the Kitchen God had been sent off at the end of the old year. The *neu* tree would stand until the seventh day of the new year, marking the end of the Tet holiday. Although people no longer raise *neu* trees, the seventh day of the new year is still a significant marker. Starting this day, people no longer say "Happy New

After Tet many people make pilgrimages to shrines and temples. This family is on its way to the Perfume Pagoda (Chua Huong) in Ha Tay province. The gold foil branches are part of the offering that they will make in the cave grotto above the temple.

Year" to those they meet. On the fifteenth day of the first month, however, families mark Tet Lai ("repetition of Tet") by placing *chung* cake on the altar for the ancestors.

Tet is changing as Vietnamese society changes in the Renovation (Doi Moi) era. Many traditions and customs related to Tet have been lost, others revived, and some transformed, and now several new traditions are in place. But the best of Tet is still alive in each person, in each family, and in the whole of society. Tet should be celebrated in such a way that it remains a symbol of the gratitude descendants feel toward their ancestors and the symbol of a harmonious society built upon harmonious families. Tet is about the journeys of individuals, families, and communities, not only of people, but of ancestors and gods as well. These journeys have both practical and magical ends. They are the link between the world of people and the world of spirits—between the past, the present, and the future.

This early-twentieth-century woodblock print portraying a Mid-Autumn lantern procession with a dancing unicorn was produced by Vo Cat Phu of Luong Noc village. It evokes very well the activity of the Mid-Autumn Festival.

THE MID-AUTUMN FESTIVAL (TET TRUNG THU), YESTERDAY AND TODAY

Nguyen Van Huy

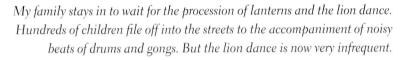

My family stays in to wait for the procession of lanterns and the lion dance.
Hundreds of children file off into the streets to the accompaniment of noisy
beats of drums and gongs. But the lion dance is now very infrequent.

—NGUYEN DANG HOP,

FORTY-SEVEN-YEAR-OLD

HANOI CRAFTSMAN

THE MID-AUTUMN FESTIVAL marks a pause in the year's journey between summer agricultural work and the autumn harvest. During this celebration, children enjoy parties and then parade around the neighborhood wearing masks and carrying paper or plastic lanterns in imaginative shapes, under the adoring gaze of their parents and grandparents. For the Kinh (Viet) and Hoa (Chinese) who celebrate this festival, the full moon of the eighth lunar month—usually September by the Gregorian calendar—signifies fertility. Originally a time when people prayed for a bountiful harvest and the multiplication of all living things—grain, livestock, and human babies—Mid-Autumn included prayers for children that were transformed, over time, into a celebration of children. In Vietnam today, children are feted at Mid-Autumn as the nation's future. This, too, can be seen as a very joyful prayer.

■ Traditions

IN ITS MOST ANCIENT FORM, the Mid-Autumn Festival celebrated the dragon who brought rain for a bountiful harvest. Men would gather to watch the progress of the moon, divining the future of the country from its color and appearance. If the moon shone with pure brilliance, then a good harvest would occur; if it were yellow, the silkworms would yield an abundant thread. Conversely, if the mid-autumn moon seemed green or blue, there would be famine in the land. Confucian scholars perpetuated the tradition of gazing at the moon, but as an occasion to sip wine and improvise poetic songs. Ambitious young men aspiring to government position hoped that on the night of the festival they would dream of ascending to the moon, as an omen of future success.[1]

Many old beliefs link the moon festival to fertility and to the fate that links destined spouses. Into the early decades of the twentieth century, young men and women used the festival as an occasion to meet their future life companions. Groups of boys and girls would gather in the courtyard of a house, taking turns exchanging verses of song while gazing at the moon. Singers who performed poorly or who could not match their adversary's verse were excluded until only one young man and one young woman remained; this talented couple claimed prizes and possibly matrimonial prospects.

These activities were not permitted to the children of rich and respectable families. Instead, the daughters of these families exhibited their talents by preparing elaborate displays of treats for their younger siblings. Any properly dressed visitor was welcome to enter the open door of the home and examine the daughter's handiwork.[2] These displays later became a central element of the Mid-Autumn Festival for all families.

By the early twentieth century in Hanoi, the festival had begun to assume its contemporary identity as a children's festival with treats, toys, and processions by gleeful children wearing masks. Even during the American War, when many children were evacuated from Hanoi to the countryside, the festival was observed. Mrs. Dinh Thi Hong Bien, a thirty-nine-year-old civil servant working in the Police Ministry, recalls, "During the war against the Americans, [on the Mid-Autumn Festival] children used to gather at the drying yard of the Farming Cooperative for a share of special treats and to fly balloons."

An old woman on a Hanoi street in 1932 smiles at the armful of hand-made toys that this boy holds. One of his toys is a paper scholar seated under a sunshade, a gift intended to inspire the child to study hard and achieve great things in life.

Today, in addition to being simply festive, Mid-Autumn celebrations foster patriotism and good citizenship. In 1945, when Vietnam threw off eighty years of foreign domination, the Mid-Autumn Festival occurred about a month after independence was proclaimed. These were difficult times, when an estimated two million people had died in a famine caused by the disruption of agriculture, a consequence of Japanese policies in Vietnam. That year Ho Chi Minh, the first president of an independent Vietnam, showed his concern for the children of Vietnam by sending them a festival letter: "Today, the Mid-Autumn Festival is yours. It is also a time for you to

Ho Chi Minh's letter to the children of Vietnam on the Mid-Autumn Festival in 1945 added a patriotic element to the festival. This Dong Ho woodblock print by Nguyen Dang Che combines Ho Chi Minh's well-known fondness for children with the festival imagery of lanterns and toys.

demonstrate your love for the country and your support for independence. You must be good, follow your parents' instructions, study hard, and love and respect your teachers and friends. You must love our country. I wish that when you grow up, you will become good citizens who are worthy of our national independence and freedom." From then on, Uncle Ho, as the grandfather to subsequent generations of Vietnamese youth, sent letters to the children of Vietnam at each Mid-Autumn Festival. Receiving this letter and carrying Uncle Ho's photograph in festival processions thus became a new custom of the Mid-Autumn celebration.

This festival is a time when bonds are strengthened across generations, both in families and communities and throughout Vietnamese society. It is also a nostalgic time, as adults remember the festivals of their own childhoods. In the words of seventy-three-year-old Nguyen Manh Cuong, a retired civil servant: "The Mid-Autumn Festival has deep cultural significance. It not only helps to shape a child's view of the world but also fosters affectionate feelings between couples and families. No matter what times we live in, the beat of drums during the lion dance and the procession of lanterns always make a strong impression on me. I like lanterns, all sorts of lanterns."

In the fall of 1999 researchers from the Vietnam Museum of Ethnology made a study of the Mid-Autumn Festival in Hanoi and surrounding villages, looking particularly at how these celebrations have changed in recent years. They collected a great many impressions from young and old, some of which are related in this chapter.[3]

Rabbit lanterns, like the one that delighted this child in the early decades of the twentieth century, can still be seen on Hanoi streets during the Mid-Autumn Festival.

■ Mid-Autumn Treats

On Mid-Autumn, I love setting out treats for younger children and going out with my friends to look at the moon.

—VU ANH HAO, SIXTEEN, TENTH-GRADE STUDENT

AT DINH TIEN HOANG SCHOOL, HANOI

FAMILIES AND NEIGHBORHOOD ASSOCIATIONS arrange special displays of treats at Mid-Autumn children's parties. Adults enjoy the beauty of these displays in the glow of festival lanterns, while children bide their time until they can enjoy the cakes and fruit. These treats not only are tasty, but they are sometimes made to be played with like toys. Pastries of roasted

This fuzzy puppy, fashioned from pomelo fruit turned inside out, is an example of the many fanciful creations displayed with Mid-Autumn treats at children's parties held by schools and neighborhood associations.

glutinous rice flour and ordinary rice paste are molded in the shapes of familiar animals. The shaggy insides of pomelo sections are fancifully fashioned into unicorns, rabbits, or fluffy puppies. The children handle these animal figures carefully and are sometimes reluctant to eat them. Children hold the image of Mid-Autumn treats, displayed in the iridescent light of multicolored lanterns, as both memory and anticipation, much as many American children think of lit Christmas trees surrounded by wrapped gifts.

Cakes and fruit in the shape of animals suggest the harmony between human beings and the natural world. Villagers from Xuan La in Ha Tay province, just south of Hanoi, are renowned for their ability to make *to he*—rice-paste creations—from a mixture of glutinous and ordinary rice paste to which natural pigments are added. Eighty-year-old Nguyen Van To, who has been modeling rice cake figures since he was six years old, recalls that in the past figures were modeled before being steamed. Today they are modeled from balls of preboiled vividly colored paste. Villagers exhibit their skill between farming seasons in cities and at festivals. In the days leading up to the festival, these talented artists can be found in the vicinity of Hanoi's Hang Ma Street, where festival decorations are sold, entertaining children by creating human, animal, vegetable, and plant figures from rice paste of different colors. They have added figures from inter-

On Hang Ma Street the day before the Mid-Autumn Festival in 2001, a couple shops for festival lanterns from their motorbike. Until 1945, Hanoi star lanterns had six points, but they now resemble the five-pointed star on the Vietnamese flag.

national popular culture to their repertory, and it is not unusual to find a rice cake image of the Japanese anime heroine Sailor Moon, for example, complete with spiked blond hair.

Handcrafted shadow lanterns, enjoyed in Vietnam since the twelfth-century Ly dynasty, were once an important part of Mid-Autumn displays in Hanoi, though today they are rarely seen outside some northern villages. Rotated by a flickering flame, one or more bands of figures, either cut out or in silhouette, make each lantern into a small shadow puppet theater. Rotating lantern figures portray legendary heroes such as Thanh Giong, who fought off Chinese invaders, and the Trung Sisters and Lady Trieu, who led insurrections against Chinese domination. Themes from more recent history have also appeared in shadow lanterns. The popular image of the mouse's wedding procession is often used.

Shadow lanterns have declined in popularity because the labor required to produce them makes them expensive and because nowadays

The simple paper party blowers on the right are made from recycled cigarette cartons. On the left is a battery-powered Hello Kitty lantern from China in the pose of a Japanese folk hero whose cheeks flash red and who beeps, "Happy Birthday to You."

the candle flame that propels the shadows is considered a fire hazard. Nguyen Van Thanh, an artisan from Van Canh commune, Hoai Duc district, Ha Tay province, told us, "I don't make lanterns anymore, since they are sold for too little money. How can one sell paper toys when plastic ones are everywhere you look?" Nguyen Van Ninh, a merchant on Hang Ma Street, confirmed, "[In 1998], during the Mid-Autumn Festival, I sold only about ten small lanterns and a few bigger ones." Today, the vendors on Hanoi's Hang Ma Street exhibit battery- and microchip-powered plastic lanterns from China, some featuring the internationally recognizable images of Pokemon Pikachu and Hello Kitty and some beeping the melody "Happy Birthday to You."

The paper scholar, a papier-mâché figure dressed in the cap and robe of a court official from dynastic times, is still found in village Mid-Autumn displays, but many Hanoi children would not recognize him. This figure represents a scholar who has successfully passed the highest civil service examination and become a government official. "We make paper scholars for children at the Mid-Autumn Festival in the hope that, like the scholar, our children will have brilliant careers," explained Hoang Nhat Tan, a sixty-three-year-old votive paper maker living in Song Ho commune, Thuan Thanh district, Bac Ninh province.

The earth god and his companion dance in a lantern procession with children carrying star lanterns during Mid-Autumn in 2001.

▪ Processions

My friends and I march off in a long procession of lanterns.
That is Mid-Autumn!

—NGUYEN TUAN ANH, NINE, FOURTH-GRADE
STUDENT AT THAI THINH SCHOOL, HANOI

CHILDREN PARADE WITH LANTERNS in the form of five-pointed stars, like that on the national flag;[4] of toads, who inhabit a palace on the moon and symbolize ascent to high position; of rabbits, who some say conceive by gazing at the moon;[5] and in other fanciful shapes. Masked figures at the center of these processions represent auspicious animals—the unicorn, dragon, and lion; they are accompanied by the Earth God, who marches with a fan in hand. Some children disguise themselves with masks reflecting their own interests and fantasies. Gentle girls often choose princess masks, while mischievous boys prefer masks of Chinese heroes known to them from movies and comic books, such as Judge Bao, who solves mysteries, and his assistant, Trien Chieu; or the Monkey, Pigsy, Sandy, and the Tang Priest, who have many adventures on their journey west to find Buddhist teachings. Tuned in to popular culture, many city children join festival parades disguised as Mickey Mouse or as Japanese animated heroes.

At the Mid-Autumn market on Hang Ma Street in 2001, this vendor's wares were handmade papier-mâché masks, including Donald Duck; plastic masks from China, including the Power Rangers; and Pikachu, an internationally recognizable figure from Japanese cartoons.

Children with a sense of humor want to be monkeys, rabbits, pigs, cats, or tigers. Masks used to be made of paper and painted with colored powder, and there were two holes at each side to tie a string. More elaborate masks were made of papier-mâché. Although some fanciful papier-mâché masks are still sold on Hanoi's Hang Ma Street during the Mid-Autumn Festival, masks are now mostly made of plastic and are in more colorful and varied shapes.

■ Toys

Toys used to be simple but impressive.
Now they boast only their variety.

— MRS. NGUYEN HONG VAN, FORTY-ONE, TEACHER IN HANOI

CHILDREN RECEIVE GIFTS OF TOYS during the Mid-Autumn Festival. Small hand drums and wooden clackers are sold in both city and country markets, and small children can be seen happily playing with these simple toys. Traditionally, many fanciful handcrafted toys and masks were produced for the Mid-Autumn Festival, especially in several villages in the northern Red River Delta, but these works of folk art have been largely replaced in the cities by mass-produced plastic playthings that now fill the festival market. Toys used to be made in several villages in the northern Red River Delta and sold in markets throughout the country. Artisans in Tu Khe handicraft village, Bac Ninh province northeast of Hanoi, and Van Canh village, Ha Tay province, still make toys by hand, and some households continue to value these products as a traditional legacy.

Traditional Mid-Autumn toys introduce children to important cultural symbols, values, and ideals. A leaping carp represents a wish for success, a paper scholar encourages a child to study hard and accomplish great things. Miniature rural scenes and familiar animals such as cows and chickens teach respect for labor and the beauty of everyday life. Toys in the form of cars, planes, and steamships reflect contemporary times.

Vietnam's craftsmen create these toys from a range of materials including pieces

Hoang Ba Kinh, age seventy-two, of Tu Khe village fashions papier-mâché unicorn masks. Although handmade toys are still sold at the Mid-Autumn market, imported plastic toys dominate the wares available for sale.

These traditional papier-mâché toys were made by Hoang Ba Kinh of Tu Khe village, who has been producing them since 1985.

of straw, plant stems, sheets of paper, pieces of string, handfuls of earth, and lumps of dough. Their methods are simple—cutting, incising, weaving, modeling, hammering, and pasting—and the toys are decorated with vegetable dyes. However, considerable skill is required to make a shadow lantern or complex paper figure. Artisans have incorporated new forms, colors, materials, and techniques into their work to meet changing tastes.

■ Mid-Autumn, Young and Old

IN A NOSTALGIC MOOD, many of our older interviewees commented on the waning popularity of handmade toys. Mrs. Nguyen Thi Chuyen, the seventy-three-year-old proprietress of a craft shop in Hanoi, recalled the Mid-Autumn market of decades past: "The area surrounding Sword Lake used to be quite busy at the approach of Mid-Autumn. At the time, we owned a tin toy shop that was usually full of tin-crafted steamships, boats, drum-beating rabbits, and butterflies. . . . Those toys all sold very well, especially the steamship." Nguyen Dang Hop, a forty-seven-year-old Hanoi craftsman, spoke of the overwhelming competition from foreign toys: "Toys of local make do not sell well in the face of those imported from China that are both cheap and attractive."

A child points to his preference for a plastic toy at the Mid-Autumn market on Hang Ma Street.

Mrs. Le Thi Thanh, a seventy-year-old retiree living in Hanoi, described the festival ambience as having been totally transformed: "In my day, toys were not so plentiful as they are nowadays, yet we managed to enjoy what we had. At the time, we only had a paper scholar, a drum-beating rabbit, a steamship, and some lanterns. We kept our toys for a long time. On Mid-Autumn night, we wore fine clothes and a lion-shaped hat. We beat drums and joined in the lion dance. With my friends, I bought fruits which I shaped into animals while enjoying the full moon. Houses are so cramped now that it is difficult to organize Mid-Autumn parties for children. Present-day toys such as guns and swords are plentiful, yet they are not wholesome. Children love splashing water, even dirty water, over passers-by with their water-projecting toy guns. In my opinion, those pranks must be forbidden."

Mrs. Dinh Thi Hong Bien, who had fond memories of wartime Mid-Autumn festivals during her own childhood, lamented that "today Mid-Autumn festivals are no longer full of meaning as they were in the past. Children do not eagerly look forward to the festival. They fail to appreciate the lovely moonlight. Traditional toys are rarely made and some lack good craftsmanship. Most present-day toys are imported. They are neither inexpensive nor educational."

A very different impression came from our interviews with schoolchildren who visited the Vietnam Museum of Ethnology. Their pleasure in the

Children eye a display of lanterns in a Hanoi shop before the Mid-Autumn Festival in 1932. The butterfly shape is no longer produced.

festival is, in many respects, similar to that expressed by their parents: they enjoy the Mid-Autumn treats, the lantern procession, and lion dances. However, their aspirations are different from those of earlier generations; contemporary children are more curious about the wider world and have added new forms of popular culture to their experience. They told us: "Our favorite toy is a water gun. All the boys in our neighborhood go out and splash water on the passers-by. When they chase us, we run away. What fun!" (seventeen-year-old boy). "Plastic masks, swords, and guns as well as electronic toys are what I like best on Mid-Autumn. I am most interested in the mask patterned after the Bonze Superior's face from Japanese anime" (sixteen-year-old boy). "I love wearing masks patterned after characters like the Monkey King [from a sixteenth-century Chinese novel popularized in film and comic books] and Sailor Moon from Japanese anime" (six-year-old boy). "I like puppets because they represent the mutual affection of brothers and sisters. Many of the electronic toys are also interesting" (sixteen-year-old girl). "On every Mid-Autumn Festival, I ask my parents to buy me storybooks. I have a great many picture books, most of which are imported. I want a collection of Vietnamese legends that will help me understand our country more thoroughly" (twelve-year-old girl).

From her mother's shoulders, a little girl happily surveys Mid–Autumn festivities in 2001.

Hmong and Kinh women bargain at a market in the mountains of northern Vietnam in the late 1990s. There is often a close relationship between calendar systems and the timing of local markets.

FOUR WAYS TO MAP

A YEAR'S JOURNEY

Chu Van Khanh, Cam Trong, and A Bao

I F WE THINK OF THE PASSAGE OF SEASONS as a journey through
time, beginning at the new year and with holidays as signposts along the
way, then by the same metaphor a calendar is a timetable for the vehicle of
time itself. In Vietnam official public time is measured by the Gregorian
solar calendar, and most national holidays are fixed by solar dates. However, most printed calendars in Vietnam have a second, smaller set of numbers, sometimes printed in lighter type, on each day of the standard
calendar. These numbers indicate a parallel but different reckoning of
time, that of the lunisolar calendar used by Vietnam's majority Kinh (Viet)
population and Hoa (Chinese Vietnamese).

The lunisolar calendar is not the only possible alternative timetable;
Vietnam is a multiethnic society, and some groups reckon significant

events through their own calendars. In this chapter we explore four different calendars: the widely used lunisolar calendar of the Kinh and Hoa and
three distinctive variants developed by the Thai, Hmong, and Muong. All
of these calendar systems are closely linked to the agricultural cycles of
these communities and most likely developed through attempts to determine optimum times for planting, transplanting, and harvesting by linking seasonal changes in the weather to the changes farmers observed in
the positions of the sun, moon, and stars as the year progressed. These calendars are also used to order many aspects of social life, from setting days
for annual festivals and special ceremonies to celebrating a wedding,
going hunting, holding a periodic market, or making a major investment.
Calendar systems have also been linked to systems of divination and medical practice.

■ The Lunisolar Calendar of the Kinh and Hoa

TRADITIONAL ANNUAL FESTIVALS such as the lunar new year (Tet),
the Festival of Hungry Ghosts (the fifteenth day of the seventh lunar month),
and the Mid-Autumn Festival (Tet Trung Thu, the fifteenth day of the
eighth month) are held according to the lunisolar calendar.[1] The first and
fifteenth days of each lunar month are appropriate times to honor ancestors
and visit temples. Ancestors' death day commemorations, held by individual
families, are calculated according to lunisolar dates. Local festivals honoring
community tutelary gods are set by lunisolar dates, usually early in the year.
Linked to the moon cycle, the lunisolar calendar is used to regulate fishing
activities, the gathering of medicinal herbs, and medical practices that link
specific times to the efficacious treatment of specific acupuncture points. In
the past, knowledgeable medical men would predict epidemics on the basis
of the lunisolar calendar system and specific climactic conditions. The calendar was also a necessary tool in determining horoscopes to predict such
important questions as matrimonial compatibility.

It is assumed that the ancient inhabitants of Vietnam had their own calendar, but knowledge of it is fragmentary, surviving only in verse and
ethnographic literature. The traditional calendar used by most Vietnamese
(and used in Korea, Japan, and Mongolia as well) originated in ancient

In anticipation of Tet in 1942, this woman listens in rapt attention to the fortune-teller's prognostication for the new year. The lunisolar calendar is an important tool in divinations, determining both personal horoscopes and auspicious days for important activities such as a wedding or the undertaking of a new enterprise.

China more than four thousand years ago. Though likely developed as a means of scheduling agricultural activities, in time the calendar became the foundation of a complex astronomically based system used to regulate many aspects of social life, from cuisine and medicine to the timing of significant events such as building a house or holding a wedding.

Commonly referred to as the lunar calendar, this East Asian system is more accurately a lunisolar calendar based on perceived movements of the sun, the earth, and the moon. The notion of the complementary forces of yin and yang (Vietnamese, *am* and *duong*)—cool-hot, dark-bright, hard-yielding, masculine-feminine, each rising to ascendancy and then declining and being superseded by its opposite—is a core principle of this system. The day, marked by the rising and setting of the sun, is the basic time unit of most calendrical systems. In the lunisolar calendar, day and night are oscillations of yin and yang. Yang dominates in the interval from sunrise to sunset, and yin from sunset to sunrise. Midnight is the peak in the ascendancy of yin, the moment that yang begins its ascendancy, as noon is the peak in the ascendancy of yang, the moment that yin begins its ascendancy. The cycle of a waxing and waning moon is similarly mapped by oscillations of yin and yang. The waxing phase is governed by the ascendancy of yang and the waning phase by yin. A moonless night marks the peak of yin, the point at which yang begins to generate. This day is the first day of the month, called the *soc* day in Vietnamese. Likewise, the year begins with the winter solstice, the peak of yin, from which yang regenerates to its peak in the heat of midsummer. While both the lunisolar calendar and the Gregorian calendar are based on the cycle of the earth's rotation around the sun, the lunisolar calendar also factors in the moon's rotation around the earth.

The lunisolar day begins one hour in advance of the Gregorian calendar, at 23:00 by international reckoning. Each day is composed of twelve time units, usually translated as "the twelve terrestrial branches." Each time unit has two halves—the first, or "lesser," half, marked by the prefix *so*, and the second, or "greater," half, marked by the prefix *chinh*. With these subdivisions a lunisolar day has twenty-four parts, roughly equivalent to the Western concept of a twenty-four-hour day. Each day is divided by a sequence of a hundred *khac*. Because twelve does not divide evenly into one hundred, a modified *khac* system developed, giving the day 108 *khac*, nine *khac* to each of the twelve celestial stems. The winter solstice, with the longest night of the year, is measured as sixty *khac* for the dark period and forty *khac* for the bright period. Inversely, the summer solstice, with the longest day, has forty *khac* for the dark period and sixty *khac* for the bright period. The vernal and autumn equinoxes have the *khac* divided evenly.

In the lunisolar calendar, a month is equivalent to a lunar cycle, but as units of time lunar months are more regular than the actual cycle of the moon. On average, an actual lunar cycle is twenty-nine days, twelve hours, and forty-four minutes in international time. This allows for thirty- or twenty-nine-day months but is sufficiently irregular to confound any regular scheme of full and reduced months. A year, measured in twelve complete moon cycles, lasts 354 or 355 days—10 or 11 days shorter than the Western "weather year" or "equinox year." Thus over the course of three years, a full month is skipped. To compensate for this gap between the lunisolar year and the weather year, a leap year with an extra intercalary month is added every fourth year.

THE *TIET KHI* SYSTEM

Tiet khi are periodic markers in the earth's annual orbit around the sun or, because the system was conceptualized by observing the sun from the earth, the sun's movement through the Zodiac. This scheme is the "solar" component of the lunisolar system. Both Eastern and Western astronomy divide the Zodiac into twelve zones of 30 degrees for a full circuit of 360 degrees. The point at which the sun enters a zone is called *trung khi*; the midpoint of the zone is called *tiet khi*. The year has twelve *trung khi* and twelve *tiet khi*. This system divides the year into four seasons: spring begins on the fourth or fifth day of the second lunar month, summer begins on the fifth or sixth of the fifth lunar month, autumn begins on the seventh or eighth of the sixth lunar month, and winter begins on the seventh or eighth of the eleventh lunar month. *Tiet khi* points also indicate the two solstices, the two equinoxes, the temperature (cold starts, cold time), and the weather (wet rain, grain rain, clear bright). The original system was based on annual climate variations in China in the region between the Yangtze and Yellow Rivers. During the long history of cultural exchanges between Vietnam and China, the Vietnamese modified and localized Chinese calendrical concepts to match climate conditions in the Red River Valley of northern Vietnam. For example, "grain rain" was changed to "heavy shower."

Since the earth actually rotates around the sun in an ellipse rather than a perfect circle, the sun's passage through the twelve zones of the Zodiac is not uniform. As a consequence, the *tiet khi* days fall at irregular intervals within each month. Generally, each lunisolar month has a *trung khi* point, but the duration of a lunisolar month (twenty-nine days, twelve hours, forty-four minutes) and of the time interval between the two consecutive *trung*

Members of the Hoa (Chinese Vietnamese) community in the Cholon district of Ho Chi Minh City (formerly Saigon) perform a dragon dance in celebration of Tet 2001. The Hoa and Kinh both use the lunisolar calendar to determine festival days, ancestor worship, and other important occasions.

khi points (thirty days, ten hours, twenty-nine minutes) cannot be fully synchronized. This gap eventually yields a month without a *trung khi* point, a month when the sun does not enter the next zone. These are leap months, and the years in which they fall are given a thirteenth lunisolar month.

Winter solstice is the official starting point for the astronomical year, the beginning of the *tiet khi* cycle by calendar numeration. However, the winter solstice falls in the eleventh lunisolar month of the conventional lunisolar calendar, with the numerated "first month" beginning more than a month later. Tet, which falls within the fifteen-day interval before or after the "start of spring" *(lap xuan)* by the *tiet khi* system, comes at a slack period in the agricultural cycle, and the milder weather is a good time for the new year ceremonies and festivities.[2]

THE CAN-*CHI* SYSTEM

Units of lunisolar calendar time are further characterized according to the *can-chi* system. The *can* is composed of ten elements: Jia, Yi, Bing, Ding, Wu, Ji, Geng, Xin, Ren, and Qu. These are the ten celestial stems, yang elements associated with the sky. The *chi* is composed of twelve elements, sometimes known in the west as the twelve Chinese Zodiac animals: Zi (Rat), Chou (Ox, Water Buffalo in Vietnam), Yin (Tiger), Mao (Hare, Cat in Vietnam), Chen (Dragon), Si (Snake), Wu (Horse), Wei (Goat), Shen (Monkey), You (Fowl), Xu (Dog), and Hai (Pig). These are the twelve terrestrial branches, yin elements associated with the earth. In Eastern philosophy, the *can-chi* accounts for the ebb and flow in the natural world: generating, developing, and decaying. The ten *can* elements are combined consecutively with the twelve *chi* elements to create a cycle of sixty possible combinations. Years are ordered and named in sixty-year cycles according to this scheme, called, in Vietnamese, the Luc thap Hoa Giap. In addition to the *can-chi* system, each of the five elements—metal, wood, water, fire, and earth— is associated with a calendar day in a regular five-day cycle.

Can-chi names are assigned to all basic units of calendar time. The twelve time units of the day start with the terrestrial branch Zi, go on to Chou, and so on, to the last branch, Hai; these are then coupled with the ten *can* elements. Therefore the whole cycle of sixty possible *can-chi* combinations for hours is repeated every five days. The days of a month have two naming systems. The first system names the days by their order: the first day, the second day, and so on. The second is the *can-chi* system, starting with Jia Zi, Yi Chou, and so on, like the name order for the years, so that a complete cycle of *can-chi* days takes two thirty-day months. Likewise, months are ordered by number—the first month, the second month, and so on—and by *chi* names: the eleventh month is Zi; the twelfth, Chou; the first month, Yin. A twelve-month year thus has a full cycle of *chi* names. The sixty possible *can-chi* combinations are completed every five years (sixty months). The fact that the eleventh month, with the winter solstice, is assigned the name Zi, the first celestial stem, reflects the perception that the astronomical year begins at this time, well in advance of the first numerical month. According to ancient Chinese myth, the first calendar began when the sun, the earth, Venus, Jupiter, Mercury, Mars, and Saturn were aligned for the day Jia Zi in the year Jia Zi, the first *can-chi* combination in the sequence of sixty.

To distinguish the similarly named sixty-year cycles from one another, the tradition is to assign each one the title of a royal reign, since the king, on behalf of heaven, "delivers the *soc* day [the first day] to the population."

These clay figures representing a goat, monkey, and rooster—three zodiac animals in the lunisolar system—were made by Hoang Ba Phat, age seventy-five, of Tu Khe village, who has made clay toys since he was ten.

The dragon, snake, and horse, portrayed here as clay toys, are the horoscope animals for children born after the lunar new year in 2000, 2001, and 2002, respectively.

The act of setting the calendar demonstrated the king's power. For example, the year 1010 was the first year of the Thuan Thien king's reign and was the year Geng Xu by the *can-chi* system. Therefore it is called the year Geng Xu of the first year of Thuan Thien's reign. The year 1011 then becomes the year Xin Hai of the second year of Thuan Thien's reign.

Since winning independence from China in the tenth century, Vietnamese kings set their own calendar, based on the Chinese prototype, and every dynasty established its own calendar office.[3] Today, the lunisolar calendar is set by the State Department of Calendar Research and Regulation under the National Center for Natural Sciences and Technology, using data available on the Internet. The Gregorian calendar was introduced to Vietnam in the early nineteenth century, under French colonial rule. The two calendars were used simultaneously, with administrative offices using the Gregorian calendar, while the Vietnamese Royal Court in Hue continued to issue the lunisolar calendar. In 1954 the new Vietnamese state established the Gregorian calendar as the sole official administrative calendar; calendar research and regulation was now administered by the Weather Bureau, which also issued a lunisolar calendar. Meanwhile, the general population continued to use a variety of systems, derived from French, Chinese, and Japanese sources. On August 8, 1967, the Vietnamese government issued Decision 121/CP, fixing Vietnam time in the seventh time zone and naming the Gregorian as the sole official calendar, restricting the lunisolar calendar to traditional holidays and historical commemorations. While the Gregorian calendar is widely used internationally and is convenient for calculating industrial production planning, the rich traditions associated with the traditional lunisolar calendar make it worth preserving.

A Hmong shaman chants during the new year celebration, Yen Chau district, Son La province, 1995.

The Hmong Calendar

THE HMONG MINORITY of northern Vietnam employs a calendar similar to the Asian lunisolar calendar used by the majority population, based on the same concept of hours, days, months, and years and distinguishing units of time by the animals associated with the twelve celestial branches of the *can-chi* cycle. It does not, however, recognize the ten celestial stems or the concept of yin and yang and the five elements—metal, wood, water, fire, and earth—used in the lunisolar calendar described above.

While the basic sequence of months is the same, the Hmong calendar is set one month in advance of the Asian lunisolar calendar. In other words, the eleventh month (Zi) in the Asian lunisolar calendar corresponds to the twelfth month (Chou) in the Hmong calendar and so on. This places the Hmong new year holiday (Tet) a month earlier than the majority population's. The Hmong calendar is cued to the agricultural activities of Hmong communities.

■ The Traditional Thai Calendar

THE BLACK THAI OF MAI SON DISTRICT, Son La province, in northwestern Vietnam have long had their own calendar. The Thai calendrical system shares the concept of hour, date, month, and year of the Eastern lunisolar calendar as derived from the *can-chi* system of ten celestial stems (called *tau ca* in the Thai scheme) and twelve terrestrial branches (called *chau pau*). However, rather than starting with Cap, which is the equivalent of Jia, the Thai system begins with Tau, the equivalent of Ren, the ninth stem. In addition, although the twelve terrestrial branches correspond to the same range of hours as in the Asian lunisolar system, the fourth branch goes by different names: whereas the Chinese call it the Rabbit, in the Vietnamese lunisolar system it is Mao, or the Cat, and some Thai groups identify it as To To, or the Wasp. Like the Kinh majority, the Thai combine the celestial stem and terrestrial branch to name the year. For example, the year 2000 was Khot Xi, equivalent to the Vietnamese Geng Chen. While the Kinh commonly shorten year names by referring to the branch only (2000 = the year Chen, or Dragon), the Thai tend to refer to the celestial stem name (2000 = the year Khot).

Different Thai subgroups living in Vietnam have different ways of reckoning months. Most Thai follow a system identical to that of the Asian lunisolar calendar, but the Thai Den (Black Thai) in the northwest of Vietnam reckon time six months behind lunisolar time. For example, January 1, 2000, by the Gregorian calendar was the twenty-fifth day of the eleventh month by the lunisolar calendar, and for the Thai Den, the twenty-fifth day of the fifth month.

The Thai calendar covers the seasonal weather cycles, agricultural activities associated with each month, and customary and religious activities. The traditional economy of the Thai is a complex agricultural production in wet paddies on the planes and dry fields on the mountains, with paddy agriculture more common. The calendar was used to regulate such agricultural activities as sowing, plowing, harrowing, clearing mountain fields, transplanting, and harvesting, linking them to specific months. The Thai Pap Mu, or "Day Book," records: "In the first month, fine rain; in the second month, interminable raining; in the third month, pelting rain squall, bringing on the water," and so on throughout the year. Since 1954 production has been regulated according to the Gregorian calendar and fixed by the Provincial Department of Agriculture and Rural Development and its district representatives. Paddies are now double-cropped. Women are more directly involved in all aspects of production, in addition to their traditional home responsibilities. The practice of burning forests to clear upland fields (swidden) has diminished; people in forested regions are involved in forestry management.

The calendar also specified days when certain activities were prohibited, days requiring specific ritual offerings, celebrations associated with planting and harvesting, offerings to ancestors, and offerings to the souls of buffalo and other domestic animals. In 1954 most of the customs and religious rites were deemed superstitious and abolished. However, Thai families still retain Pat Tong or Xen Huon ancestor ceremonies. The Pat Tong ceremony is performed every five days by noble families and every ten days by commoner families on days with the stems Huong or Hai. The Xen Huon ceremony is performed annually in the first month.

With the exception of the Thai Den, all Thai subgroups have adopted the Eastern lunisolar calendar used by the majority population and celebrate the new year according to the lunisolar date. They also celebrate the Kin Pang festival in the first month and mark the fourteenth day of the seventh month with a holiday very similar to the Festival of Hungry Ghosts, which the majority population observes on this day.

▪ The Muong Bamboo Calendar

THE MUONG, WHOSE SETTLEMENTS are concentrated primarily in Hoa Binh province, developed a bamboo calendar called Sach Doi, which is even more distinctive than the other variant lunisolar calendars. Although local and regional cultural exchanges have altered their calendar concept, there is very good evidence to show how the system originally functioned and how it embodied the Muong understanding of the natural world.

The Muong calendar is called the Sach Doi (or Khach Doi) because it is based on the movement of the Doi star and the moon. The Doi star is the grape-shaped twinkling star conglomeration known in the West as the η-star (Pleiades) in the constellation Taurus (Tua Rua or Rua in Vietnamese) and as the Mao star in Chinese astronomy. In Vietnam farmers have fixed the start of summer planting on the day the Tua Rua rises at dawn.

The Muong calendar is inscribed on twelve flat sticks of bamboo, to record the twelve months. There are three sections on each stick. The month is inscribed on the first section with a distinctive symbol. Days are indicated by small grooves engraved on the edge of the stick in the second section. The third section indicates natural events and auspicious and inauspicious activities associated with different days: rain, typhoons, successful fishing, and inauspicious commerce (one should avoid purchasing or exchanging goods on these days). During the days of Ngam Doi, "Doi Star Coming," days when the moon overcomes the Doi star, good opportunities may come from outside the community, but it is important to avoid doing important work. In some localities additional events are marked on the sticks: days for visiting guests, days for hunting strong animals, and days when ghosts and malevolent spirits are ascendant.

Days are divided into sixteen time units, each corresponding to approximately one and a half hours, loosely demarcated by the course of a day. The day starts at *ca cay* (cock-crow), followed by *hieng lang* (dawn), *loi tha*, *trua det* (about midday), *trua ca* (near midday), *nua ngay* (midday), *khuong tuong*, *khuong pan*, *lan loi* (sunset), *vang mat* (fading light), *giat dau* (deep sleep), *cau nam*, *kham tay*, *khay uoi*, *khuoi a*, and *lan la*.

On each stick there are thirty grooves for the thirty days of the month, divided into three "weeks." This system of weeks is similar to the traditional Kinh (Viet) month of three weeks of ten days each—the first, the middle, and the last "week"—which correspond to the *cay* "week," the *loong* "week," and the *coi* "week" of the Muong calendar. The *loong* week is notable for the grooves engraved on the edge of the bamboo stick. Traditional markets were held every ten days—in other words, once a week in this calendar system.

The Muong now use the lunisolar calendar, which they call the mandarin calendar, as a reference point, but they map it according to their bamboo calendar, counting days of the month later and the sequence of months earlier than the lunisolar calendar. The first day of the month follows the first moonless night, the day when the crescent moon appears on the western horizon while the sun sets. Thus, the Muong first day (Cay 1) corresponds to the second day of the month by the lunisolar calendar. Muong months generally are one month ahead of the lunisolar calendar. Muong groups in western Vietnam count their months three months in advance of the lunisolar calendar, in the central region, two months in advance, and in the eastern region

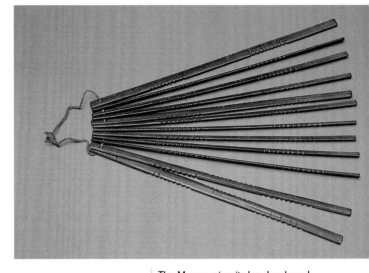

The Muong minority has developed a unique calendar system, reckoning time along the joints incised on strips of bamboo to determine favorable and unfavorable dates for such activities as agriculture, fishing, hunting, marriage, and funerals.

only one month in advance. The first month of the lunisolar calendar corresponds to the fourth month of the Muong calendar, but along with most of the citizens of Vietnam, the Muong celebrate the start of the year in what some Muong communities recognize as the fourth month.

The Muong divide the year into twelve months of twenty-nine or thirty days, based on their observation of the moon. A folk verse describes the phases of the moon:

> Day 1, *it looks like the herb leaf,*
> Day 2, *it looks like the* chit *leaf,*
> Day 3, *it looks like the crescent,*
> Day 4, *it has a bright nimbus.*

The month in which the moon overpasses the Doi star is the first month of the Muong year. If the twelve-month cycle begins again in a month when the moon is distant from the Doi star, this becomes a leap month and is attached to the previous year; the next month then becomes the first month of the year. Although Muong leap years do not correspond to lunisolar leap years, they occur with roughly the same frequency; every nineteen lunisolar years have seven leap years, each with thirteen months.

The Muong calculate auspicious days, inauspicious days, and days for sowing crops according to a scheme mapped on the index finger, middle finger, and ring finger of the left hand. The joints of these fingers, except the middle joint of the middle finger, form eight sectors of a square. The months are counted on these sectors, beginning with the bottom joint of the middle finger and proceeding clockwise to the bottom joint of the ring finger. The sectors are named as follows:

The first sector, *thuom ngang*, indicates the first month.
The second sector, *cay trong*, indicates the second and third months.
The third sector, *thuom trong*, indicates the fourth month.
The fourth sector, *kim trong*, indicates the fifth and the sixth months.
The fifth sector, *khoa ho*, indicates the seventh month.
The sixth sector, *kim tha*, indicates the eighth and ninth months.
The seventh sector, *thuom tha*, indicates the tenth month.
The eighth sector, *cay tha*, indicates the eleventh and twelfth months.

Every sector has auspicious or inauspicious time spans, and events undertaken during those times must be approached accordingly. Days and time units are similarly mapped. In the inauspicious *thuom ngang*, for example, the time of ghosts and unfavorable spirits, people avoid any important enterprises other than ceremonies conducted by shamans. The letter *thuom* means blood, so this is an extremely bad month for departures, marriage rites, and house construction, though it is good for hunting. If a person cannot avoid these activities in the month *thuom*, they should be conducted in the days and time units of the Cay sector. The *thuom trong* sector is bad for activities inside the house, while the *thuom tha* sector is bad for outdoor activities, including travel. The *thuom ngang* and *khoa ho* sectors are considered generally bad, so no significant activity should be undertaken at these times. The *cay trong* sector is best for such events as marriage or house construction. The *cay tha* sector is best for travel and commerce. The shamans apply this system with some flexibility, each using his own method of interpreting the circumstances surrounding events.

Within Vietnam, as we have seen, time maps are diverse. While the Gregorian calendar provides both a unifying national and international means of reckoning time, the alternative paths are encoded with rich cultural meanings and are one means of signifying and perpetuating distinctive ethnic identities.

A Hmong woman casts a ball through a hoop held high on a bamboo pole at a Hmong new year festival in 2000. This game is a part of the new year celebrations in several northern minority communities.

This dish of Vietnamese origin from the fifteenth or sixteenth century was found in Indonesia. For centuries Vietnamese ceramics were traded throughout Southeast Asia and as far west as the Middle East.

BAT TRANG:

A POTTERY VILLAGE

AND GLOBAL NODE

6

Nguyen Anh Ngoc

Mats from Nga Son,
bricks from Bat Trang,
cloth from Nam Dinh,
silk from Ha Dong.

THIS FAMILIAR VIETNAMESE PROVERB testifies to the long tradition of ceramics in the Red River Delta from the fifteenth century, when Vietnamese ceramic ware was sold throughout Southeast Asia, a significant amount reaching as far west as the Middle East. Indeed, among Western connoisseurs, the best-known piece of Vietnamese ceramics is probably a vase in the Topkapi Museum in Istanbul. Ceramics were tailored to the needs of varied customers. Large painted plates from Vietnam were used for communal dining in Muslim households in Southeast Asia. Polychrome tiles of Vietnamese manufacture have been found on several buildings in eastern Java.[1] Commenting on the range of wares recovered from a fifteenth-century shipwreck outside the port of Hoi An, ceramics expert John Guy writes that many of the items "would not have been out of place in a well-appointed Middle Eastern household, and could have been transmitted through the system of trading networks that linked Tonkin to the Mediterranean."[2]

Today the village of Bat Trang on the Red River is the center of a revivified global ceramics industry producing both traditional Vietnamese wares and products that meet the specialized needs of distant customers. Large ceramic planters from Bat Trang factories can be seen in American garden supply shops, sets of Japanese-style dinnerware are sold in Tokyo department stores, statues of Kwan Yin and the three gods of good fortune are shipped to Taiwan, pastel flowerpots are produced to fill custom orders from Denmark. At the same time, the shops that line the main street of Bat Trang are fairly bursting with a dizzy array of tiles, ashtrays, incense pots, and a great variety of cups, bowls, and dishes produced for Vietnamese use.

The village of Bat Trang has been designated a tourist site by the Hanoi city government. Situated on the Red River, six miles from central Hanoi, Bat Trang was originally part of Thuan Thanh prefecture, Bac Ninh province, but has been absorbed into the administration of greater Hanoi. Bat Trang potters trace their roots to the pottery village of Bo Bat in Thanh Hoa province, claiming that their ancestors moved to Bat Trang about six hundred years ago. The history of Bat Trang village is inseparable from the history of Thang Long royal city (now Hanoi), which was built with bricks and tiles produced at Bat Trang. Bat Trang wares are even mentioned in folk poetry.

Bat Trang is an excellent location for ceramic production. White kaolin clay is transported from neighboring provinces, and boats on the river can bring supplies and carry wares to widely dispersed markets. Given these favorable conditions, potters became adept at producing cheap wide bowls and other simple domestic pieces as well as artistic wares. The Bat Trang kilns reached their first peak of productivity at the end of the eighteenth century and beginning of the nineteenth, before being overshadowed by foreign competition under the French.[3]

The commune of Bat Trang is composed of two adjacent villages, Bat Trang and Giang Cao, both of which are engaged in ceramic production. The population of the commune is 6,600, distributed among 1,600 households. Of these, 1,300 households, or 81 percent of the total, are directly

Bat Trang ceramics await transport to markets. Bat Trang's location on the Red River facilitates the import of supplies and the export of finished wares.

involved in ceramic production, with members working for dozens of local companies; other village households include many truck drivers, dealers, and clerks and are thus indirectly part of the ceramics industry. Giang Cao, though primarily agricultural until the recent market boom, has produced some ceramics ever since the nineteenth century. In Bat Trang village proper, 90 percent of the households are involved in ceramic production, largely for export. The growth of the Bat Trang ceramics industry, fueled by the opening of new markets in Korea, Taiwan, Japan, the United States, Australia, and Western Europe, has helped create new jobs not only for the villagers but also for workers from the neighboring villages and even neighboring districts of Van Giang, Gia Lam, Thuan Thanh, and others. The ceramics industry makes a huge contribution to the economic and social development not only of Bat Trang but of the surrounding region. Each year the commune produces around seventy million items, including domestic wares, fine handicrafts, and building materials, which are marketed both at home and abroad.

The Bat Trang communal house was built in 1719–1720 during the reign of King Le Du Tong and is dedicated to Bach Ma, the patron god of the ceramics industry, and to Luu Thien Tu and La Thanh Mau, who are revered as the founding ancestors of the village. According to local legend, the two were descendants of the Nguyen line and, in the manner of culture heroes, taught the local population the art of ceramic production. The communal house holds twenty-four incense burners to commemorate the twenty-four lineages that have lived in the village, but of the nineteen still remaining, only the Nguyen, as descendants of the founders, are allowed to enter the communal house by the middle door.

Both men and women are proficient potters, although most typically men do the heavy work of preparing the clay, making molds, and readying the kiln for firing. Women typically pour slip into molds and apply glaze and painted decoration. The most valued skill is potting or shaping wares. In the past this was done solely by women, but today both male and female artisans are respected for their high level of skill.

The Bat Trang ceramics industry has been marked by innovation. With the discovery of a new source of kaolin clay, potters began to use more efficient chamber kilns in the 1930s and 1940s and upgraded their basic bowls to coarse porcelain. They also began to produce more diverse products, including figurines and statues.[4] With the expansion of the market under the "open door" (Mo Cua) policy from the late 1980s, these trends have continued as potters have continued to introduce new technologies and to develop their skills in reproducing antique wares and developing new products. This has contributed to the quality as well as the quantity of Bat Trang ceramics.

The flowering of the local ceramics industry has also brought unanticipated problems. Coal-burning kilns have proliferated, bringing serious pollution. Villagers began to notice that the potted plants in their gardens were dying because of the toxic air. Today, the storied coal-burning kilns in Bat Trang village are gradually being replaced by more expensive but far more efficient gas-burning kilns. The tall kilns and the walls decorated with drying pats of coal—memorable features of the Bat Trang landscape—will soon be a thing of the past.

The dynamism of Bat Trang ceramics is best demonstrated by the people who contribute to the industry. In the remainder of this chapter, I will introduce four important figures: Le Van Cam, a master artisan who, although officially retired, is hard at work executing new wares, some in imitation of antique ceramics and some totally innovative; Ha Thi Vinh, a

A bicycle covered in white ceramic dust stands in stark contrast to the building behind it, which has been blackened with pats of drying coal. Coal furnaces and blackened walls were once a hallmark of Bat Trang, but today more efficient gas-burning kilns have all but replaced their coal-burning predecessors.

successful businesswoman whose factory sells goods worldwide; and Nguyen Van Phuc and Pham Thi Yen, ceramic workers who commute to Bat Trang from a neighboring village. Their stories exemplify the vitality and variety of experiences and visions associated with the production of Bat Trang ceramics.

■ The Master Artisan

BAT TRANG HAS PRODUCED MANY ARTISANS, and conversely, many artisans have contributed to the present success of the pottery village. Le Van Cam, a veteran potter of seventy, recalls with feeling that he began his apprenticeship with an old artisan in Bat Trang village when he was thirteen years old. Every time the foreman left his potter's wheel unoccupied, the little Cam, intelligent and curious, sat down to practice modeling on his own. After many efforts, he succeeded in making a teapot that was comparable to that of a proficient potter. He soon got himself hired in the workshop of a certain Mr. Thinh, an old Bat Trang villager. In 1945 Le Van Cam continued his work in ceramics while taking part in a youth movement to promote a revolutionary way of life. When the French War began in 1946, Le Van Cam joined the regular army and lost a leg during a battle in 1950. After the war he and some friends founded a pottery cooperative, and he became the manager, becoming a successful administrator despite the fact that potting was his first love. The cooperative, making mainly crockery, was then in the vanguard of small companies in Hanoi.

Le Van Cam retired in 1979 and set up a private enterprise. At first he faced a lot of difficulties. He could not afford to build a furnace six feet high but eventually managed to build a small furnace and a slip tank with loans from his friends. While making articles for everyday use he studied different kinds of glaze and in the early 1980s managed to reproduce an antique glaze and produce a teapot along antique lines that had great market appeal. Many antique dealers began to buy the pieces he made, reselling them as antiques at the highest possible price. Within two years Le Van Cam had enough money to build a new house. Now famous far and near, he is repeatedly invited to participate in exhibitions, and a piece imitating a

This jar, produced by master artisan Le Van Cam, was inspired by antique forms but executed in his own design. It demonstrates mastery of technique as well as consummate creativity. Early twenty-first century.

lamp stand made during the Mac dynasty (1527–1592) won a gold medal at the 1987 exhibition in Hanoi. He was subsequently awarded the title "outstanding artisan."

Le Van Cam pours his heart out to me:

This fortune results from a lot of effort. I must devote all my energies to studying models and decorative patterns from ancient and present times. I must go in quest of ancient ceramics to be studied, and sometimes I stand still for hours before museum pieces to observe the decorative designs. I take an interest in ceramics in temples, pagodas, and private houses. We always recall an old saying of the Bat Trang potters, "First is the bone, second is the skin, and third the furnace." The bone is kaolin clay that must be well worked, or else the product will crack. The skin means glazing, which often calls for the touch of a gentle woman who is clever with her hands. The furnace means that the fire must always be kept alive. This phase of work is quite important to the quality of the product. Other pottery owners and I all have a good command of every link in the chain of the production line, but each of us specializes in a job. I specialize in modeling pieces and glazing.

His old age and efforts devoted to researching and passing on professional skills to the new generation compel Le Van Cam to leave the management of his business to Le Van Thu, his eldest son. Since Le Van Thu is both a skilled worker and a good manager, the business has become increasingly prosperous. His two gas furnaces turn out a steady stream of products, many destined for export. Both Le Van Cam's younger son and daughter have a gas furnace as well, and both have done well in business. His grandson, still at school, also studies pottery and has produced some original models. Mr. Cam shows me a collection of amusing figurines—an elephant, a horse, a frog, and a chicken—made by his grandson. When asked about passing on his skills to his children, Le Van Cam says:

They watch me working, and imitate me. Their quick minds and their passion for the profession help them to do well. My second son is very good at imitating old-time ceramics, in some respects even more skillful than I am. My eldest son is both a good worker and a good manager. He is somewhat bossy and resolute, but this may be necessary for our profession. His busi-

This blue-and-white plate was fashioned by Le Van Cam; a Bat Trang glazer added the traditional dragonfly motif following his instructions. The dragonfly and the taro plant are rustic motifs, evoking the countryside of Vietnam. These motifs and the antique-style crackle over-glaze are often seen on Bat Trang wares, but it takes considerable skill to produce a large plate of this quality. Early twenty-first century.

ness has made considerable headway, and he now can purchase a building worth 200 million dong [approximately U.S. $13,000]. This large pottery business is due to his hard work, creativity, and resoluteness. My children have come to maturity and are becoming owners of their own pottery enterprises. As for my grandson, I always try to convey to him a love for the profession and the skills handed down by our forefathers. I encourage him to study industrial arts so he can become an even better worker than the present generation, and I believe in his success.

▪ The Businesswoman

HA THI VINH, FORTY-FIVE YEARS OLD, is manager of Quang Vinh Ceramics and China Company, one of the most prosperous companies in Bat Trang. In this slender, wan woman is hidden an uncommon energy. Born in the pottery village, she inherited many professional practices from her parents, both well-known potters, and her neighbors. As was typical during her childhood, she and her friends went to work in one of the ceramics cooperatives in Bat Trang and learned the craft from senior workers. Mrs. Vinh says, "In the ceramics and china cooperative of Bat Trang I was charged with the task of supervising articles for export. I had to work with the Technology Section to create models acceptable to foreign markets, so I knew very well what I was doing and my business career has made considerable headway."

With the Open Door and Renovation (Mo Cua, Doi Moi) policies advocated by the government in the late 1980s and with the new market economy taking off, Mrs. Vinh stopped working for a state-owned enterprise. She set up My Hanh Enterprise, specializing in articles for export. Ten years later, this small enterprise had grown into the big Quang Vinh Ceramics and China Company, with workshops extending over 32,291 square feet. Its staff, 176 strong, includes forty technicians specializing in clay kneading, molding, designing, glazing, and firing. Molds are prepared carefully in secret to secure a monopoly for the company's products. Glazing is also very important. Japanese and Scandinavian customers are very partial to Vietnamese traditional glazes. Mrs. Vinh holds that not only the modernization of production, but also the old saying "First is the bone, second is the skin, and third the furnace," are critical to maintaining high quality. In her interpretation, the fineness of the bone (clay) and the skin (glaze) is owed to each worker's hands and brain.

Apart from professionals, Quang Vinh also hires many seasonal workers. Her company contracts work to more than one hundred households scattered through all of the nineteen lineages in the village. In addition, Quang Vinh has numerous smaller workshop affiliates. The mother company develops the molds and glazes, then puts the production into the hands of these affiliates. Each affiliate has ten to fifteen workers, which means that Quang Vinh has created jobs for thousands of people. According to Mrs. Vinh, the company and its affiliates cooperate closely with one another, sharing troubles and joys. She maintains that the company always fulfills its promises to customers to maintain its reputation.

Aware of developments in technology and marketing, the company has established solid markets in the United States, Japan, Korea, Taiwan, and Denmark. Quang Vinh has participated in exhibitions in Texas, Cologne, and Osaka. It is noteworthy that inexpensive and well-executed Vietnamese pottery has penetrated the market in Japan, which is itself a major ceramics producer. According to Ha Thi Vinh, Vietnamese ceramics made in Bat Trang in general and those made by Quang Vinh in particular have

This spouted *kendi* was made at Bat Trang during the 1990s in imitation of antique wares. *Kendi* were common items of export for the Southeast Asian market in the fifteenth and sixteenth centuries. Blue glaze against a background of gray-white clay is often seen on ceramics from the Red River Delta.

unique characteristics; models are simple but elegant, combining traditional and contemporary design elements, so they attract the attention of many customers.

In the future Quang Vinh's workshops will extend over 69,965 square feet, allowing for a great increase in production. The company is now cooperating with about twenty major merchants in Bat Trang. Quang Vinh Company also acts as a middleman, buying pottery from local manufacturers and selling to customers that it has located independently. In addition, the company has made an effort to reduce pollution from its kilns.

Mrs. Vinh's global vision includes her children. Her eldest son assists her in managing her large enterprise. Her daughter is studying business in Australia. Her youngest son is learning Chinese in Beijing and will study ceramics and porcelain manufacture in Kwangxi province. Mrs. Vinh recently made a trip to China to survey the ceramics and porcelain industry. "We propose to contract with our Chinese partners for two lines of production in order to raise the quality of our products. I hope that my children will come to maturity in business. They will not only take traditional skills into account, but also assimilate up-to-date technology to push Quang Vinh ahead."

Bicycle loaded, this woman will deliver pottery to market. Her bicycle is specially fitted to hold the weight of the ceramics and maintain balance as she pushes it, steering with an attached pole.

Although she is both a worker and a manager, Mrs. Vinh does not neglect household duties. "I am one of the first-rate cooks of the village. I was carefully trained by my mother. All women must know how to cook and do needlework. When I was growing up, men never entered the kitchen, so women were in charge of all cooking. Bat Trang food is quite delicious. Bat Trang women are good at both ceramics and at housekeeping."

According to Mrs. Vinh, Bat Trang potters must make the most of traditional skills while learning new technology from other countries, and Bat Trang must do business in the contemporary global market if it is to develop further.

■ The Workers

EACH DAY IN THE LATE AFTERNOON, crowds of workers spill out on motorcycles, bicycles, or on foot onto roads leading from Bat Trang to Gia Lam, Thuan Thanh, and Van Giang. They are full-time and seasonal ceramics workers, ranging from eighteen to fifty years in age, earning their living at the companies, enterprises, and private kilns of Bat Trang. Mingling with the crowd, I chat with a young couple. The husband, Nguyen

Performing one of the highly skilled jobs at a ceramics works, this woman paints decorations on a vase before it is fired.

A market booth is stacked with blue-and-white Bat Trang incense burners and imported Chinese bowls. Early 1990s.

Van Phuc, thirty-three years old, kneads clay. The wife, Pham Thi Yen, twenty-eight, paints decorations on pieces before the final firing. They live in Xuan Quan commune, Van Giang district, Hung Yen province, and both have worked in Bat Trang for seven years.

Phuc says, "At first, I worked for a brick kiln in Xuan Quan, where the work is arduous and the pay low. I moved on to a pottery works, where I had an advantage over inexperienced people. However, the work in a Bat Trang pottery workshop involves much more skill and effort. Kneading clay is an important phase of production. That is why the saying goes, 'First is the bone, second is the skin, and third the furnace.' Clay for making bricks can be found on the spot, but kaolin for ceramics must be bought from a remote province. It must be carefully leached from the sand, or else the pottery will be cracked. So the worker must be strong, diligent, and careful."

I ask, "How much do you earn each day? Are you employed regularly?"

Phuc replies, "I earn 35,000 dong [a little more than U.S. $2] each day, and there is plenty of work, but I am only a seasonal worker. I must return to my village at harvest time."

His wife also goes home at harvest time, working in Bat Trang only during the agricultural off-season. At first she did unskilled work, earning 15,000 dong a day (about U.S. $1). Intelligent and hardworking, she decided to learn drawing. Four months later she had become a skilled painter and was hired by a Bat Trang limited liability company. She was paid 20,000 dong a day in the first year and 25,000 dong the next year; now, as an experienced worker, she earns 30,000 dong a day. Nonetheless, she must stop working for the company at harvest time. "My family has four people—my mother, my husband, and my four-year-old daughter, in addition to me, but we have only about 16,146 square feet of farmland on the riverbank. Harvests are uncertain. Since my husband and I work in a pottery company, my family has enough to live on. Bat Trang ceramics have made life easier for many families in the villages, and we think well of this trade. Though still a farmer, I never forget pottery. I must train myself to draw fine designs on ceramics."

We continue our conversation until we come to Xuan Quan commune, across an irrigation canal from Bat Trang. Saying good-bye to the young couple, I return to Hanoi, much impressed by the pottery commune of Bat Trang. It has grown from a traditional pottery village to the present Bat Trang commune, producing goods that are successfully marketed at home and abroad.

Red Yao women in the Sapa market embroider and socialize during a lull in the flow of prospective customers. The women's richly embroidered clothing is a testimony to their skill. (All photos this chapter from the late 1990s.)

SCENES FROM

THE SAPA MARKET

Claire Burkert

E ARLY THURSDAY MORNING Cu Thi Pa, age fifty-five, arrives ahead of most of the ethnic minority women who sell handicrafts in Sapa market in Lao Cai province, near the China border in northern Vietnam. In the 1990s, Sapa's scenic mountain setting and traditionally dressed women drew ever larger numbers of tourists whose presence created a market for locally produced handicrafts. As Mrs. Pa waits for customers, a few vans with tourists are arriving before the busy weekend. She and the other Hmong women who wait along the main street are hoping to sell the few cushion covers, shirts, blankets, and other items that they have hand-stitched in their villages during the week. Materials for making one cushion cover cost Pa less than 20,000 dong (U.S. $1.50), but she can sell it for 60,000 (U.S. $4.00), so it is worth the time she spends in the market.

Mrs. Pa encourages a young Japanese tourist to buy a blanket that she made from the cloth of a batik Hmong skirt. She herself does not wear skirts, the traditional dress of her group of Hmong consisting instead of a tunic (*shao khua*), jacket, and short pants. Rather, the decorated cloth comes from Flower and Blue Hmong groups who live in other nearby districts. She buys chemical dyes in the market and overdyes the cloth at home, bringing new life to the faded cloth. For her blanket, she has used a bright green chemical dye because, she says, "Foreigners like this color." The blanket is a new product, copied from the ones Vietnamese traders have recently begun to display in their shops along the main street.

The Japanese tourist shows no interest in the blanket, and so Mrs. Pa returns to sit with her basket on the steps of a café that offers fruit shakes. From here she can keep an eye on tourists who amble between the market stalls and handicraft shops at one end of the street to popular Vietnamese and Italian restaurants at the other. All morning she beseeches each passerby, but her luck comes only when an American tour group strolls by on their way to lunch. "*Pantalon joli*, buy from me," she cries, greeting them with a pair of trousers. "*Chapeau?*" she inquires, waving a hat, then again tries to capture their attention with a jacket, stretching to hold it against a tall woman's shoulders. "Jacket, *joli* jacket?"

"How many times do you think I need to wash it to get the dye out, Greg?" the woman asks her companion, because their guidebook describes how the dye in Sapa clothing runs and runs. The woman bargains the price down from 100,000 dong to 70,000 dong (U.S. $5.00) and then rejoins her tour group with her purchase. Mrs. Pa follows her down the street, calling, "You buy blanket from me—hey, you buy blanket?" She holds the blanket up to the restaurant window. The tourists are hot and want cold beers, not blankets. But at least she has sold one jacket, and so Mrs. Pa also takes a break to enjoy a bowl of noodles in the market.

Later in the day, a group of Hmong women from Mu Cang Chai district arrive by bus with their rice sacks of old skirts. The afternoon finds Mrs. Pa standing outside one of Sapa's many Vietnamese handicraft shops. Inside, a Mu Cang Chai trader shows one skirt after another to a Kinh woman who holds a stack of bills. They bargain over each skirt, the Kinh woman paying out 30,000 or 40,000 dong (U.S. $2–$3) per skirt, a skirt that could have taken well over a month to make. The Hmong woman protests, receives

Tourists in the Sapa market examine the ribbon bracelets a Black Hmong girl is trying to sell them. Hmong girls in the Sapa market learned to make these bracelets from other tourists.

10,000 dong more, and the skirt is tossed onto the pile behind the Kinh trader. The trader's shop has an ever-increasing mound of skirts, as well as heaps of plastic bags stuffed with pieces of Hmong embroidery, Yao embroidery, Hmong collars, hemp cloth, and other materials for making handicraft products. The business is big: the Vietnamese trader has clients in Hanoi and Ho Chi Minh City (formerly Saigon) to whom she sends large shipments of ethnic minority materials. She also has buyers in Thailand, Singapore, France, Mexico, Japan, and the United States for whom she and other family members sew clothing, blankets, cushion covers, and other items from the traditional cloth. She organizes about forty ethnic minority traders to collect skirts and collars and whatever else she needs for her ethnic handicraft business. The sewing machine is busy all day, and even male family members pitch in to undo the hundred pleats of old skirts and to help cut the cloth to make new products. The shirts are made according to Western sizing. The cushion covers have standard sizes, with openings large enough to put cushions inside. The blankets fit Western beds. The orders for products created and sewn by Kinh traders are multiplying each year, and the network of suppliers of ethnic cloth is increasing accordingly.

When she has gone through all the skirts, the Kinh trader helps the Hmong woman trader stuff the remaining ones into her large rice sack and to lift it a few paces from the shop. Immediately Mrs. Pa and other Hmong women gather, pulling out the skirts, bargaining with the trader. When the women return to their villages, the skirts will be transformed into cushion covers, bags, blankets, and jackets. Hence a shoulder bag sold on a Sapa street may have a unique life story. Take this one, for example: Once a girl in Mu Cang Chai carefully crafted a skirt before the new year festival (Tet). After Tet the girl was married, and she wore the skirt in the fields for two years until it became soiled and worn. A Hmong woman trader from Mu Cang Chai bought it from her and took it by bus to Sapa in a bag of skirts. Cu Ti Pa bought the skirt, took it home, disassembled it, and dyed the cloth bright blue. Following a design she had seen in a Kinh handicraft shop, she cut the cloth and hand-sewed it into a handbag, adding part of a Yao sleeve, bought in the market from a Yao woman trader, for decoration. Finally, the bag was sold to a tourist in the market who took it home to San Bernardino, believing it to be a fine example of a traditional accessory from northern Vietnam.

Mrs. Pa has copied all of her products from Kinh traders, but the cutting and use of old pieces of cloth require her own inventiveness. In fact, her cushion covers have openings too small for cushions. Her hand-sewn shirts are made in only one size, and the narrow lengths of batik cloth composing them are awkwardly pieced together. Her business is minuscule in comparison to that of the Kinh shop owners, yet from time to time she manages to sell her creations, because, stitched together as they are by her own dye-stained hands, they come from what one Sapa hotel advertises as the "authentic world."

This same four-star hotel arranges special "Beaujolais weekends" among the "colorful ethnic minorities" during which tourists are offered the opportunity to picnic in a minority village and perhaps purchase some handicrafts. According to anthropologist Jean Michaud, during the period of French colonization French residents and summer visitors visited villages to buy the handicraft of the local Yao and Hmong, who made their subsistence living then, as they do today, on agriculture. Outside exchange with the minorities ceased in the late 1940s, during the First Indochina War, when many of the French buildings in Sapa were destroyed. In late 1979 Sapa was further damaged by shelling during a border war with China. In the 1970s, Sapa was newly settled by the Kinh (Viet), but the town did not open to foreign tourists until the early 1990s.

A Hmong woman prepares vats of commercial dye to refurbish old batik in colors that she hopes will appeal to tourists.

Since Vietnam's opening to tourism, the town has boomed, becoming one of Vietnam's most popular tourist destinations and also one of the most vital centers of Vietnam's handicraft trade. Accordingly, the Kinh population has been rising steadily. (Hmong make up about 50 percent of the population of Sapa district, Yao 25 percent, and Kinh 15 percent; in addition are the Giay and a small percentage of Xa Pho.) Today, most civil servants in Sapa are Kinh, and shops, hotels, and tour businesses are also owned by Kinh people, increasingly marginalizing the ethnic minorities economically in their own market town.

Since the 1990s, the market has expanded to include a huge central building with a lower open area for stalls selling prepared foods and fresh produce and meat. Upstairs, vendors sell goods the ethnic minorities need for their handicraft work, including thread, cloth, and beads. In addition, there is a large hall with space that can be rented by local and nearby traders.

Over the years, authorities, mainly Kinh, have introduced different measures to prohibit street selling. It has been said that local people should not sell on the streets because they bother tourists or because they might be hit by one of the jeeps, buses, trucks, or motorcycles that zoom up and down the main road at unregulated speeds. At times, policemen have confiscated the baskets of older women who regularly sell on the street. Now a number of these women sell inside the large hall mentioned above, paying 1,000 dong a day for rent. Making a colorful display along the wall are the blankets they have created from Hmong skirts, following the recent innovation by Kinh traders.

Traditionally, ethnic minorities have come to Sapa market not only to buy and sell, but also to mingle; for them, the market is a social event. By Friday many people are leaving their villages to come to the market. In particular, Yao girls—who, unlike the Hmong girls who frequent the market, are at home most of the week—hop on motorcycle taxis in their villages, eager to join the market activity. In the late afternoon, many of them gather on the steps of the central market building to meet and see what the others have brought to trade.

On this Friday, several Yao and Hmong women surround one ethnic Lao woman from a village near Tan Uyen, a town south of Sapa. She is selling silk that women of her village have spun by hand, and the women are gathering to feel the quality of the material. Silkworms are not raised in Sapa, where the climate is harsh most of the year, and silk thread is a precious commodity. The finely embroidered clothing of the Yao requires at least two hundred grams of fine silk thread. A Yao girl who is engaged to be married must stay at home to make several sets of clothes before her marriage. The groom's family makes gifts of one or two kilograms of silk and

In addition to benefiting from tourist traffic, Sapa is an active local market. These Hmong women display hardware and ribbon that they have purchased in China.

indigo-dyed cloth, and on her wedding day she wears all of the sets of clothes she has made for herself, showing off her wealth and skill. A Yao song tells how a girl's embroidery skills are a measure of her worth:

> *She was very skillful in embroidery since she was a child.*
> *She is such a good girl, worth silver.*
> *My family wants you to be our daughter-in-law.*
> *I want you to sew for us.*

Several of the young Hmong girls of Lai Chau village, more than an hour's walk south of Sapa, are also setting off to the market on Friday afternoon. Fourteen-year-old Mo takes a cap to sell for her neighbor, Mrs. Dua, putting it in her basket along with some cushion covers her mother made.

Mrs. Dua remains behind, hoping to attract tourists who trek through the village. Inside her house, she has a table with a number of colorful hats and cushion covers. On a string on the wall next to the family altar hang shirts she has made for the tourist trade, as well as one traditional indigo-dyed long outer vest with an intricately appliquéd and embroidered collar. Mrs. Dua has learned to use collars to decorate cushion covers and hats. First she dyes the collars in indigo or chemical dye to make them look old because she knows that foreigners like old things. The hat that she has given Mo has a collar around the headband. It is also made of scraps of old hemp cloth. Mrs. Dua would never use new hemp cloth because it is too valuable, its production being extremely time-consuming. Hmong women in Sapa commonly have hemp fibers wound around their hands, not wanting to lose a moment joining hemp fibers to make thread for weaving.

Hemp-making is a process Mo doesn't worry about yet, although she knows that in a few years, after her marriage, it will be her task to make hemp cloth for the family. But now it is a sunny Friday in April, and Mo is free. In Sapa, she joins friends who have stayed in the market all week. By Friday there are gangs of young Hmong girls, and they are finding tourists to befriend for the weekend. Mo approaches a girl who already sports a "Sapa *pantalon*," wide cotton pants with a trim of Yao embroidery, hand-sewn by Mrs. Pa. "Where are you from? Oh, California—I have a friend there—his name is Ted. What is your name?" Sometimes Mo's mother chides her for having too much fun in the market and not doing enough

A Red Yao woman purchases Chinese-made ribbon to use on made-for-tourist goods while a Hmong girl plays one of the mouth harps she will try to sell to tourists. Preteen and young teenaged Hmong girls spend a great deal of time in the market cultivating friendships with travelers from Europe and the United States.

selling. Mo and her friends make and sell trinkets, which include traditional mouth harps wound with Chinese ribbons bought from women traders from Bac Ha; imitation ethnic jewelry, purchased from Giay traders; and woven friendship bracelets, which she learned to make from tourists. Mo plays with her friends into the evening, doesn't think about selling yet, and then stays overnight, sharing a bed with several girls for 1,000 dong each in a guesthouse where older traders such as Mrs. Pa also stay.

Mo and her friends are the subject of study by anthropologist Duong Bich Hanh, who sits with them in the market or watches television with them at night in their guesthouse and wonders about the future of these Hmong girls. It is not yet known if they will marry and return to their villages or how long they can remain on the streets of Sapa innocently making friendship bracelets and decorating mouth harps. Their future is part of the evolving story of the market in Sapa, as unpredictable today as next year's new trend in Sapa handicraft.

Eight o'clock Saturday morning finds the cement steps of the market building clogged with Yao and Hmong women trading with one another, and a long line of French tourists with video cameras who are trying to pass through the activity. Three Yao women from Tan Uyen have yellow, green, and red pompoms dangling from their headdresses and ornamenting their intricately embroidered clothing. They are selling two sleeves to a Yao man whose daughter is soon to marry. There are Red Yao from Bat Xat district, distinguished by their tall turbans of printed red floral Chinese cloth, trading with the local Red Yao, whose red headdress is perhaps even more elegant, made of as many as twenty layers of red cloth trimmed with silk fringe and silver coins and bells, sitting on her head like a pompadour. There are other differences in the embroidery and style of their clothing, too, and these differences the women also spend time examining and appreciating. It may be that here on weekends, on these very market steps, new embroidery patterns are learned and remembered. The Yao of Sapa, for instance, claim that the embroidery pattern of their belts is borrowed from the style of the Bat Xat Yao, whose distinctive motifs include a bird, the spirit of thunder, and a tiger paw. One can imagine that the patterns of embroidery of each Yao community have evolved continually this way over the past hundreds of years.

A Bat Xat Yao woman appears with a rice sack full of finely embroidered back flaps, the most important part of a Yao woman's clothing. Her flaps are worn but still beautiful, their motifs including pine and banyan trees, and many fine rows of peach and plum flowers. Yao and Hmong women gather around her to bargain for her back flaps. Mrs. Pa is among the first to select one, and she knows already that she will make two bags and one cushion cover with it and have a few scraps left for a hat. Mo also buys a flap to take back home to her mother.

The little children in Sapa, some carried on the backs of the women selling handicraft, are dressed with much attention. Many of the babies and toddlers wear carefully decorated hats. Coins are attached to ward off evil, and cardamom, sewn into small triangles of cloth, is attached to hats to protect a child's health. In addition to coins and beads, one Hmong toddler has a hat with a rat jaw amulet, a pull tab from an aluminum can, and the plastic end of a battery. A Yao baby wears a hat covered with silver studs and a 1958 French coin, while his mother sells a hat made from an old Yao trouser leg to a tourist who needs to cover his balding head under the hot April sun.

San Mai, a Yao child of six, has come to the market with her mother and already speaks two sentences in English: "Buy from me" and "How old are you?" She holds up bracelets to tourists while her mother sells an

This Hmong child wears a cap decorated with French-period coins. Both the coins and their configuration have talismanic properties intended to protect the child.

Hoping to attract a buyer's attention, an elderly Hmong woman holds up a baby carrier made from batik and appliqué work.

old embroidered sleeve to a Hmong woman who thinks she can use it to decorate a handbag.

Batik baby carriers displayed along one railing are still made by Hmong women from a village fifty kilometers away from Sapa. A local Hmong woman examines each one over and over again, lifting them in her indigo-stained hands, which are wrapped in hemp thread. She examines not only the stitching but also the batik patterns. The batik motifs represent a variety of elements important in Hmong life: a device used for winding hemp, a bird's eye, a crab, a plow, a pig's foot, a trough, and chicken feet (boiled chicken feet are commonly used in divination).

At the base of the market steps vendors are selling chicks, which are carried home in plastic bags, as well as plums and sugarcane. On this hot April day, the constant noise of the ice cream vendors' horns, made out of plastic detergent bottles, adds to the commotion caused by vehicles arriving with tourists from the night train. By 9:30 most of the local people are eating ice cream, many holding two sticks of melting ice cream at once. It is as if the ice cream marks a break between selling among themselves and the rest of the day, with its push to sell goods to the latest wave of tourists, who are beginning to emerge from hotels and restaurants after finishing breakfast.

Meanwhile, local shopping continues. On another set of steps, people taste rice alcohol sold by Giay traders, sipping from the caps of large plastic jugs before siphoning off the clear liquid into their own bottles. Also from the Giay traders they buy imitation Yao and Hmong jewelry made in China, which they can resell to tourists at a profit. Down in the food market, they purchase meat, potatoes, cucumbers, and tomatoes, which they then drop into their back-baskets. Hmong people buy bunches of special leaves and roots used for herbal medicine from Hmong traders. From Hmong traders from Bac Ha, near the train station and the Chinese border, Hmong girls are buying ribbons with which they will decorate the mouth harps that they sell to tourists. At a Kinh handicraft shop on the road, where disco music blares from Chinese speakers, a Hmong man sells a traditional pan flute and purchases some wicks for oil lamps. A Kinh grandmother bargains for a Hmong flute for her grandchild; a Yao grandmother bargains for a plastic rattle for her daughter's new baby.

By 11:30 it is extremely hot, and local people are taking breaks in the food stalls. Here Sang Mai's mother buys her rice, while other Hmong raise toasts of rice wine. The tourists drift into restaurants for a cold drink. Some handicraft sellers cluster near the restaurants, holding their creations up to the windows. For the rest of the afternoon and into the evening, the selling continues. After dinner is a good time—the tourists have had some beer and don't mind joking with the traders. At night, some Hmong are singing in a local bar, and both local people and tourists come

Although the glare of tourist attention on the so-called love market has
curtailed courtship activities in Sapa,
this Hmong boy and girl find a quiet
moment together.

to see. This entertainment has become a substitute for the fabled "love
market" of Sapa.

The "love market" was what originally drew tourists on weekends. In the
past, young boys and girls, both Yao and Hmong, met each other on Saturday night to sing love songs. Later they became shy and carried radios to
play cassettes of songs. And because the gaping tourists did nothing to
enhance the mood of love, eventually they made neither music nor romance
in the market at all. But still occasionally—perhaps not even on a weekend—one may hear a Yao couple standing some distance apart on Sapa's
main street, singing a beautiful song.

Sunday is noticeably quieter in Sapa. Yet one notices many well-groomed
young Hmong. Some of the Hmong girls call this "boyfriend-girlfriend
day," and it is for this reason that boys and girls wear their best clothes to the
market. They can also be seen at the local photo studios primping in front
of tiny mirrors, then posing stiffly for the Kinh photographer who does a
steady business making photos that are displayed on the wall of every village
house. Best clothes for Hmong girls may be decorated with bright synthetic
thread, Chinese ribbons, and strings of plastic beads. When dressed up, the
Hmong girls and boys have collars standing tall, showing the elaborate
embroidery at the back of their heads. Best clothes for Yao girls include
their first red headdress, adorned with tassels, beads, and bells to attract the
attention of boys. Each girl also wears a belt and a purely decorative baby

On Sunday morning in Sapa, Hmong girls, their embroidered collar bands up for display, primp in front of a mirror outside a photographer's shack.

carrier, both of which have bright red tassels. They also adopt new accessories, such as tiger-printed scarves from China, which have the same yellow, orange, white, and black colors as the silk embroidery of Yao clothes.

On Sunday tourists often depart Sapa to go to Bac Ha, another market town, before catching the night train back to Hanoi. After making their own purchases in the market, many of the handicraft traders also leave the market to return home. Tan Ta May, a thirty-nine-year-old Yao woman, summarizes her business dealings, clearly understanding the economics of her trade: "When the client is generous, I can get from 300,000 to 500,000 [U.S. $20–$30] for a set of clothes; otherwise I can get just 200,000 dong to 300,000. If lucky, I can earn over 100,000 dong, including investment and profit; otherwise I earn no money at all. Last week I bought two pairs of trousers for 160,000 dong [together], and then this weekend I sold them for 100,000 dong each. This morning I sold a necklace for 50,000 dong which I bought at 40,000 dong, so the profit was 10,000 dong [U.S. $0.50]. I spent some money on fertilizer, oil, and salt, but the rest I have to keep for capital."

The careful embroidery on these Hmong collar bands is proudly displayed on social occasions, when the collar is arranged to stand tall behind the neck.

As her tourist friends from California board the bus to Bac Ha, Mo sells a few bracelets, making 10,000 dong profit on each. Then late Sunday afternoon, after spending time with her girlfriends watching boys in the market, Mo walks back to her village on a beautiful winding mountain road. She will spend a few days going to morning school and helping at home before returning to the market on Thursday.

Mrs. Pa buys some pork in the market and returns home satisfied. Now she will spend Monday through Wednesday making some new products, and this time she will dye the skirt cloth blue because she's observed that foreigners prefer blue to green.

Mrs. Pa, among other Hmong and Yao women, and the young Hmong girls have increased their livelihoods considerably through the making and selling of tourist products. How traditional skills as embroidery and hemp-making will be preserved in the effort to make products for tourists cannot be foreseen. Certainly, it is likely that Kinh traders will continue to benefit more from the trade of used garments than will the ethnic minorities. Some handicraft projects carried out by Craft Link, a craft organization working in Sapa with women like Mrs. Pa, aim to help ethnic minority women revive and use traditional skills to make new products to increase their income. In the meantime, a unique Sapa style is ever evolving. Hmong and Yao women play a vital role in the reimaging of their traditional clothes,

This Hmong girl intently embroiders a collar band.

and the Sapa market provides continual inspiration. Furthermore, a collar, a skirt, the tail of a jacket, and a pair of sleeves are now seen as commodities of value. Whether the makers and sellers of handicraft are local ethnic minority women, young girls, or Kinh traders, it is sure that the reuse of traditional clothing will continue, and Sapa style will continue to change and be traded for years to come.

One of a set of paintings used during the Yao initiation ritual in Khe Mu village, Son Ha commune,
Bao Thang district, Lao Cai province. Initiates must
be certified by the highest deity, Ngoc Thanh, that
they have committed no serious misdeeds in their
previous lives. The painting represents messengers
dispatched to Ngoc Thanh.

THE YAO INITIATION CEREMONY IN THE NEW MARKET ECONOMY

Ly Hanh Son

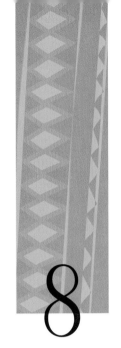

D
URING THE COURSE OF HUMAN LIFE, a person experiences many ceremonies on his or her journey from birth to death. Birth rituals, funerals, and weddings are common in all societies. Most Yao men, however, also take part in another ceremony, one marking their mastery of important ritual knowledge. This ceremony, called the Qua Tang or Chay Xay by different Yao groups, is known as the "candle-lighting ceremony" in Vietnamese because of the lighted candles that are placed on the body of the initiate during the ceremony. In this ceremony, the initiate is provided with a new name, spirit protectors, and a certificate of participation.

Despite seven centuries of residence in Vietnam, the Yao have maintained many distinctive cultural practices, including the Qua Tang ceremony, a ritual unique to them. However, the Renovation (Doi Moi) policy of 1986 brought significant changes in the material life of Yao communities, raising the question of whether the Yao can maintain their cultural traditions as they journey into the new market economy. The fate of the Qua Tang ceremony is an excellent lens through which to regard this question and to assess the ability of ethnic groups to adjust their cultural practices to a changing environment. While many scholars have written about the Yao Qua Tang ceremony,[1] I am the first to have studied it since the development of the market economy in Vietnam. In this chapter, I will focus on the ceremony as practiced by the Yao Tien of Mit village, Tu Ly commune, Da Bac district, Hoa Binh province, where I have done extensive fieldwork. I have chosen this area because of the many changes that have occurred here as a result of the development of the market economy.

■ The Yao in Vietnam

THE YAO ORIGINALLY MIGRATED TO VIETNAM from China over the course of several centuries, with the earliest group arriving in the thirteenth century.[2] In the past, the Yao in Vietnam were nomadic mountain hunters and horticulturalists who lived in the mountains and practiced shifting cultivation (swidden). Today they live in mostly settled communities practicing forestry, fruit tree cultivation, and animal husbandry, enjoying an improved standard of living. In 1989 there were 473,945 Yao in Vietnam, and by 1994 this number had grown to 527,524.[3] Most Yao inhabit the central and northern highlands, where they are concentrated in Ha Giang, Tuyen Quang, Yen Bai, Lao Cai, Cao Bang, and Quang Ninh provinces. In Hoa Binh province alone, there are 10,373 Yao.[4] Ethnologists have classified the Yao as several distinct subgroups based on cultural practices and language.[5] The Yao Tien are identified by the embroidered indigo shirts worn by the men and the long indigo tunics worn by the women. The several coins suspended on a beaded string from the back collar of a Yao Tien garment are the source of their name, *tien*, meaning "money" in Vietnamese. The Yao Tien live in both the northeast, mostly in Tuyen Quang and Bac Kan provinces, and northwest, mostly in Hoa Binh province, where they are most numerous in Da Bac district.

■ Mit Village

MIT VILLAGE, WHICH IS INHABITED solely by members of the Yao Tien, is seven kilometers from Da Bac town and two kilometers from the center of Tu Ly commune. As a result, residents have seen a lot of economic development and have interacted with other ethnic groups. Forty-two years ago, the present site of Mit village was still old-growth forest. In 1956 there were only three Yao Tien households in the village, and in 1957 only six, living apart from the sparsely populated Muong villages in the area. In 1960 government policies establishing agricultural cooperatives and mandating permanent agricultural settlement brought the Yao into working relationships with their Muong neighbors. Since the development of a market economy, and especially since 1990, the Yao Tien have had many more opportunities for cultural interaction with other ethnic groups.

In 2000 Mit village had forty-one households, making for a population of 239. The village highway was widened to accommodate car and truck traffic in 1991 with aid from Oxfam Belgium. The village also has schools, housing, electricity, and water tanks built with government assistance. Government programs have provided funding for the development of forestry and gardens and for the expansion of land for agriculture and animal husbandry. Consequently, wood products, fruits, and sugarcane are produced for the market. By 1997 one village household had a grinding machine, nine had motorbikes, fifteen had television sets, and thirty-six had radio–cassette players.

With economic development and the concomitant improvement in living standards, many outward signs of Yao life disappeared. In 1997, only six households in Mit village still lived in traditional Yao houses; the rest lived in Kinh-style housing furnished with modern beds, wardrobes, tables, sofas, sewing machines, and rice-threshing machines. Moreover, only middle-aged and older women still wear Yao clothing; the rest are undistinguishable from the majority population in their dress, and young girls wear Kinh-style clothing. Furthermore, Mit villagers use the Vietnamese language rather than Yao, even for religious ceremonies and poetry. However, living separately from the neighboring Muong, Kinh, and Thai, and administering their own land and village, the Yao have continued to maintain their cultural practices in less visible areas, such as

These small square paintings are fastened to the foreheads of ritual officiants and initiates to signify the deities' presence and protection.

laws and beliefs. They continue to marry only within the Yao Tien, organize themselves by a clan system, and practice traditional rituals, including the Qua Tang ceremony.

■ The Qua Tang Ceremony in Mit Village

THERE ARE THREE LEVELS OF QUA TANG ceremony, based on the number of candles that are placed on the body of the initiate—three, seven, or twelve. Because the Yao were formerly nomadic and there were few ritual masters to monitor the content of these rituals, each Yao group in each region has somewhat different understandings of the necessary ritual, and ritual knowledge has to some extent been lost. Today the twelve-candle level is rarely performed because it is very complicated, requiring quite a few ritual masters who have already themselves undergone the twelve-candle ritual. In Mit village, as in Yao Tien communities elsewhere in Hoa Binh province, many people hold the Qua Tang ceremony only at the three-candle level—which itself is far from simple.

In contrast with Yao Tien of the northeast, Yao Tien boys in Mit village take part in the Qua Tang Ceremony at the very young age of nine or ten, with preparations beginning a year earlier. According to custom, the eldest son must take part in the ceremony first, and a household with several sons of nearly the same age must make preparations for several ceremonies at one time. Because each household holds its own Qua Tang ceremony, the burden of preparation is on the family, especially the parents. Whether this preparation period is long or short depends on the family's wealth. It takes only six or twelve months to prepare for the three-candle ceremony, but higher levels require from two to five years of preparation. Preparation for the three-candle ceremony includes the following: raising two pigs weighing sixty-five to one hundred ten pounds, making women's clothing for the initiate, brewing *hoang* alcohol, and gathering or buying rice, incense sticks, and paper money. While brewing *hoang* alcohol, the household does not eat sticky rice or fried meat or consume alcohol because these three items are for the spirits. If they are consumed before the Qua Tang ceremony is finished, the ancestors and the spirits will not be satisfied with the offerings provided during the ceremony, thus rendering the Qua Tang rituals not only worthless but also unlucky for the family.

The Qua Tang ceremony is always held on November 11, December 12, or January 1 (lunar calendar) in the initiate's home. These months are also when the Yao celebrate weddings and funerals. The date for the Qua Tang ceremony must be selected carefully so that it does not occur on an ancestor's death anniversary, on the first day of thunder in any month (and on that day of the month during the rest of the year), or on days that will be unlucky for the initiate. Before the ceremony, the family sends someone to invite the fifteen designated participants: two ritual masters who lead the celebration, one dancer, three young men and three young women, three ritual masters who read poems to the Yao ancestors, and three servants.[6] None of these people can be relatives of the initiate.

The Qua Tang ceremony as a whole can be divided into two main parts: the Qua Tang itself and a Yao ancestor worship ceremony. Each is very complex, and I will explain only the major sequences. The first step of the Qua Tang ceremony is to arrange the altar, hang the ceremonial pictures, and pray to the ancestors and spirits asking them to participate. There are two altars for this ritual, each with one incense burner, four small bowls of

In December 2000, in Khe Mu village, Lao Cai province, a thirteen-year-old initiate climbs to the top of a ladder from which he can descend only by jumping into a net suspended below. His body falls, but his soul travels to divine realms. He will then be ready to learn the Taoist teachings appropriate to the first level of initiation.

alcohol for the spirits, one bowl of rice, one bowl of water, and one bowl of incense sticks. In addition, the altar of the lead ritual master has three small bowls that hold the candles to be used in the ceremony. The Qua Tang ceremony takes place in the middle of the house as determined by the position of the main door. Ten ceremonial pictures belonging to the primary ritual master and the secondary ritual master are hung above the altars. After preparing the altar and the pictures, the servants thoroughly sweep out the house to "frighten away" all the "misfortune" and keep the Qua Tang ceremony rites safe. From this moment to the end of the rites, all household members and participants in the ceremony must carefully observe a number of taboos. For example, all male participants must wear indigo hats or turbans, women must avoid wearing white turbans or white clothes, and both men and women must abstain from flirting, using obscene language, or quarreling. In addition, everyone, especially the ritual masters, must wear traditional clothes. There are two types of ritual masters' attire. The first is called *tom lui* by the Yao Tien and includes one skirt, one hat, and one belt. In addition, the primary ritual master must bring a ritual robe called a *lui doa* for the ancestor worship ceremony.

The two main ritual masters, wearing ritual robes, skirts, and hats, begin by asking the ancestors and spirits to take part in the ceremony. Then the initiate and his father sit behind them as a report on the boy's life is submitted to the spirits. After that, the host and all participants who know how begin dancing, performing several traditional dances accompanied by drums, gongs, bells, and singing.[7] The next step is the candle ritual. A small chair is placed near the two altars in the middle of the house, and the ceremonial subject takes a seat. The primary ritual master then uses his spiritual powers to "drive out" the boy's misfortune. Next, the two ritual masters and the initiate's father each place a small bowl with a lighted candle on top of the boy's head and on his left and right shoulders. A few minutes

A Taoist master's paper hat showing the Three Pure Ones of the Taoist pantheon—Pearly Azure, Upper Azure, and Supreme Azure—who together control human destiny.

The back view of this Taoist master's paper hat has, possibly, a depiction of the deity who governs souls' fates in the underworld. The horse-headed and cow-headed figures guard the entrance to the underworld. Yao ritual specialists wear a variety of hats depending on their own rank and the particular ceremony or prayer they are performing.

later, the three servants come and stand next to him to keep the candles from falling. The two leading ritual masters and the initiate's father dance slowly around him ten to fifteen times while the initiate, assisted by three men who have already experienced this ritual, balances the candles on his head and shoulders. This is called the *vay tang* ceremony and serves to increase the initiate's courage and cleverness. Following the candle lighting, the candles are removed and the initiate is given a lunar name, spirit protectors, and tools.

In the second part of the Qua Tang ceremony, the secondary ritual master guides the initiate in performing more than ten Yao traditional dances. At the end of some of these dances, they offer sticky rice cake and the initiate's cup of alcohol to the ancestors and spirits. They will do this for more than four hours, playing musical instruments such as drums, gongs, and bells and singing. The dancers wear square portrait paintings of Yao deities bound around their foreheads with string, which confer the spirit's protection on the initiate and also contribute to a jubilant atmosphere. Then the initiate's relatives and all others who know how will start to dance and pray to the ancestors and spirits to win their support for the Qua Tang ceremony. In interviews, the Yao in Mit village said that this part of the Qua Tang ceremony demonstrates the Yao art of dancing in couples, in groups, or alone. Finally, the invited dancer puts on ritual masters' clothing and performs over twelve dances while offering ritual cakes and his cup of alcohol to the ancestors and spirits. At the conclusion, the two main ritual masters, the dancer, and the three servants perform a ritual to bid the spirits farewell, and all musical instruments, altars, and pictures are put away.

The second half of the Qua Tang ritual is for ancestor worship. Again, the first step in this ceremony is to arrange the altars and ask the ancestors to participate. There is an altar for ancestors of the subject's family, an altar for recent ancestors, and an altar for distant ancestors. Once the altars are arranged, two pigs are sacrificed and cleaned, and the entire carcasses are placed on the altar. Tissue paper is cut to make paper money.

Offerings placed on the second and the third altars include one cleaned pig (unboiled) lying on its side with its entrails and liver intact, five small bowls of spirit alcohol, one bowl of water, one bowl of rice, and one bowl for incense sticks. After the altars are prepared, the primary ritual master puts on the special *lui doa* robe and a high cloth hat coated with resin and invites the Yao ancestors to participate in the ceremony, while the three young men and three young women who have been specially invited stand behind him, bending their knees and bowing from the waist and singing to the spirits.

After this, one more altar is arranged in the middle of the house near the ancestral altar; on it are placed three bowls of cooked and roasted pork, three bowls of vegetables, a bottle of alcohol, six bowls with six pairs of

During a Yao initiation ceremony in Phuc Loi commune, Yen Bai province, in 1997, the host and all participants who know how perform several traditional dances, accompanied by drums, gongs, bells, and singing. The vests worn by the initiates are modeled on women's clothing.

chopsticks, and a ritual book called the *tom sau*. The two main ritual masters, the dancer, and the three additional poetry-reading ritual masters sit behind the altars and recite poems written in the *tom sau*, to the accompaniment of two small bells. After praying to the ancestors and spirits in order to win their support for the whole family, the ritual masters burn incense and perform the ritual of bidding farewell to the spirits. At this point, the Yao ancestor worship ceremony and the full three-candle Qua Tang ceremony are completed.

This brief description omits a great deal of detail, and a seven- or twelve-candle Qua Tang ceremony would be even more complex. The three-candle rituals that I observed in Mit village in the northwest are essentially the same as those of the Yao Tien in the northeast, the primary differences being that in the northeast, young men usually undergo this ritual at the time of their marriage.

■ The Qua Tang Ceremony and Cultural Practices

THE QUA TANG CEREMONY PLAYS an important role in maintaining Yao cultural practices and in strengthening the Yao community in general. The deities of the Yao—the village spirit, the rice spirit, and the spirit of poultry and domestic animals—are invoked in the ancestor- and spirit-worshiping ceremonies. One of the primary goals of the ceremony is the creation of a dialogue between the initiate and the ritual master with the ancestors and the spirits. The ritual master gives the initiate an underworld name, spirit protectors, and a certificate of participation in the Qua Tang ceremony and advises him to lead a moral life. For this reason, after the ceremony, the initiate enjoys a new social stature in the Yao community. Initiates of the Qua Tang ceremony are fully recognized as Yao descendants by the Yao ancestors, are allowed to conduct ancestor worship, and may learn ritual methods of curing disease and driving out malevolent spirits.[8] Through my interviews in Mit village, I learned that a man who has undergone the Qua Tang ceremony can also serve as a ritual master and lead the ceremony for others, officiate at funerals, choose auspicious days for important tasks, and be buried accompanied by drum rhythms to send his spirit back to China. Mit villagers believe that a boy who has undergone the Qua Tang ceremony is recognized by the spirits. Thus, he can make religious offerings and worship, carry out any other rituals related to the spirits, and perform exorcisms without any risk to himself or his family. He can do this because he has won the ancestors' and spirits' support and his spirit helpers' protection during the Qua Tang ceremony and the ritual masters have ritually cleansed him of his past mistakes.

The Yao in Mit village and other regions believe that men who have undergone the Qua Tang ceremony can be considered adults with the right to discuss important issues with the village elders, to be the first sower of the harvest season, to bring fire into a new house, to bring furniture to a new house, to be matchmakers, and to escort a bride to the bridegroom's house. They also believe that only Qua Tang initiates understand what it is to be a good person who can master and follow traditional habits and customs.

As we have seen, not only Yao beliefs and customs but also literature and visual and performing arts are a part of the Qua Tang ceremony. During the ceremony, especially during seven- and twelve-candle rites, many artisti-

The primary Taoist master uses his powers to "drive out" the initiate's misfortune before lighting candles on his head and shoulders. Phuc Loi commune, Yen Bai province, 1997.

cally valuable pictures are displayed. During these rituals, many Yao groups, such as the Yao Quan Chet and the Yao Thanh Phan, display twenty-four pictures portraying different aspects of their spiritual life, including their conception of the cosmos, various spirits, and even pictures of the kitchen spirit.[9] The Yao in Mit village display pictures related to the Qua Tang ceremony itself, including the spirits that the initiate addresses. The ceremonial clothing worn by the ritual masters and the initiate are another artistic aspect of the ceremony. The ritual master's *tom lui* robe is particularly valued. The act of sewing such a robe is reported to the ancestors and spirits, and when it is completed, it must be presented to them. Traditional patterns have beeen handed down from generation to generation and must be followed lest the ritual master, the tailor, and their relatives be punished by the ancestors and spirits. As a result, ritual master clothes, especially the *tom lui*, are nearly identical in all Yao groups.

Most dances performed in the three-candle ceremony require the ritual masters to sing (or another experienced singer if the ritual master cannot sing), holding bells in their right hands and short sticks in their left hands; these dances are accompanied by gongs and drums. In seven- or twelve-candle ceremonies, additional dances are performed with traditional musical instruments, including drums, gongs, cymbals, and bells, creating a jubilant atmosphere. Instead of singing, the dancers mime Yao methods for such activities as turtle catching, preparing for a journey, hunting, escorting the bride to the bridegroom's house, and dancing in religious ceremonies. All these dances without singing are performed during high-level Qua Tang ceremonies. The performers of the songs exchanged between three young couples and the six men who recite poems during the Yao ancestor worship rituals must also be highly skilled. The singers have to perform thirty-six songs on such topics such as natural beauty, love, successful harvests, and morality.[10] The poems from the *tom sau* that the six men recite are about the origin of the Yao people and their subsequent exodus from China.

But while the Qua Tang ceremony plays an important role in preserving and transmitting Yao cultural practices, it is not without some negative features, such as the huge amount of labor and money spent on it. Belief in the power of spirits inhibits modern and progressive behavior. The ceremonial system also subordinates Yao woman to their husbands, who, having undergone the Qua Tang ceremony, have a higher position in Yao society.

■ The Effects of the Market Economy on the Qua Tang Ceremony

IN THE PAST, AS A RESULT of poor economic conditions, the Yao Tien not only broke the age regulation for the three-candle level ceremony but also began holding the ceremony for three boys at once at the home of the head of the clan, in order to save money. They did this because the honor accorded to a clan is based on the number of men who have undergone this ceremony. By 2000 higher incomes again allowed the Yao Tien to hold the ceremony for only one person. This continues to place a heavy burden on the individual families, who have to prepare offerings and invite ritual

One of several scroll paintings used during an initiation in Khe Mu village, Son Ha commune, Bao Thang district, Lao Cai province, this painting represents figures in the Taoist pantheon.

masters for each son. However, because both the parents and the community consider it important, the Qua Tang ceremony is held for all Mit boys at the proper age. In this respect, the market economy has in fact contributed to the perpetuation of the Qua Tang ceremony. Moreover, the government's policy of encouraging the maintenance and preservation of ethnic cultures has also played an important role in maintaining the Qua Tang ceremony of Mit village and of the Yao in other regions. In Mit village today, rapid changes in economic life and interaction with other ethnic groups have also improved ethnic consciousness. Yao today value the Qua Tang Ceremony as a precious cultural legacy.

Nevertheless, the new market economy, while bringing positive changes to the material life of the Yao, has also affected the material components of the ritual. In the past, Yao ritual masters created the ceremonial paintings, but after 1986 they began to buy them in the market. The bells and knives that used to be made by Yao blacksmiths are also bought in the market, as are the candles used in the ritual. In the past, the ancestors ate wild squirrel meat, which the Yao hunted, and sticky rice from mountain swidden fields; today they are offered lowland sticky rice from paddy fields or from the market and cooked pork, the product of expanded animal husbandry.

Some cultural knowledge is maintained by a tenuous thread. Old ritual masters can read the poetry written in the *tom sau* in Chinese ideographs, but the young, schooled in the national script, can only chant along, following the lead of the older ritual masters. Even so, in Mit village in 1998 there were seventy-two men over the age of nine, and all of them had undergone the Qua Tang ceremony. Parents of eight- or nine-year-old boys feel that they must make preparations for their sons' ceremonies however burdensome the preparation. If not, they will be spoken of with scorn and considered base people who do not love their children.

Yao ritual lore is contained in texts written in an ideographic system based on Chinese but distinctive to the Yao. Today, young Yao cannot read these texts and must chant their contents from memory, but a full Taoist master is expected to read and write Yao script.

A wedding party in Ho Chi Minh City (formerly Saigon) in June 2001; the bride and groom pose with both sets of parents under a heart-shaped sign reading, "The bride goes to her husband's house."

WEDDINGS AND FUNERALS IN CONTEMPORARY VIETNAM

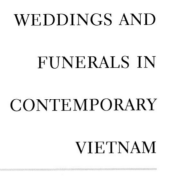

Shaun Kingsley Malarney

■ Visitors unfamiliar with Vietnam who travel to Ho Chi Minh City (formerly Saigon) in the early winter are often surprised when they see small processions of people, laden with trays of colorful food and gifts, traveling around the city in cars or pedicabs. Visitors to Hanoi may be equally puzzled when they are passed by a bus adorned with floral wreaths full of people wearing white headbands and in whose open door stands a person throwing small red and white cubes onto the road. For the Kinh (Viet), the majority population of Vietnam, such events are routine. The procession is a group from a prospective groom's family traveling with gifts to the bride's family in order to formalize wedding plans. The bus is full of mourners who are traveling from the home of a person who has recently died to a cemetery, and the person standing in the door is throwing out symbolic gold ingots that the deceased's soul will use to find the way back from the cemetery to his or her former home.

Weddings and funerals, along with their obligatory processions, feasts, and rituals, constitute common and significant journeys that almost all Kinh make. They mark journeys through a lifetime—the expected transition from childhood to adulthood usually signified by a wedding ceremony, and the transition from a living being to a deceased family ancestor through funerary rites. The Kinh also mark the beginning and end of the calendar year with ceremonies. The year begins with Tet celebrations, when families invite the souls of their deceased ancestors to partake of food, drink, and good cheer, and concludes with the "wedding season" in late autumn, when couples, processions, and highly decorated vehicles move across communities to celebrate new unions. To experience the world as a Kinh is to enter a reality in which weddings and funerals are not simply disconnected events that periodically enter one's life, but are, instead, profoundly significant events woven into the everyday experience and texture of time and existence.

■ The Social and Historical Background of Wedding and Funeral Rituals

EVERY SOCIETY HAS TOPICS THAT SEIZE the social imagination and are fond subjects for discussion. The French can discourse in remarkable detail on the relative quality of different wines, while the Japanese display a similar ability to discuss the virtues of different rice varieties. In Vietnam a guaranteed way to begin a conversation is to ask, "What are your weddings and funerals like?" The listener will likely be surprised at the amount of information imparted about the number of guests at the average wedding or funeral feast, the type and quality of food and drink served, the size of the gift expected from each guest, the dress of the participants, the ritual order, the exemplary cases—when things were done well—and the opposite cases, when things were done improperly. Most Kinh have an extensive knowledge of these subjects, and their opinions are often equally strong. Weddings and funerals are not simply rituals that should be performed: they should be performed in very definite and morally appropriate ways.

A coffin leaves the deceased's house near Song Day, with mourning relatives following behind. Food for the deceased is placed on the coffin, along with candles—seven for a man, nine for a woman, who have seven or nine souls or vitalities, respectively. April 1992.

Social interest in weddings and funerals has a long history in Vietnam. Until the early twentieth century, the Kinh mandarinate was active in writing regulations on the proper conduct of weddings and funerals. The premodern state, in fact, had a Ministry of Rites whose officials were responsible for developing and disseminating primers that described correct ritual conduct. The government was assisted in this by elite scholars who published their own officially approved primers, such as the renowned *Tho Mai Gia Le* (Manual of Family Rites), written by the scholar Ho Si Tan in the 1500s. These texts were often inspired by documents written in China. Official interest in weddings and funerals was strong because the state regarded them as events that could be used to advance officially approved ideas and values. Two ideas central to the state's vision were the frugal consumption of resources and the public display of filial piety by the living toward their deceased ancestors. A display of filial piety was particularly important at the funeral rites held immediately after death and the series of prescribed commemorative rites held later on such occasions as the anniversary of a death. The state reasoned that if families conducted funerals and other rituals in an officially acceptable manner, the rituals would play a vital role in maintaining public support for filial piety; in other words, by nurturing proper (hierarchical) human relationships, the kingdom would enjoy harmony, peace, and prosperity.

After the Vietnamese revolution began in the mid-1940s, the new government instituted reforms governing weddings, funerals, and other ritual practices. Similar to the approach of their predecessors, the revolutionary authorities sought to create a set of rites that would publicly restate officially endorsed virtues, such as gender equality, the building of the new socialist society, or the persistent virtue of frugality. Officials in northern Vietnam vigorously enacted these reforms from the mid-1950s to the late 1980s, while in the southern and central regions they were implemented in a more limited manner from 1975 until the late 1980s. An unexpected similarity between the revolutionary reforms and their prerevolutionary antecedents lay in the inability of state officials to persuade the population to implement the full range of prescribed ritual practices. For centuries, mandarins had complained that people in villages across Vietnam diverged from official dictates on a number of points, particularly on their alleged profligate use of resources in their rituals. In the second half of the twentieth century, Vietnamese officials would echo these complaints, and they are still easy to find in the official press today.

The reasons for opposition were quite simple. For one, Vietnam is culturally diverse, and although the country shares a basic structure for ritual practices, there is still a wide range of local variation. In fact, it is not uncommon to find slight differences in the conduct of weddings and funerals in two adjacent villages, and even greater differences can exist between urban and rural areas or between geographical regions. These variations are often socially significant markers of local identity, so many Kinh have resisted official attempts at ritual standardization, seeking instead to preserve elements of local pride and tradition. Perhaps more important, many residents opposed aspects of the ritual reforms because they interfered with their ability to fulfill important moral obligations to friends, neighbors, coworkers, and family members. For many, these obligations were paramount, and efforts were made to properly fulfill them, even at the cost of antagonizing government officials. Nevertheless, despite this opposition,

A wedding party in Hanoi poses for a formal portrait in 1936.

official reforms had both their supporters and successes, particularly with regard to the simplification of ritual practices. Any serious review of contemporary wedding and funeral practices thus illustrates the impact socialist reforms have had throughout the country.

■ Wedding Journeys

KINH ARE FOND OF COMMENTING that a wedding is a "work of the family": although a wedding will join a man and woman as husband and wife, reaching that stage must involve the participation of both their families. Courtship in contemporary Vietnam is a relatively open activity, more so in urban than rural areas. The Law of Marriage and Family stipulates that to marry, men must be twenty-two and women twenty years of age, but many couples marry at younger ages. Before the 1950s, Vietnam had a high rate of arranged marriages, but today most marriages are voluntary. Yet to describe the contemporary situation as completely voluntary disguises two important aspects of contemporary practice. First, when a couple decides to marry, they usually seek out and take seriously their parents' opinions of the match; strong parental opposition in some cases ends marriage plans.

Second, in many areas, most notably in rural areas, parents will often suggest or "introduce" potential marriage partners for their children. Usually the parents choose the potential spouse through a family they know, or in some cases the potential groom's family will consult a matchmaker who will make suggestions. The children have the legal right to refuse such unions, but in a good many cases marriages are formed after these introductions. This practice was common in all regions of the country during the American War years (1964–1975), when soldiers, while home on leave, hastily married women introduced to them by their parents.

Getting married is an expected rite of passage in Vietnam. Visitors to Vietnam are often perplexed by the number of times that Kinh ask whether they have "built a family yet," but the question underlines the importance of marriage in marking a person's transition to adulthood. The follow-up question for those who are married—whether they have any children— illustrates the other widely held expectation that those who marry will have children. Although in recent years the government has encouraged married couples to have a maximum of two children, for many couples a large family with many children is very desirable.

There is perhaps a greater desire to have sons rather than daughters because sons carry on the family name and the eldest son will assume responsibility for the aged parents and take over the family ancestral cult. "Daughters are the children of others" is a commonly quoted adage. In some cases this adage has been misinterpreted to mean that Kinh families do not value their daughters. But daughters are highly valued in all homes, and many parents, with a nod and a wink, will tell you that daughters take better care of aged parents. The adage refers instead to the fact that almost all women spend but a limited time in their parents' home; when they marry, they embark on one of the defining journeys of their lives, the departure from their parents' home and the resettling in their husband's or his family's home. Once a woman takes up residence with her husband, she becomes a child of that family as well. She addresses her mother- and father-in-law as Mother and Father, and they address her as Child. From that moment on, many of her most important responsibilities are to her new family, although her ties to her own mother and father will never be severed.

A Hanoi bride and groom pose for a studio portrait before their wedding in September 2000. "Hollywood"-style wedding portraits with professional makeup and romantic backdrops are a part of many urban weddings.

A couple's decision to marry initiates a lengthy process of exchanges between the bride's and groom's families. While the marriage will ultimately involve the bride's leaving her home and moving in with her husband, before that stage is reached it is important for the groom's family to demonstrate its commitment to the bride, her family, and the marriage by meeting the family and giving them a series of different gifts. There is no standard manner of conducting these meetings and exchanges for all Kinh.

Considerable variation exists, not only between geographical regions and urban and rural areas, but also between elites and non-elites.[1] Also, the revolutionary authorities, particularly in northern Vietnam, implemented a number of reforms designed to simplify wedding practices, and in many communities in the north these reforms continue to have an influence. Finally, accompanying Vietnam's rapid economic development has been a significant amount of cultural innovation and improvisation that has brought about new ways of getting married, with notable changes in dress styles and the gifts exchanged between families.

Nevertheless, some general patterns are apparent. Once a couple has asked for and received permission to marry, one of their first tasks is to consult with their families regarding an appropriate time for the groom's family to pay a visit to the wife's family for a "pre-engagement ceremony" *(le dam ngo)*. In the past, this rite was called the "seeing the face" *(xem mat)* ceremony in some areas, as it was sometimes the first time a bride and groom saw each other. On this occasion, the groom's family brings a set of simple gifts, such as areca nuts and betel leaf, to the home of the bride. Upon arrival at the house, the groom's family formally asks permission to enter. The bride's family invites them in, and the gifts the family has brought are placed upon or before the family ancestral altar. Before any further activities are initiated, members of both families stand before the ancestral altar and perform a brief set of rites for the ancestors, the purpose of which is to announce the coming engagement and gain the ancestors' approval. After these rites are concluded, the families formally discuss their shared desire for the couple to marry. Before the groom's family leaves, the gifts are divided up; although these gifts were intended for the bride's family, politeness demands that a portion, though always less than half, be returned to the groom's family. This ritual relates to the desired relationship between the families. Historically, the Kinh have preferred marriages between families of roughly equal status, though a husband with a slightly higher status than the wife (but not the reverse) was acceptable. By sending some of the gifts back with the groom's family, the bride's family publicly asserts that significant status differences do not exist between them.

In some communities in northern Vietnam the pre-engagement ceremony has been dropped, but where it has been retained, its performance means that now the two families will not entertain any other marital possibilities. The next event in the traditional sequence, still retained throughout

Seven young women in Vietnamese dress are on their way to deliver seven boxes of betrothal gifts to the home of the bride. As a sign of betrothal, the groom's family brings gifts of food and drink to the bride's family. The cakes are then distributed to friends and neighbors to announce the couple's engagement.

the country, is the engagement ceremony *(le an hoi* or *le dam hoi)*. In terms of structure, the engagement ceremony is similar to the pre-engagement ceremony: the groom's family visits the bride's family with gifts, rites are performed before the ancestral altar, and then the groom's family returns home with part of their gifts. However, several important distinctions exist. The weeks leading up to the engagement ceremony are a time of serious negotiation. One of the first issues to resolve is the day for the ceremony. Despite the socialist government's efforts to secularize social life, many families consult an astrologer to determine an auspicious date for the ceremony. Once that issue is settled, the families must determine what gifts are appropriate for the groom's family to bring. Given that at this ceremony's conclusion the couple will be "engaged" *(dinh hon)* or, as is often stated, a "husband and wife who have yet to marry," the type and quantity of these items are a more sensitive issue than in the pre-engagement ceremony. In addition to the standard areca nut and betel leaves, families might bring alcohol, tea, tobacco, fruit, or cakes, although the exact nature of these items can vary considerably between an impoverished Red River Delta farming village and the Saigon elite. At the ceremony's conclusion, the bride's family distributes many of the gift items to friends, neighbors, and kin in order to announce the engagement.

Historically couples remained engaged for three years or longer in rural areas, but in contemporary Vietnam engagements are generally shorter, often lasting only a few months. As the end of the engagement approaches, the families must negotiate a wedding date, which is usually held on

Young men carry betrothal gifts into the bride's home in the old quarter of Hanoi in the fall of 2000. The rented lacquer cake boxes are covered with cloths of auspicious red.

another astrologically auspicious day. More important, they must also negotiate the size of the set of gifts the groom's family will give to the bride's. Of all the pre-wedding negotiations, these have always been the most difficult. Some Kinh argue that the gifts given at this point, known as the *thach*, serve as a form of compensation for the loss of the bride and the labor she would give to her family, since the bride leaves the family home on her marriage, taking up residence in her husband's home. Hence the nature and number of the gifts are especially important. Others reject this argument and claim that the difficulties derive from the bride's family's need to demonstrate its status and the value of its daughter by receiving a large gift. In any case, in the weeks leading up to the wedding the two sides negotiate a set of gifts to be given just before the wedding. Again, these gifts vary by region, though they usually include such items as pork, tea, alcohol, rice cakes, tobacco, money or gold, and particularly areca nuts and betel leaves. After receiving these gifts, many rural residents redistribute a portion of the rice cakes, areca nuts, and betel leaves as wedding invitations. Urban residents often prefer paper wedding invitations.

The elders of the two families en route between the bride's house and the groom's house during a Hanoi wedding in 1936.

Weddings in rural Vietnam usually take place over a three-day period; in the cities this is sometimes shortened to one day. On the day before the wedding or perhaps a few days before, the groom's family delivers the gifts to the bride's family. By this time, both households will have begun in earnest to clean up their homes and make them ready to receive guests. The evening before the wedding is a jovial time in both homes as kin, friends, and neighbors who have received invitations visit the home to announce their intention to attend the wedding or its feast. Historically, these pre-wedding gatherings demonstrated the social differences between the bride and groom. The house of the latter was often quite animated, and the guests who arrived were obliged to bring with them a predetermined gift, usually money, although rice or other commodities were acceptable. These gifts then helped the groom's family cover the costs of their wedding feast the next day. The bride's gathering was always smaller and more sedate, and guests did not bring gifts because the gifts from the groom's family largely covered the expense of their feast. With these differences in practices, it is fair to say that the marriage of a son was celebrated more than that of a daughter, but in recent years these differences have been reduced in many communities; the gatherings at the brides' homes have become larger and more jovial, and in some cases the brides' families have also begun to accept gifts from their guests to help pay for the wedding feast.

In Tam Nong district, Phu Tho province, in 1999, a country bride rides off to her new home on the back of the groom's bicycle. Before her departure, the groom's family and representatives promised to care for her like a daughter under their roof.

In rural areas the bride's and groom's families both hold feasts in their homes on the morning of the wedding day. Of the two, the groom's feast is always more extensive and generally has a larger guest list. After the feasts, the wedding journey begins, the symbolically most important part of the proceedings. Unlike their Western counterparts, traditional Kinh weddings do not involve an officiating clergy with the authority to declare the couple husband and wife (Christian Kinh weddings are exceptions). Many regard the official registration that makes a marriage legal in the eyes of the state as little more than a bureaucratic formality. Instead, social recognition of the new marriage is conferred first by the authority of the ancestors, whose permission must be asked, and then by the senior kin on both sides. The final stage of this process begins when the groom conducts brief rites at his family's ancestral altar to ask permission to bring his bride back to his home. He then leaves his house, and he and his guests form a procession that will travel to the bride's home. How he gets there varies. In some communities, procession members walk, in others they travel by car, bus, or even, in the

Mekong Delta region, by boat. At the bride's house, the bride and groom jointly propitiate her family ancestors and ask their permission for her to leave their home. Afterward her senior male kin give laudatory speeches to acknowledge the new marriage. The entire procession, now joined by the bride and some of her guests, then returns to the groom's home, where the ancestral rites and speeches by senior male kin are repeated. Following these speeches, the couple have become husband and wife, and a reception that usually lasts into the night begins at the groom's home. The next morning the bride and groom again return to her family's home to pay their respects to her parents and bid a final farewell to her former home.

This description is a brief sketch of the basic features of marriage and wedding practices. Above this deeper structure rests a bewildering number of possible variations, particularly in terms of clothing, gifts, food and drink, invitations, and overall ritual structure. Not only have such variations long existed, but new ones keep appearing as Vietnam continues to make its postsocialist transition. Nevertheless, despite such variations, the authority of the ancestors and the passage of people and objects between the two families remain the core of wedding practices.

■ Funeral Journeys

THE CENTRALITY OF ANCESTRAL ALTARS in wedding ceremonies demonstrates a basic feature of Kinh social life: the dead are intimately woven into the world of the living. Not only do most family homes have ancestral altars where the spirits of family ancestors reside, but the souls of the dead are also present in shrines, temples, and communal houses, and their names adorn cities, streets, and buildings. The dead, in a way, live on everywhere in Vietnam. For the Kinh, the final social transition that all individuals make is from living to dead. At death, the corporeal body dies, but the soul lives on, becoming a component of the ancestral spirit. Once that happens, the soul is poised to make the defining journey of its postcorporeal existence, but what that journey will be and the quality of the existence the soul will subsequently enjoy depend upon the actions of the living.

This paper motorbike and red Toyota were sold in Ho Chi Minh City in 1995 as *hang ma,* votive goods burned for use by the dead. Innovations in *hang ma* production reflect the changing material aspirations of the living.

Kinh describe weddings as "works of amusement" *(viec hy).* Funerals and other rites surrounding a death are described as "works of filial piety" *(viec hieu)* because one of their main dimensions is the expression of filial piety paid by the living toward the deceased. All Kinh are expected to display filial piety toward their senior relatives, particularly their parents. Children display filial piety while their parents are alive by being respectful and taking care of them, especially in their old age. The death of a parent, however, is one of the defining moments that every child faces. With the parent's passing, the child must organize an appropriate funeral that publicly demonstrates the child's piety. To do otherwise shows the child to be a significant moral failure and risks censure from kin, friends, and others.

One of the reasons moral failure is associated with an inappropriately conducted funeral relates to the overarching goal of all funeral rites. With death, the soul leaves the body but is not yet at rest; it wanders around the area in which it died. In order for the soul to achieve lasting peace, the living must conduct rites that will facilitate its journey from the place where the soul left the body to what is known in the vernacular as the "other world" *(the gioi khac).* The other world is similar to the one in which we live in almost every detail. The dead eat food, wear clothing, and use gold and money. During funeral ceremonies, the living bring the soul back to an altar where the funeral is being conducted, usually in the home where the individual died, and then perform a set of rites that will send it across to

A daughter, distinguished by her cotton mourner's hood, keeps vigil by a coffin.

the other world. A Kinh may say that the soul is at peace once it reaches the other world, but in fact the dead must continue to be provided for if they are to live a happy and satisfying afterlife. As a result, the living continue to perform rites, such as the annual death anniversary ceremony in which they provide the dead with the food and items, *hang ma,* that they need in the other world—clothing, money, jewelry, hats, houses, animals, all made of paper or bamboo. The living offer these items in their rites, then burn them. The objects are transported via the smoke to the other world for use by the dead. The nature of these items provides one of the most interesting manifestations of social change in Vietnam. In the 1990s people were content to provide quite basic *hang ma* items, such as bicycles and local currency; ten years later some families are offering motorcycles, refrigerators, and even cars, while others prefer to burn copies of the American dollar, which is regarded as a more stable currency than the dong.

As with weddings, funeral rites exhibit a tremendous amount of variation across Vietnam, and no single pattern is practiced in all localities. Again, part of this derives from regional and sociological differences that predated the revolution, part is from the varying acceptance of revolutionary reforms introduced in the post-1954 period, and part is from the changes associated with the country's recent economic improvements. Nevertheless, deeper patterns can be identified that inform practices throughout the country. Of primary significance, the organization and conduct of a funeral is a family

A votive paper pair of white high-heeled shoes, sold in Hanoi in 1991, when white pumps were popular on the streets of the capital city.

responsibility. The ideal way to die is quietly, in one's home; not only is the person's soul comforted when it leaves the body in familiar surroundings, but all subsequent funeral rites can be held in the family home as well. When someone dies outside the home, the casket is not permitted to be brought back inside, and the funeral must be conducted with the casket outside the door. Soon after death close family members procure a casket (unless the deceased had already chosen one), clean the body, and then place the body into the casket. At this point family members also set up a small altar near the casket on which they place an urn for incense sticks and perhaps candles or a photograph of the deceased. This altar will serve as the main site for rites dedicated to the deceased.

In rural communities, news of an individual's passing often spreads quickly, and people soon begin to visit the deceased's home to offer their condolences and provide assistance. The next major stage of the funeral is the "distribution of the mourning headband" rite. In the hours immediately after death, a senior family member conducts a rite in which white cloth mourning headbands are distributed to family members genealogically junior to the deceased. (In some communities different-colored headbands are distributed, the color indicating the individual's genealogical distance from the deceased. In some communities, too, relatives supply their own headband rather than relying on the deceased's family.) This rite marks the transition of family members into a state of mourning. Although many of the restrictions formerly placed on people in mourning are no longer strictly followed, such as prohibitions on marrying within a certain number of years depending on one's relationship to the deceased, many people still take their state of mourning seriously and will, at least in the initial months, avoid attending such celebratory events as weddings or other public displays of joy or levity.

A few hours later the family begins the funeral's *phung vieng* phase. This phase derives its name from the two main acts it contains, a visit to the deceased's home *(vieng)* and the presentation of gifts while there *(phung)*. Unlike weddings, where people attend by invitation, attendance at a funeral is voluntary, although in many cases there are very strong moral pressures to attend, particularly if one had a close relationship with the deceased or his or her family. People often arrive at the deceased's home in groups, usually composed of close relatives. In rural areas, people normally bring incense sticks and a tray of food that usually includes cooked rice and either pork or chicken. When people arrive in the home, they make the symbolically important declaration to the family that they have come to "divide the sadness" *(chia buon)* of the grieving family. This metaphor almost perfectly encapsulates the social ideals behind funerals. The loss of a family member is obviously a devastating experience that generates tremendous sadness, but by coming to the deceased's home in the hours after death, friends, relatives, neighbors, and others appropriate some of that sadness and take part of it away with them, thereby lightening the burden of those who grieve. Kinh often comment that the best funeral is one in which dozens, if not even hundreds, of guests participate. Such a number not only provides a public statement of the esteem in which the deceased was held but also helps lighten the pain of the family's loss.

After entering the home and greeting the family, guests present their trays of food and then propitiate the deceased's soul with lit incense sticks before the casket and specially constructed altar. The presentation of the food gifts is another symbolically critical component of funeral rites. As with weddings, feasting is an essential part of the funeral process. During the *phung vieng* phase, the deceased's family collects dozens of trays of food, along with such gifts as fruits and money. These gifts then provide the foundation for the feast that the family holds the following day. Here again, the logic behind these gifts deeply engages people's social ideals regarding funerals. The deceased's family is suffering a tremendous loss, but by contributing food and labor, people come together as a community to provide the essentials and help defray the costs of the funeral. If all goes well, a family will have to shoulder only a minimal financial burden.

Feasting also mobilizes another aspect of the moral conceptualization of the ideal Vietnamese society. In Vietnamese social life, one of the most prized types of social relations is the "sentimental" *(tinh cam)* relationship. Having sentiment with another implies many things, but foremost among them is a feeling of warmth and affect, a sense of unity that transcends any status differences and an abiding conscientiousness in which one will willingly make personal sacrifices to assist the other. Having sentimental relations with many people and families is a highly prized attribute, the importance of which is stated in the comment one regularly hears that "Vietnam is a poor country, but very rich in sentiment." Families and individuals that have sentimental relations with the deceased or the family are expected to contribute gifts of food, money, or labor to funerals. This act maintains the sentimental relationship and places an obligation upon the receiver to reciprocate in the future if the giver's family has a funeral. The failure to bring gifts to the funeral can lead to a rupture in social relations. The same mechanism obtains with the giving of gifts at weddings, although Kinh strictly separate their wedding and funeral debts. It is difficult to underestimate the importance of these exchanges in social life. For centuries Vietnamese governments, both Communist and non-Communist, have labeled the gifts exchanged in these contexts, which can be quite significant, as wasteful. However, families in communities throughout the nation value the exchange of these gifts so highly that they willingly ignore official dictates.

During the first evening after death, most homes holding a funeral are filled with guests who keep the aggrieved company and help out with the funeral arrangements. In many homes the family will also sponsor a rite that formally begins the process of sending the deceased's spirit to the other world. These rites take a variety of forms and can involve a variety of ritual specialists, but all share the goal of securing the presence of the deceased's spirit in the home as a properly tended ancestor, not a wandering ghost, and preparing it for its journey to the other world. In some cases these rites conclude in an hour, while in others they continue throughout the night. Which rite is performed often depends on the deceased's personal preferences. If the deceased was an active Buddhist, the rites will likely involve a

As an expression of filial grief, the daughters and daughters-in-law of an eighty-year-old man have leaped into his grave. Tam Nong district, Phu Tho province, 1999.

monk or nun; other people might request rites performed by a spirit priest *(thay cung)*, an indigenous spirit specialist.

Almost all families are careful at this point to place a tray with lit incense sticks and several bowls of rice porridge on the ground or on a table outside their home. This offering provides a glimpse into the consequences of an inadequate funeral. According to Vietnamese cultural ideas, an inadequate funeral angers a soul, which then becomes a malevolent ghost *(con ma)*. Unlike well-cared-for ancestors residing in the other world, ghosts are doomed to remain in the world of the living without a regular supply of the items needed to subsist and prosper. They angrily roam the earth searching for food and are particularly attracted to carelessly performed funeral or ancestral rites where they can sneak in and steal the bounty dedicated to a family ancestor. The rice porridge rite provides these ghosts with something to eat, thus preventing them from entering the house. One of Vietnam's most poignant contemporary problems is the tens of thousands of soldiers, from both north and south, who died in battle and never received proper funeral rites. Although the wars are over, this army of wandering souls remains, and scores of families continue to search for the bones of their lost loved ones so they can perform appropriate funeral rites and give the souls their final peace.

A funeral procession crosses a bridge on its journey from the village to the grave, 1992.

On the morning after the death, the family begins preparations for the journey of the casket to the gravesite. As with weddings, the social transition of the main actor, the deceased in its casket, is marked through a large procession in which it is escorted from its home to a new locale. Removing the casket from the home is always a painful experience, often accompanied by crying and even loud wailing. Again, no single type of procession is found across the country, but all processions have three common features: the casket is preceded by a "death car" *(vong xa)*, a small palanquin upon which the deceased's name or picture and an incense urn are placed; the casket is placed on some type of palanquin or trolley and carried to the grave site by nonkin; and most of the people in the procession follow behind the casket. Two interesting points of variation lie in the attire of the deceased's sons and daughters and their position in the procession. Unlike other guests, who wear their mourning headbands, sons and daughters often wear distinct mourning dress that includes a white tunic made of coarse fibers and special headgear. Daughters wear a peaked cheesecloth cap, and the eldest son a "straw hat" *(mu rom)*, a turbanlike cap usually made of wound straw; he will also carry a mourning staff. Some communities dictate that sons

Dress and head covering indicate a mourner's relationship to the deceased at this Hanoi funeral in 1994. The two men in the center of the photograph are sons, as indicated by their gauzy tunics and turbans of banana leaf and dry rice stalks. The woman on the right, in a gauze tunic and hood, is a daughter-in-law. The man on the left, wearing a simple white band, is probably a grandson.

and daughters must walk before the father's casket but behind the mother's. Some communities also expect the oldest son to push against the casket as it moves in the procession, while daughters must lie on the ground to impede its progress. These practices demonstrate the children's filial piety and reluctance to part with their parents.

Family members bid farewell to the casket at the gravesite in another tearful moment. After the casket is in the ground, family members throw dirt onto the coffin and then the grave is filled in. This usually creates a small mound on which family members and others will place lit incense sticks as they say farewell. Mourners typically disperse at their own will, in contrast to the organized procession in which they traveled to the gravesite. The family then returns home to complete the final preparations for the funeral feast. Soon dozens, and in some areas hundreds, of guests arrive at the house to remember the deceased and show their sympathy for the family. The feast marks a death, but the event's inherent sadness is tempered by a celebration of the deceased's life, and people eat and drink well. When the feast is over, friends and family help clean up and remain at the home to provide company for the grieving family. On the next day the family will hold another small feast for those who were unable to attend the previous day. At its conclusion, the three days of funeral activities are finally over.

In contemporary funerals, photographs of the deceased have replaced wooden ancestor tablets inscribed with the deceased's name and titles. The photograph in this funeral in Que Nhon in 1988 would have been carried back from the grave and installed in the house as a site for offerings to the deceased, now an ancestor.

The obligation to care for the deceased's soul does not conclude with the funeral. Most families hold another rite on the thirty-fifth, forty-ninth, or hundredth day after death, dedicated to securing the soul's transition to the other world. Usually called the "raising up of the soul rite" *(le sieu hon)*, this can be performed at home or in a Buddhist temple. When performed in a temple, the family leaves a small photograph that will be permanently displayed. From that point on, the deceased will "eat of the Buddha's good fortune" *(an may cua Phat)*, which means that every time people make food offerings during rites in the temple, the soul will partake of them, thereby receiving continual sustenance.

The next major ritual obligation of the family toward the deceased is the performance of the first death anniversary ceremony. Some elderly Kinh comment that until recently the Kinh were far more concerned about remembering a person's date of death than his or her date of birth. This was true because every year the deceased's family is obliged to congregate on that day and conduct rites for the deceased. The largest of these rites, in which several dozen people might participate, takes place on the first and third death anniversaries. On these days the family, usually led by the eldest son, conducts rites in which it invites the deceased's soul to return home to enjoy the offerings made for it on the ancestral altar. This pattern is repeated on all other occasions in which the living conduct rites for the dead, notably at the turning of the lunar new year (Tet Nguyen Dan), when

This elaborate paper and bamboo "funeral house" was made to cover a tomb, 1992.

the ancestors are invited back for an extended stay. In some areas of northern Vietnam the final journey of the dead takes place with the secondary burial, when, three years after the initial burial, family members return to the cemetery, exhume the casket, remove and clean the bones, and transfer them into a smaller urn for reburial. For many northerners this is an important obligation, although it is rarely performed in the south. Once it is completed, people feel that the deceased is finally at rest.

■ Conclusion

WEDDINGS AND FUNERALS, despite the numerous variations in how they are performed in Vietnam, are tremendously important events. At one level they are vital social occasions that mark journeys to a new social status, be it married person or family ancestor. At another they provide an occasion in which the living come together, repay old debts, renew their relationships, and celebrate a new marriage or the life of a beloved family member. Perhaps most important, they are contexts in which the living reassert and revitalize their moral relationships, first to those who are with them now, but also to those who have come before them. As the Kinh make their own journeys through their lives, their paths along the way are marked by the many weddings and funerals in which they participate.

At the tomb site of Cam Van Oai, a distinguished Thai nobleman and official, mortuary *(heo)* trees have been erected to assist his soul in its ascent to the sky to live with the ancestors. Mai Son, Son La province, 1933.

OTHER JOURNEYS

OF THE DEAD

Luu Hung, Nguyen Trung Dung,
Tran Thi Thu Thuy, Vi Van An,
and Vo Thi Thuong

THE QUESTION "What happens when we die?" is probably universal. In response, cultures around the world have produced diverse answers, articulated through the prayers, songs, and ritual acts performed during funerals, mortuary rituals, and public and private commemorations of the dead. Death rites function on two levels: explicitly, as a symbolic or ritually efficacious means of easing the dead into another state of being; and implicitly, as a series of procedures over an interval of time that guide kin and community through a process of grief and mourning. It should not be surprising that many peoples describe the transition of the dead through the metaphor of a journey. The Kinh rituals described in the previous chapter, in particular the funeral procession, are themselves often enacted as ritualized journeys from the living community of household and village to the grave.

Because death rituals touch on a fundamental human condition, they are richly enacted in many societies, where a funeral may be an occasion to express core social values and affirm significant social relationships. It is no surprise, then, that death rites have been avidly studied by ethnologists. In this chapter, we present the responses of five ethnic communities to the question "What happens when we die?" The Muong, Thai, and Hmong are concentrated in the north of Vietnam; the Giarai are a Central Highlands people; and the Khmer, having ties to the majority population of Cambodia, live in the Mekong Delta of the south.[1]

■ The Travels of Multiple Souls

THE QUESTION OF EXISTENCE after death becomes more complex when belief holds that the living body is animated by multiple souls. According to the Muong, each person has ninety souls or animating forces (*wai*, or *via* in Vietnamese), which are distributed throughout the living body. At the time of death, the souls are combined into a single *ma* (*hon* in Vietnamese), a wraithlike entity that must travel across the cosmos to reach the Land of the Dead (Muong Ma), guided by a ritual specialist called a *mo*. Thais who have lived in close proximity to the Muong similarly hold that the living body contains several souls or animating forces (*khoan* or *van* in Thai dialects), which change into wraiths, or *phi*, after death. The *phi* travel to three different domains: one remains with the family as a protecting ancestor, one lurks in the graveyard as a "cemetery ghost," and the rest are lead by the *mo* priest to the next world.

The Hmong recognize three separate souls: the principal one in the fontanel; the second in the navel, governing the body and its internal organs; and the third in the chest. When one of these souls becomes detached from the body, the person falls sick, and if a soul is completely lost, the person dies. At death, the three souls all leave the body and go off in different directions. The first soul flies to heaven to see the ancestors. The second also flies to heaven to inquire about the death of the human body, but then returns to the human world where it resides in the tomb. This soul sometimes comes back from the grave to disturb the living. The third soul reincarnates as another living form. In Muong, Thai, and Hmong

Mourners in a Thai community in Son La province in 2000 wait for the funeral procession to pass. The different wraps of their white turbans indicate their relationship to the deceased.

funerals, a dramatic recounting of a soul's journey is an important part of funeral rites. For the Giarai, in contrast, mortuary rites mark the end of the relationship between the living and the dead, and for the Khmer relatively simple rites punctuate another reincarnation on the path to ultimate release.

■ The Muong Journey to the Land of the Dead

MUONG MA, THE LAND OF THE DEAD, is a mirror image of the world the deceased has left behind. There are mountains, rivers, fields, houses, and villages, but in this dark world, night and day are reversed. Although there is a road to this unseen world, not every soul can reach Muong Ma. The soul must be led by the *mo*, the master of ceremonies who chants texts to lead the soul during the funeral. The *mo*, whose role is hereditary, is the only person capable of communicating with supernatural powers and

A huge catafalque, made of paper and bamboo, is placed on the gravesite at an elaborate Muong funeral. Hoa Binh province, 1932.

leading the soul to the other world, mediating between the soul, the living, and the inhabitants of other worlds. Traditionally, two *mo* would perform a funeral; the primary *mo* would come from another village, but the secondary *mo* could be the deceased's fellow villager. In the past, moreover, some *mo* served only rich and noble families, while other *mo* held rites for ordinary people.

Since the soul *(ma)* is newly born when the body dies, it is not yet accustomed to its new situation and not yet ready for the *mo* to lead it. First the *mo* must destroy the relationship between the soul and the living by cutting a thread tied to the coffin. Next, the *mo* uses his power to force the soul to accept its new status. In subsequent rites, force will not be necessary: the *mo* will simply persuade the soul by instructing it about death and its new situation, and the soul will accept the *mo*'s guidance voluntarily.

The *mo*, standing in front of the coffin, recites a variety of mourning chants, including those that guide the soul on its journey to the Land of the Dead and to the Heavenly Court. The soul is thus never alone in its journey but always guided and supervised by the *mo*. A third partner to this journey is the "servant" *(chi chuoc)*, who carries the dead's belongings. During the funeral, the servant assists the *mo* by burning incense, pouring alcohol, or beating gongs. The servant is an ordinary villager without the *mo*'s magical powers, but he comes from a family that has filled this role in previous generations. Thus, there are three invisible travelers on the jour-

Relatives return from the burial ceremony at a Muong funeral.

ney described in the *mo*'s chants: the *wai* souls of the *mo* and the servant and the newly transformed *ma* soul of the deceased.

In the texts chanted by the *mo*, the soul makes its first journey to the Land of the Dead and is led before the ancestors to be accepted into their community. The road reaches only from the home of the deceased to the burial ground, but the way is unfamiliar to the soul. The soul's second journey is a final visit to familiar places in the village that must be left behind. This poignant journey, described in *mo* texts, reveals the attachment of the Muong to their own land and village.

Now the soul is led home to prepare for its journey to the Heavenly Court to hear God's judgment. This is a difficult trip, not only for the soul but also for the *mo* and the servant because the road to Heaven is long and there are many obstacles. Various supernatural forces will attack them along the way. The *mo* helps the soul to overcome all challenges and protects the soul so that it is not afraid. Once they reach the Heavenly Court, the soul stands trial for the "many crimes" it committed in life, such as consuming the meat of animals and mistreating domestic animals. The souls of these animals level complaints against the soul, but God's judgment is very tolerant; the soul will be allowed to reincarnate.

The soul again returns to the coffin to prepare for a final journey to the Land of the Dead. Wealthy families might keep the coffin at home for several days so that the soul can receive its inheritance—in the form of household utensils and tools specific to the deceased's gender. These goods are placed around the altar so that the deceased can organize its new "life" in the Land of the Dead. This is a difficult parting because the soul must bid farewell not only to its family and fellow villagers but also to its cattle, poultry, houses, and intimate possessions. Then it is time for the final procession to the burial ground.

In the past, a Muong funeral could last several days—in wealthy families as long as twelve days—with the deceased's close kin waking the coffin in shifts, but now most families bring the dead to the cemetery within twenty-four hours of his or her last breath. Performed over a single day and night, the *mo*'s recitations are necessarily abbreviated, but he still chants the most essential parts, never omitting the first journey to the Land of the Dead and the journey to the Heavenly Court.

■ Hmong Journeys with a Shaman

THE HMONG RELY ON A SHAMAN to show them the way to the other world. While the shaman's recitation is not as long and elaborate as that of the *mo*, the shaman's performance is combined with several ritual acts to suggest the ascent of the soul to the sky and the journey of the ancestor to the grave.

The community learns of a death when shots are fired and a horn is blown. The family places the washed and dressed corpse on a bamboo bier or in a coffin symbolizing the horse that carries the dead to the ancestors. Placed in front of the house spirit's altar, the body is tied to the bier with hanks of hemp fiber. A rope of hemp, tied to the bier, is run through the roof of the house. The soul uses the rope to ascend to the celestial abode of the gods and ancestors, which is fragrant with blossoms and delicious herbs.

A shaman is requested to "show the way" *(khua ke)* to the deceased. Without this assistance, the soul of the deceased cannot find the ancestors. The shaman speaks of the origin of the universe, the cause of death, and the dangers confronting the soul as it journeys to join the ancestors. He also tells of a cock that serves as guide for the dead, and recites additional legends and customs concerning funeral practices. The shaman then places a stick wound with a long length of hemp fiber in the hand of the deceased, explaining that

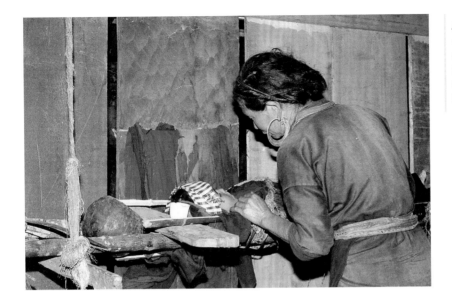

A Hmong mother or kinswoman comforts a dead child. The child's soul will climb toward the sky via the hemp rope at the left of the bier. Mu Cang Chai district, Yen Bai province, 2000.

the dead cannot ascend to the level of the ancestors without this hemp cord. The shaman puts traditional Hmong hemp shoes on the deceased's feet and recounts how each person must go on foot to find the land of his or her ancestors. He also explains that the ancestors will not recognize the soul unless the deceased arrives dressed in traditional Hmong hemp clothing.

After the shaman has "shown the way," musicians perform a mourning song on long bamboo pipes and a drum, describing how the soul of the deceased says farewell to the house spirit, the door spirit, the main post spirit, the kitchen spirit, and the room spirit and then journeys to the ancestors.

Late at night, some Hmong men "drive back the enemy," running seven circuits around the house if the deceased is male and nine if the deceased is female. This act recalls the original journey of the Hmong people to the south, harassed by Chinese armies. Reliving this history, the Hmong perform this rite three times a day to protect the soul of the deceased. The man who leads the way holds a torch, followed by those holding a knife, a cutlass, and a gun. A shot must be fired and the horn blown after each circuit.

The following morning, before the corpse is carried from the house, a man stands next to the door of the house and shoots an arrow with a small bow, aiming at the sun so that it cannot shine into the eyes of the dead and blind the soul on its journey to the ancestors. The bier is carried to an open area where a platform has already been erected. In the middle of this open space the drum, bamboo pipes, and a wooden bird are suspended from a small tree. The tree symbolizes the connection between the living and the dead and the link between the earth and the sky realm of the ancestors. This is a temporary resting place, where a buffalo or ox is sacrificed and a final meal shared with the deceased. In an auspicious hour, chosen by the shaman, vigorous young men will run with the bier to the grave where it will be interred. The tomb will be tended with more offerings three days later, and thirteen days after the interment a rite will be performed to help the third soul reincarnate.

■ Black Thai Journeys Assisted by Kin

THE THAI ALSO HOLD THAT DEATH is only the end of life in this particular world; the soul lives on with the ancestors (*dam chao*) in Heaven (*pha*). Thais hold funeral rites solemnly and carefully to meet the requirements of custom and because the observance of sacred death rites is an important event in the life of a community. The rituals observed by the Black Thai of the northwest are more typically Thai, less influenced by the culture of the Muong or Kinh than are the death rituals of other Thai communities in Vietnam. Among the Black Thai, funeral rites of the nobility differ from those of common people in scale and procedure, but they share the same basic procedures and purpose of easing the deceased from the household and village realm of living people to the realm of the ancestors.

On the first day the deceased is washed with warm water steeped with fragrant leaves. The corpse is dressed in fresh garments, its hair is combed, and it is placed in the coffin. Nobody is allowed to weep yet because "the spirit would be awakened." Once three rounds of bullets are fired to announce the bereavement, kin gather and sit around the coffin weeping. The eldest son tears down the partition in front of the house spirit's shrine to show that ordinary family life has been ruptured. The deceased is offered steamed glutinous rice, boiled chicken, and wine, his first meal as an ancestor. When most of the guests have departed, the family has a practical discussion about the funeral. The oldest kinsman on the deceased's father's side is chosen as chief mourner and empowered to determine the procedures the family will follow.

On the second day kinsmen perform different tasks, based on their relationship to the deceased. Kin who share a common ancestor with the

The cremation site at a commoner Thai funeral, Yen Bai province, 2000.

deceased within five generations wear mourners' clothing and receive con-dolences. More distant kin who share a common paternal ancestor are responsible for seeing that the rites are carried out according to custom. The sons of the deceased and his male relatives by marriage—the deceased's brothers-in-law and sons-in-law and other men related to the lineage by marriage—do the work of slaughtering buffaloes, killing pigs, weeding the path to the grave, preparing the bier, fetching firewood, setting up the funeral pyre, and carrying the coffin. The oldest son-in-law of the deceased's lineage *(khuoi coc)* assumes an important role in the funeral, and he and his wife receive gifts of clothing from the deceased's family. It is the "stock descendant-in-law" who aids the dead man on his journey by reciting the story of the soul's forthcoming journey. He speaks of the historical journey of the Thai people who migrated to this village from a distant homeland, which the deceased will visit on his way to the sky. He describes how the soul will travel through a familiar landscape until it reaches an imaginary river (Ta Khai) separating this world from the land of the dead. The deceased crosses the river by boat, ascends a high mountain, and continues up into the sky.

The skull of the deceased is retrieved from the cremation site and placed on a tray covered with a red cloth. Mai Son, Son La province, 1933.

On the third day the corpse leaves the house for the forest of spirits (*pa heo*). The coffin is taken out by the front door if the deceased is the father and out the back door if it is the mother. The catafalque is then laid on the coffin, and the funeral procession starts out. The sons-in-law are at the head, followed by male descendants; the coffin comes next, with its designated bearers who are affines or lineage affines; male and females relatives follow; and unrelated villagers bring up the rear. Although a widow walks behind her husband's coffin, as a wife follows her husband, a husband never walks behind his wife's coffin and does not go to the graveyard. The coffin and the catafalque are put onto the funeral pyre in the forest of spirits, and the eldest son-in-law lights the fire. After the pyre has caught fire, the male in-laws take off their mourning turbans and place them on the ground before returning home. The descendants remain in the graveyard until the fire goes out.

On the fourth day the male descendants and descendants-in-law pick up the bones from the pyre and wash them with wine. The bones are bagged and placed into an earthenware jar covered by a plate with a hole in it. A silk string, drawn through the hole, enables the soul to leave the jar. Once the jar is buried, the primary mourner gives the first son-in-law a white buffalo if the deceased is a father or a black buffalo if the deceased is a mother. The buffalo is sacrificed so that the deceased can resume farming in the next world, and the mourners hold a feast with the buffalo meat.

A mortuary hut is built in the forest of spirits, and *chao pha* and *heo* trees, made of decorated bamboo poles, are erected as a bridge for the soul's ascent to the sky. If the deceased is a man, both a *chao pha* and a *heo* are erected; if a woman, two *heo* trees. The *chao pha* tree, which can be put up only by men, is twelve arm spans high for a noble and six for a commoner (who in the past were not permitted to erect any trees). The *heo* is a pole hung with 120 decorative banners for nobles, 60 to 80 for commoners. Models of a horse with wings, which men ride to the sky, or a banana flower, which women ride, are placed at the top of the *heo* tree.

A *chao pha* tree is erected beside the tomb at the end of a Thai funeral as a bridge for the soul's ascent to the sky. The *chao pha* tree is raised only if the deceased is a man. Yen Bai province, 2000.

On the fifth day children and relatives of the deceased bring food to the grave. From the sixth to the twelfth day, they make these offerings every two or three days. Then the soul is called to take its place in the family's ancestral shrine. According to custom, Thais mourn a deceased father or mother for three years during which singing, marriages, and house building are prohibited. At the end of the three years of mourning, the family of the deceased treats kin and neighbors to a dinner to mark the transition back fully into the world of the living.

■ Sending Off the Dead:
The Giarai Rite of Abandoning the Tomb

THE GIARAI OF THE CENTRAL HIGHLANDS also send their dead on a journey but not until many years after the death. They see each mortal as having a soul (*mngat*) that is transformed into a spirit (*atau*) after death. After departing from the village world, the dead live a parallel existence in a village of spirits situated where the sun sets. The Giarai Arap describe the land of the dead as a typical Giarai village governed by a white-tailed eagle and a monkey. The Giarai Mthur speak of a deep cave to the west reigned over by Lady Tung and Lady Tai. In the remote past, the living could enter the cave and visit their ancestors, but when the cave became too crowded, Old Man Koi Doi blocked the mouth with a huge tree trunk to separate the world of the dead from that of the living.

In the village of spirits the deceased Giarai lives another full life, dies, and will eventually return to the world of mortals. After its second death in the village of spirits, the spirit turns into a spider that Lady Tung and Lady Tai allow to move about on the earth's surface. It is transformed into a dewdrop that seeps through the earth; it then enters a newborn child and becomes its soul. The Giarai also say that when Lady Tung weaves a new weft into the fabric, a baby is born, and if one of these threads breaks, someone dies.

Until they make their initial journey to the village of spirits, the Giarai dead reside in the village graveyard. Giarai have typically buried several corpses in a common grave, sometimes in the same coffin made from a hollowed tree trunk, although this practice is dying out. When another mem-

The Giarai dead lead a parallel life in the land of the ancestors, presided over by a monkey village chief as imagined in this sculpture placed beside the mortuary hut. Late twentieth century.

ber of the family died, perhaps several years after the first bereavement, the coffin was unearthed to receive another corpse and was reburied. A single coffin may have held three or four corpses. In the past, only kin were buried together, but later unrelated corpses could be placed in the same grave, though not in the same coffin. A grave can hold dozens of coffins. The coffin of the first deceased in the grave is buried in the middle, with other coffins on each side, forming a row of parallel biers with the heads of the dead facing the setting sun.

Until the rite of abandoning the tomb (*po-thi*), which might take place more than ten years after death, the dead in the graveyard are still considered present in the lives of their fellow villagers, who wish to prolong the moment of departure. Families are very attached to their dead relatives. They tend them every day, feeding them offerings, cleaning their graves, and mourning their loss. On the last evening of each month, villagers hold a feast in the graveyard, make great libations, and chat with one another in the graveyard in a demonstration of the community's feelings toward the dead and the members of village households in mourning.

People cease mourning through the rite of abandoning the tomb, a huge event that has both religious and festive elements and allows the mourners to finally say farewell to the dead. Tomb abandonments are held by households with relatives in a common grave, but all villagers take part in it. Crowds of people from other villages also participate in the festival, taking the occasion beyond the village.

Preparations for this ceremony are made long beforehand. At least one month before the rite, trees and bamboos are cut down to set up a new mortuary hut that will be sumptuously decorated. The roof may be decorated with painted designs or designs woven from bamboo strips. Imposing figures carved out of large tree trunks are placed around the tomb, including statues on the verge of copulation and pregnant figures, suggesting future regeneration, figures performing everyday activities to suggest the parallel world of the spirit village, the monkey ruler of the spirit village, and even such eccentric figures as soccer players and U.S. soldiers.

All manner of relations come to mourn the dead at the mortuary hut. Families provide for their dead by giving them not only the new and lovely mortuary hut but also cattle and pigs to be sacrificed, liquor, water, food, and a variety of model implements made of wood or bamboo. Banana trees and sugarcane are planted next to the mortuary hut, and a live baby chick is fastened to it. Some people believe that this chick will show the way to the spirits. Throughout several days and nights, villagers slowly march in single file, counterclockwise, around the mortuary hut, with musicians beating drums and gongs in the front and men, women, and children dancing behind. When a dance is finished, that group of dancers will pause to eat, drink beer made from several grains, talk, and possibly sleep before dancing again, but other groups of dancers maintain the procession. Groups of

This mortuary sculpture portrays a woman with a rice mortar, suggesting both everyday life and preparations for the mortuary feast. Late twentieth century.

visitors from other villages join in, hitting their own sets of gongs, adding to the intensity of sound and motion. In Giarai Arap villages, the dancers make a circuit of the graveyard, led by two animated men who are smeared with mud, wearing masks made from banana leaf sheaths and dressed in banana leaves. Some believe this pair represents ancestors who have come to meet the spirits.

Hitting drums and gongs, Giarai mourners circle the tomb, bidding farewell to the dead who are journeying to the land of the ancestors. The fence around the mortuary hut and several mortuary sculptures are visible in the background. Central Highlands, 1936.

Villagers and outsiders who have come to offer their condolences and say farewell to the spirits contribute beer, rice, and chickens and share a communal dinner in the graveyard.

The widow or widower is emancipated by a bath in a stream. He or she can now change into ordinary clothing and comb his or her hair. Marital relations with the deceased are now terminated, and remarriage is permitted. The dead have been sent off on their journey to another place.

▪ Khmer Cremation

IN CONTRAST WITH THE ELABORATE RITES described thus far, Khmer funerals seem simple and matter-of-fact. The Khmer, followers of Theravada Buddhism, believe in reincarnation and accept the death of a loved one as the resumption of a journey through multiple existences toward a realm of bliss. When death approaches, relatives might seek out a renowned monk, or *achar*, who says a few words of comfort and murmurs a short prayer for the repose of the deceased. When death occurs, the *achar* closes the eyelids and announces the bereavement by beating a drum. He lights three candles, one at the head of the deceased and one at each side of the body, symbolizing the Buddha, virtue, and devotion to Buddhism. After sliding a silver coin into the mouth of the deceased, he helps the relatives wash the body in scented water, clothe it in new garments, and cover it with a length of white material. The dead person's face is covered with a white veil.

Four more monks are summoned to keep watch over the body and pray for the soul of the deceased. The corpse is wrapped in a length of cloth, then tied up with three thin slips of white material, thus separating the body into three parts representing three worldly ties: to one's spouse, to one's children, and to one's estate. After the body is put into the coffin, the hair of the mourners is closely cropped. They dress in white to keep watch over the coffin and listen to the prayers recited by the monks. These rites are all performed within a day, although in wealthy homes they may last for several days.

The *achar* chooses a lucky day for cremation, avoiding Tuesday, Thursday, and Sunday, when the man-eating demon roams free. The funeral procession, sometimes including a band, is led by monks who chant prayers as they walk, followed by the *achar*, who holds a small shovel used to gather up the bones after cremation. A flag with a small terra-cotta pot suspended from its shaft is carried in the procession. The pot is broken next to the pyre; it may be left there or offered to the *achar*. Behind the *achar*, the deceased's daughter carries a tray of food offerings for the *achar*; coconut milk, used to wash the bones recovered from the cremation, and wine, to wash the hands of those who gather up the bones.

One of the deceased's daughters strews the path with steamed glutinous rice that will sustain the soul in the next world. Relatives and neighbors follow behind. The coffin is carried around the pyre three times and then laid on it with the dead person's head facing west, where he may rest in peace and see his ancestors. The *achar* removes the coffin lid and uncovers the dead person's face to let everybody say one more farewell. Relatives of the deceased hold flowers or incense sticks in their hands, palms pressed together, and pray while the monks recite a sutra. Flowers are strewn over the pyre, and the *achar* and a son or a granddaughter of the deceased light the fire. Four people stand at the pyre to keep the fire alive.

Khmer monks listen to a sermon at Wat Doi in Soc Trang province during the New Year, 2001. In common with Thai, Lao, and Burmese, Khmer are Theravada rather than Mahayana Buddhists.

In front of all the people, the most senior monk *(luc krou)* gives a Buddhist robe to one of the sons or, in the absence of a son, the chief mourner. The person who receives the robe immediately dons it, becoming a monk. He will enter the temple for at least several years after the funeral, depending on his personal and family circumstances. For the Khmer, becoming a monk is a responsibility but also an honor that the mourner undertakes out of respect for the deceased.

Five or six hours after lighting the pyre, the fire is extinguished with water, and the *achar* gathers up the charred bones. The family washes them in coconut milk, and the eldest son carries them home. If there is no living son or if he is disabled, the deceased's grandson, his daughter's son, or the son of his oldest brother fulfills this task. That night the family of the deceased places the parcel of bones before the monks. Then the family serves a meal to the relatives and the monks to express its gratitude. The bones are held in a metal or ceramic jar, bamboo tube, or dried coconut shell depending on the family's circumstances. The container is placed on the Buddhist altar at home or committed to the temple's care. Every year all families who have entrusted bones to the temple's safekeeping hold a common ceremony, and the monks pray for the souls of the dead.

In the past, corpses were cremated in the open air, the temple garden, or a secluded spot. Today many temples have crematoria with high chimneys to protect the environment from pollution.

A crowd gathers at the gate of the communal house in Yen So village in the Red River Delta during the festival honoring the tutelary god and local hero Ly Phuc Man in 1995.

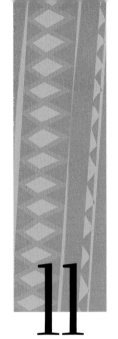

THE VILLAGE
GOD'S JOURNEY

11

Nguyen Van Huy, Nguyen Anh Ngoc,
Nguyen Huy Hong, and
Nguyen Trung Dung

THROUGHOUT VIETNAM ELABORATE local festivals are held to invoke community tutelary gods and to ask for their protection and blessings. After a long period of prohibition and neglect, many of these festivals were revived during the 1990s. In northern Vietnam in the Red River Delta, festivals are usually held just before the spring planting season, and they carry a wish for a prosperous agricultural year. Along the south and central seacoast, the festivals of fishing communities include prayers for safe and successful fishing. A costumed procession with ornate palanquins is the most spectacular element of many festivals, enacted with the pomp and formality of a king's or dynastic official's progress through his domain. These processions signify that the local tutelary god, represented by an inscribed wooden tablet, is being carried in state from his own temple to

This palanquin carries the tutelary god in the festival of Nanh village, Ninh Hiep commune, Hanoi. The elaborate red-and-gold lacquered vehicle approximates the palanquins used to carry high officials in dynastic times.

the communal house where the festival is held, that local deities are being invited to the festival, or that local dignitaries are approaching the deity with a petition for the community's well-being.

In this chapter we present three variations on the festival theme, one from the Red River Delta, one from the central coast, and the third a festival procession in miniature, enacted by water puppets.

■ A Festival in the Red River Delta

IN YEARS PAST, THE PEOPLE OF HANOI enjoyed spring festivals held in Bac Ninh province to the east and Ha Tay province to the west. One of the most spectacular was the Gia Festival, held by the village of Sau Gia (also known as Gia or Yen So village), Yen So commune, Hoai Duc district, Ha Tay province, about nineteen miles from Hanoi. Held on the tenth day

A distinctive feature of the Gia Festival in Ha Tay province is the reenactment of a heroic battle against foreign invaders, led by a commander who impersonates Ly Phuc Man. Youths from the community are trained in traditional military exercises; their mock battle is the liveliest part of the festival.

of the third lunar month to commemorate the death anniversary of the village tutelary god, Ly Phuc Man, the Gia Festival's procession was renowned throughout the region.

According to a memorial stele dated 1728 and housed in the village temple, Ly Phuc Man was a native of Gia village. In the sixth century, during the Ly dynasty (542–601), he fought successfully against foreign invaders on the southern border of the country. He died a hero's death in the fight against the northern Luong invaders. To pay homage to this hero, Yen So villagers installed Ly Phuc Man as their protective deity, building a temple in front of the legendary site of his grave. The elaborate Gia Temple that we see today dates from the eleventh century, though it has been repaired and renovated many times.

An ethnographic report on the Gia Festival from 1937, written in French by the ethnologist Nguyen Van Huyen, relates how the two neighboring villages of Yen So and Dac So combined with Gia village to enact a festival with care and splendor.[1] A full festival was seventeen days long and had three main parts: temple rites, military exercises, and processions. In the temple itself, rites of offering incense, flowers, and food while addressing the tutelary god were carried out according to strict ritual procedures. The military exercises (*nghiem quan*), unique to the Gia Festival, were the liveliest part of the proceedings. In this mock battle, enacted under the direction of a commander in the role of "general," nearly one hundred young men in traditional uniforms with ancient armaments in their hands lunged and parried with one another, advancing and falling back following military rules. In this manner the valiant deeds of Ly Phuc Man and his troops were reenacted.

Following the *nghiem quan*, these costumed troops headed the procession. Processions were the central activity of a festival day, as the ritual officiants went in pomp to the temple to make their offerings. Strict rules regulating how Dac So and Yen So villages were to conduct their processions were inscribed on a stele dating from 1855 and housed in the temple. Both villages made offerings on the first and the last days of the festival, but for the rest of the festival, they alternated, one village going to the temple in procession on even days and the other on odd days. Unlike the custom in some other festivals, here the festival palanquin did not carry a tablet inscribed with the tutelary god's name. Instead it held the *so*, the ritual texts that would be read in the temple.

The full procession was more than half a mile long. Participants marched along a dike through the rice fields, starting from Gia Communal House (Quan Gia), where Ly Phuc Man is enshrined, to the Temple of Literature (Van Chi) in Yen So village, where the texts were written, then placed in a box and set on the palanquin. The box was then carried back to Gia Communal House. Alternatively, the procession went from Dac So Communal House to the Temple of Literature of Dac So village, to Gia Communal House, and back to Dac So Communal House.

The Yen So procession in 1937 included a palanquin decorated with green branches bearing a drum and gong and a palanquin bearing altar fittings and the written invocation to the tutelary god. Villagers in military garb bore horns, staffs, lances, maces, fans on sticks, lanterns, folding fans, parasols, canopies, and sunshades to shield the palanquins, two signboards bearing the inscription "Infinite Sacredness" *(Thanh linh)* and "Eternal Majesty" *(Vuy vien)*, and other paraphernalia. A musical ensemble and two rows of five carefully selected elders were led by an elder in the garb of a general to represent Ly Phuc Man. Everyone in the procession wore colorful costumes. Teenagers carrying flags wore brown tunics with red belts and brown turbans but were barefoot. Festival officials *(ky muc)* wore blue or brown tunics, brown turbans, cloth shoes, and hats like those worn by dynastic officials. People carrying offerings wore brown tunics with high

At the Gia Festival in 2000 a petition to the tutelary god Ly Phuc Man is carefully placed in a lacquer box and set on a special palanquin, where it will be carried in the festival procession.

collars and wide sleeves. Elders wore red tunics with large, long sleeves that reached to their knees, blue belts, and large vermilion straw hats.

As elderly villagers remember it, the last big festival was held in Yen So village in 1944. From that time until 1990, neither the Gia Festival nor any other village festival was held in the Red River Delta. This was in part a consequence of the two Indochina wars, but also a consequence of the official perception that village festivals honoring tutelary gods were "superstitious," that the elaborate organization required to enact them was a waste of time, money, and labor. The area around Gia Temple witnessed many changes in these years. During the nine-year resistance (1946–1954), Gia Temple was burned by the French army on the eleventh day of the first lunar month in Dinh Hoi year (1947) and totally destroyed. During the first years of the resistance, it was used as a medical station for injured soldiers who were transported from the Hanoi front. During the second resistance (1964–1975), the covered wings where old people used to sit during the festival were turned into storerooms for the cooperative.

However, the memory of the festival and the villagers' gratitude for the protection of its tutelary god were transmitted to younger generations in various ways. Annually, villagers organized a small ritual to pay homage to Ly Phuc Man. Although there was no festival, people preserved the temple and burned incense to the tutelary god, even in the most difficult days of war. The temples in the Gia Temple complex were all rebuilt once before the major restoration projects of the 1990s. Whenever there was a big event in the village, such as sending off troops or receiving an official commendation, people offered incense and flowers to the village god.

For several decades, Yen So village did not celebrate any village festival, devoting every effort to the resistance or to basic survival. With the Renovation (Doi Moi) policy in the late 1980s came a new impulse to revive village festivals throughout the northern delta. The economic condition of the villagers improved in the reopened market economy, and people felt a need to revive their traditions. In 1999 Nguyen Ba Han, a seventy-year-old villager, told us that many believe that "their lives have improved through the help of the spirits, so they feel that they should contribute to the renovation and conservation of temples and the provision of offerings and festival paraphernalia such as armaments, flags, fans and gongs." In addition to the government's investment in the conservation of heritage sites, the villagers' voluntary contributions to the restoration of the temple were a decisive factor in the revival of the Gia Festival. For example, Tran Thi Cuc, a resident of Hanoi born in Gia village, contributed 100 million dong (nearly U.S. $7,000) to rebuild the central temple in 1997, and in 2000 she contributed another 20 million (nearly U.S. $1,400). Nguyen Van Vi, a local resident, has continuously given equipment and expensive utensils to the temples. Nguyen Ba Bach, born in the village but now living in Australia, also sent money to conserve the temples.

The revival of the village festival began with the refurbishing of the temples in 1986, supported by villagers and other people of goodwill. The upper temple in the Gia Temple complex was inaugurated in 1990, and this was also the occasion for reviving the Gia Festival. From 1990 to 2000,

During the festival of Co Loa, just outside Hanoi, community elders prostrate themselves during formal rites honoring the tutelary god. Offerings are made and an invocation is read, asking the deity's blessings on the community. Early 1990s.

the festival was held four times. During that decade, the Gia Temple complex was rebuilt step by step: the lower temple in 1995, the middle temple in 1998–1999, and Tam Quan Gate in 2000. At the 1992 Gia Festival, the government designated both Gia Temple and Gia Forest as heritage sites. In 2000 the festival welcomed the new millennium. Each time the festival was organized, more of it was revived, maintenance work on the temples continued, and the elaborate old rites were again practiced.

This ultimately successful revival has not been easy. "By the time we were able to revive the Gia Festival," said Nguyen Dang Hoan, the forty-year-old chairman of the People's Council of Yen So commune,

> *many people questioned the wisdom of this course. "Aren't rites and processions superstitious?" Many people questioned the propriety of wearing traditional tunics and turbans again, especially the soldiers, who were accustomed to wearing uniforms. The local leaders, but not just the local leaders, were divided in their opinions. In 1981, General Vo Nguyen Giap, who was the vice prime minister at that time, visited Yen So village, and he advised the local people that they should revive the festival in a major way, including the procession and the military exercises, to pay homage to the people's hero, Ly Phuc Man. His support helped sustain the will to revive the Gia Festival. However, we had to wait for the right conditions.*

In 1990 the prospects for revival were dim. By this time, most villagers had only hearsay knowledge of the festival, based on the fragmentary and imprecise memories of the handful of old men who had participated in their youth. Sometimes one said one thing and another said something else, and no one knew who was right and who was wrong. Many discussions were held among the villagers, especially with old people, in an effort to find the right solution. But this village was more fortunate than many others, since its festival had been carefully documented in the 1937 ethnography mentioned above. Nguyen Ba Khanh, chairman of the People's Committee of Yen So commune since 1989 and head of the Gia Festival organizing committee since 1990, relates:

> *It was lucky that the ex-minister of education, . . . Nguyen Van Huyen, made such a careful and detailed study on Gia Festival. During the second war of resistance he was evacuated to Yen So village, and he gave the villagers a copy of his monograph. It is our priceless treasure. We had to find a translator and make a careful study of this book. We considered it our handbook for reviving the Gia Festival, containing all the details from conducting the procession to the military games, to clothing, to ritual songs.*

In the first days of the revival, almost nothing remained of the festival accoutrements except a palanquin in the temple. Costumes, ritual clothing, and paraphernalia used in the procession had been burned long before. The leaders of the revival decided to launch a campaign to motivate all the villagers to participate in the preparation of the festival. As a result, village families produced all of the costumes for the four or five hundred people who would take part in the procession and more than three hundred flags, all within twenty days.

The chairman of the commune's People's Committee heads the festival's organizing committee, which is divided into a section for ritual and a section for games and entertainment. The Old People's Association, under the direction of the commune's Protocol Committee, organizes the rites in the temple, the procession, and the military exercises. Performances of songs and dramas as well as games and athletic events, including wrestling, soccer, volleyball, human chess, badminton, swinging, a shooting match, and cock fights, are also a part of the festival. These well-attended activities are organized by the commune's Cultural Committee.

Rehearsals for the procession and military exercises begin officially on the fifth day of the third lunar month in anticipation of the festival's opening on the tenth. The four or five hundred teenagers who participate must practice often and follow strict rules. The most important task is to find people to participate in the procession. Each village has the responsibility for recruiting participants, according to strict criteria. Anyone who has committed a crime such as drug use or theft cannot participate, nor can any member of that family enter the temple. The youths who carry flags must have good grades in school and must also be from good families. The men who carry the main flags must be from "cultural families" (*gia dinh van hoa*), a title issued by the People's Committee of the commune indicating families of good character who uphold social norms and whose children respect their elders and do well in school. It is considered an honor to have a family member take part in the procession and participate in the festival; if a family is barred from the festival because a member violated village rules, the family will carry that sorrow for the whole year. If members of such a family should dare to participate in the festival, they would feel that they were committing an offense against their tutelary god and their fellow villagers. Thus the festival fosters village morality and community spirit.

These red-and-gold lacquered standards are part of the elaborate paraphernalia carried in the Gia Festival. The signboard indicates that the power of the deity extends far and wide.

The Gia Festival of today has changed a great deal owing to changes in the mindset of the local leaders as a consequence of profound changes in the social and political conditions of village life. The most significant change lies in the spirit of equality that now infuses the festival. In the past, women did not have the right to serve in the festival, but in 2000 one-quarter of the thousand participants were women. Old women now have the right to sit as equals with old men in the communal house, though they usually yield this privilege to the old men. Also in 2000, for the first time in the history of the Gia Festival, a woman participated as a member of the organizing committee, and she was an equal contributor in every respect. The festival no longer discriminated between local people with genealogical roots in the village and newcomers. All residents seventy years and over, even if they have moved to the village from the south, are considered elders and can sit in the most respected places in the communal house, and all people over seventy-five wear red tunics.

In the past, the festival was held annually and took fifteen days with another fifteen of rehearsal, but now it is held over three days once every five years. The young men who take part in the military ceremony used to be chosen according to membership in local men's fraternal associations based on residence, kinship, or common interest (*phe giap*), but now they are chosen by village residence, and the schoolchildren are chosen by the village school. The commander of the military exercises used to be appointed by rank, but now the Veterans' Association assigns a veteran who is an experienced drill commander; this means that the practice is much more efficient, requiring only three or four days. The traditional systems whereby delegations were ranked and ordered in the procession no longer exist; instead, the delegations are now organized according to age. In the past, there were three palanquins, one for the tutelary god and one for each of his wives, who were honored as goddesses. Today, there is one palanquin for Ly Phuc Man and a second one bearing a picture of Ho Chi Minh, the hero of the Vietnamese people in the new era. Ritual texts have been amended to reflect the current situation of the village. The revival and maintenance of meaningful traditions in a new society is necessarily a creative act requiring both respect for old ways and flexible accommodation to new values. In the words of fifty-two-year-old Nguyen Tuan Mac, a leader in the festival revival, "The festival created an opportunity to recall the achievements of a hero from the past. Through participation in the festival, people were educated about proper human relationships and about the need to help each other in the community. Spiritually, by participating in the festival, people seemed to receive magical forces to overcome the obstacles they face in life." Despite the forty-five-year hiatus and the many changes in the modern festival, this was always the meaning of Gia Festival.

The tutelary god's palanquin leaves the communal house during the Gia Festival in 2000.

■ A Festival on the Central Coast

FISHERMEN ALONG THE central and southern coasts of Vietnam venerate the spirit of the whale, called by the reverential name Ngu Ong, or "Sir Fish." Festivals in honor of whale spirits are celebrated in many coastal fishing villages. In Man Thai ward of Son Tra district in Danang, the Cau Ngu Festival is held in the first lunar month, at the start of the spring-summer fishing season.

Villagers in Man Thai recall that the festival has a long tradition, stemming from at least the time of Emperor Gia Long (r. 1802–1820), who first recognized the veneration of whale spirits. Despite disruptions during wartime, the festival in Man Thai has been revived since the 1980s; a large festival is held every three years, with smaller observances in the intervening years.

Offshore fishing is a major economic activity along the central coast of Vietnam. Just as festivals in the Red River Delta are associated with agriculture, festivals along the central coast are appeals for a good catch and safety at sea. 1999.

For the fishermen of Man Thai, Sir Fish is a sacred deity who protects them as they venture out upon the open sea. Before fishing boats were equipped with motors and radios to monitor weather reports, the sea was a dangerous and frightening place, and fishermen depended on Sir Fish during storms or calms. Fisherman Le Van Ta, seventy-four years old, remembers going fishing at the age of twelve with his older brother, then fifteen. The winds were blowing fiercely, carrying the young boys from Da Nang to Quang Ngai. For two days and three nights, winds carried the boys along helplessly, until, Ta recalls, "I heard a sound like 'khit, khit' from under the boat. On this side we heard 'gwap' and on that side 'gwam.' The boat was steadied and lifted. Sir Fish thus saved our lives and carried us to Sa Huynh." His neighbor Nguyen Van Trieu, sixty-two, recalls how, when he was also only twelve years old, "I was going with my father to Bai Bac. We used as many as eleven or twelve oars. I was sitting next to the net, when suddenly there were very strong waves. I saw two whales, each twice as big as we were, swimming back and forth. . . . It was the whales who saved us, guiding us to Bai Bac. I saw this when I was a child, when the fishermen just used oars; they didn't have motorboats as we do today." Almost every fisherman in Man Thai has a similar story of how Sir Fish came to his rescue at a time of great peril.

The sighting of a whale—living or dead—brings good luck to fishermen, who can expect to have a bountiful catch that day. The appearance of a dolphin augurs no good, because the dolphin incarnates the soul of a man who died by drowning and became an evil spirit, causing harm to fishermen. Fishermen dread catching a whale in their nets, as Le Van Ta explains: "When a whale is caught in the net, it is usually so weak that it dies immediately. If the boat is far offshore, the fishermen will leave the net at sea, . . . they dare not bring it home because they are worried about their safety." A whale that dies near the shore and is not the unintended victim of the fishermen's nets is considered an omen of good luck. The first person to catch sight of the carcass of a whale, either on the high seas or washed ashore, is considered the eldest son of Sir Fish and must go into mourning for the deceased whale. Not only he but his entire village will have good fortune for many years thereafter. Le Van Ta continues, "The person who finds him wears a red mourning band, as if he were the oldest son of the whale, [as if it were] his own parent's funeral. It seems like fate, like destiny, for a whale to die near the shore. Many are injured somewhere and cannot survive. On shore, the villagers will bury them."

Villagers treat the carcass of a whale with all the respect they would give to a deceased person. "If he dies in a village, that is an event of utmost importance to the village. When the sun and sky go dim, it means a whale has died somewhere. As he dies, the heavens are sad," Le Van Ta explains. Once the carcass is ashore, it is washed in alcohol and wrapped in a red shroud. Villagers place papers on the mouth of the dead whale to saturate them with its saliva and then set the papers out to dry. Later, they will burn the papers and use the ash mixed with water to cure children of asthma. If the deceased whale is small, the fisherman will carry it along the shore in a funeral procession. Fisherman Tran Van Tan, seventy-six years old, remembers how one such procession was accompanied by a family of whales swimming along the beach with the cortege, bidding a last farewell to the departed. The carcass is carefully shrouded and buried in a sand dune near the sea. An altar is set above the grave. Every afternoon before starting out to sea, fishermen burn incense sticks on the altar to pray for peace and good luck.

Three or four years after burial, the deceased whale becomes the honored focus of the Cau Ngu Festival. In a parallel to the traditional funerary

The bones of beached whales are carefully tended in a mausoleum that is also a temple to the protective spirit of the whale. Vicinity of Danang, 1999.

practices observed for humans, the whale's bones are exhumed at the start of the whale festival to be carried in procession to the mausoleum, where they will be venerated for years to come. The mausoleum itself is a shrine of three bays, the central one containing an altar with a box to hold the bones of whales, topped with an incense burner, a large vase, and a tray for wine and other ritual objects. The mausoleum, which has a guardian who supervises worship, is opened only on festival days and during the lunar new year. In the courtyard of the mausoleum trees may not be cut, children may not play, and leaving trash is prohibited. Women may not enter the mausoleum, especially the central bay. The rituals enacted here are men's responsibility, perhaps because in this part of Vietnam only men do deep-sea fishing.

Tran Van Tan explains that the Cau Ngu Festival is one of many ritual acts intended to safeguard fishermen on the dangerous seas.

> We fishermen are very superstitious because it is our job to go offshore, facing the winds and waves. We attach great importance to the worship of Sir Fish. We often hold joint rituals for all the boats of the locality before going fishing. Every year, when we have luck in our fishing, we give some pigs as votive offerings to the sea, the deities, so that they help us in our work, thus helping our wives and children. Each individual tries to save three to five million dong [approximately U.S. $200–$350] for a ritual to protect his own boat.

In the first lunar month of 1999, the villagers of Man Thai celebrated a large Cau Ngu Festival honoring a whale—ten meters long—that had beached three years earlier. The festival began, following tradition, on the twenty-fourth day of the first lunar month (March 10 that year), but for several days beforehand the entire village helped with preparations, positioning tables and benches, cleaning the mausoleum, and making ready for the coming crowds. On the first day of the festival, the whale bones are typically disinterred from their first burial plot, washed with wine, dried in the sun, wrapped in red paper, and carried on a bier to the mausoleum. On the occasion of the 1999 festival, however, when the whale's grave was excavated the villagers saw that the flesh had not yet rotted away and the bones could not be removed. Undaunted, the villagers determined that the sand surrounding the whale's corpse could also be a medium for the whale's spirit, so they wrapped some sand from the grave in the red paper; this they placed on the bier and carried in procession to Sir Fish's mausoleum. They reburied the whale's corpse with the same ceremonies they had observed when the whale was discovered on the beach.

The festival continued on the twenty-fifth day of the first lunar month (March 11 in 1999), which was the first day of the spring-summer fishing season. The entire community—men and women, young and old—met in the mausoleum courtyard. Community leaders and representatives of the fishermen's cooperative, along with delegates from neighboring villages, addressed the throng by loudspeakers. (Such speeches were a new element: in the past, people simply gathered at the temple to pray for a good fishing season.) After this gathering, the fishing season was officially open.

Following the meeting, villagers went out with a *kieu huong*, a palanquin bearing a pot of burning incense and a formal letter inviting all of the local deities to the festival. The curling column of incense smoke established communication with the spirits. The palanquin was carried from the whale mausoleum to temples and various sacred sites—the local communal house *(dinh)*, the Buddhist temple, the seaside graves of whales, and various small shrines maintained for drowned fishermen—returning to the mausoleum after each visit. With the *kieu huong* as a sort of spiritual taxicab, the procession gathered up all of the local spirits so that they might join the festival. That evening there was a performance of *cheo ghe*, a local form of singing and dancing that evokes the lives of fishermen.

The third day (the twenty-sixth day of the first lunar month, or March 12 in 1999) was the most important day of the festival. At three o'clock in the morning, the incense palanquin was carried to the village Literary Association to collect the written text that had been prepared for the whale spirit and bring it back to the mausoleum. Before dawn, the biggest ritual was held, with offerings made to the whale spirit, the tutelary god, and the souls of drowned fishermen. Participants asked the spirits to give the fishermen a plentiful season and protect them from misfortune and thanked the spirits for attending the festival. When offerings are made at the shrines to drowned fishermen, girls of fifteen or sixteen perform *cheo ghe* songs to comfort their souls. Their songs describe the fisherman's life on the sea and celebrate the ocean vista. These songs are essential to the ritual, and if a community does not have its own singers, it must hire them from a neighboring community. In the afternoon, there were races in round boats and games of tug-of-war. On the evenings of the twenty-sixth, twenty-seventh, and twenty-eighth days of the first lunar month, classical sung drama *(tuong)* was performed.

During the festival, every house has a lively atmosphere and every villager is eager to participate. The courtyard of the mausoleum is packed with people during the rituals and the evening performances. Those in attendance pray for peace and prosperity, for a good catch, for safety on the open sea, and for everyone's good health. As elsewhere, the festival is an

During the Cau Ngu Festival in Man Thai ward, Danang, in 1999, fifteen- or sixteen-year-old girls, here carrying painted oars, perform *cheo ghe* songs describing the fisherman's life on the sea and celebrating the ocean vista.

occasion for reaffirming the bonds of friendship and neighborhood. As Le Van Ta explains, these bonds now extend over several continents: "Everyone contributes to the great celebration. Not only the local people, but also the overseas Vietnamese. We spent 30 million dong [U.S. $2,000] on the 1999 ritual, and part of the sum was from the donations of Vietnamese in the U.S., Canada, and Australia. Before they left, they had also participated in the Cau Ngu ceremony. They still follow the customs after going abroad." Dang Van Kha, seventy-two years old and a leading organizer of the festival, says with great feeling, "The Cau Ngu Festival will exist forever because it is our spiritual life."

■ Procession in Miniature: Water Puppets at the Chua Thay Festival

IN NORTHERN VIETNAM, performances of water puppets are often a part of festival entertainment. The puppetry tradition is found throughout the Red River Delta in the provinces of Thai Binh, Nam Dinh, Ha Tay, Hai Duong, and Bac Ninh and in the Dong Anh district of Hanoi, where broad repertories of stories and old techniques are preserved. Manipulated by strings or wires that run under water, the puppets appear to be swimming,

WATER PUPPETRY is an original Vietnamese performance art with close links to the Vietnamese life-world of water, wet-rice cultivation, vil-

■ VIETNAMESE
WATER
PUPPETRY

Nguyen Huy Hong

lage life, and other forms of folk performance. Water puppetry has a nearly thousand-year history in the north, where it has been performed since 1124; in the south it has been performed since 1975.

Water is the essential element of water puppetry. A liquid capable of reflecting light, water provides a stage on which illusions include changing reflections of the sky, clouds, trees, and landscape. On this natural liquid mirror, everything, including the coarse, stiff movements of the puppets, is smoothed and shimmers with vitality. Water also hides all the secrets of the puppetry performance, including the underwater strings or wires that move the puppets. Water puppets appear and vanish in a flash.

Water plays an important role, both positive and negative, in the life of the Vietnamese people. Not only do floods rank first among the four terrible disasters—floods, fires, thieves, and invaders—but water is also the most essential factor for wet-rice cultivation, more important even than seeds, hard work, and fertilizer.

Most water puppetry troupes are concentrated in the Red River Delta around Hanoi, where the tradition may well have been invented. The puppets that soak themselves in water and mud are akin to the

boating, transplanting rice, riding on horseback, or dancing on the very surface of the village pond.

Tu Dao Hanh, who lived as a monk at Thay Temple (Chua Thay) in the eleventh century, is regarded as the founder of this unique tradition of puppetry. Enshrined in that temple, he is regarded as the village tutelary god. During the Thay Festival, his inscribed tablet is carried in state in the festival palanquin. When puppeteers perform during the Thay Festival, they do honor to Tu Dao Hanh, their founder and patron deity, by replicating this ceremonious procession in miniature. However, instead of using a miniature version of the inscribed tablet and palanquin, they carry a tiny copy of the image of Tu Dao Hanh that sits in the temple. Tu Dao Hanh rides in the puppet procession upon a carved lotus flower, signifying his Buddhahood.

Red River peasant paddy farmers who are well acquainted with "soaking their bodies in water in this life and their skeletons in water after death."

Water puppeteers are often middle-aged farmers, familiar with the plow, hoe, paddy rice, and soil. They contribute a great deal of money and effort to the establishment of puppetry guilds and associations to maintain the puppets. They also volunteer their time, practicing plays in order to make their villages and hamlets merry. The community spirit of water puppetry is clearly evidenced in the careful preparation of each bamboo string and rope, each bamboo pole and wooden plank. The puppeteers protect their "creation" very strictly by transferring their art only to their sons, to ensure a pure, undiluted line of transmission. Without the care and protection of these village guilds, folk water puppetry could not survive.

The puppets' movements are manipulated by pulling and pushing strings and poles to operate the submerged control mechanisms. Traditional folk water puppetry machines are made of bamboo or wood and fixed on the top of a pole. A rope is used to control and manipulate the puppets' bodies. Other parts of a puppet's anatomy are manipulated by smaller ropes. The techniques used to make the water puppetry machines aim to maximize the liquidity, resistance, and buoyancy of water in order to animate the puppets. It would not be wrong to call this theatrical form "the art of village ponds."

Wooden water puppets made in Binh Phu commune, Ha Tay province, carry the image of the monk Tu Dao Hanh, said to be the founder of their art. Early twenty-first century.

The water puppet troupe of Binh Phu commune, Ha Tay province, performs a festival procession in miniature. Water puppets are manipulated by strings and wires concealed underwater. The puppeteers are standing in water behind the screen in the small pavilion several feet back from the action. 2000.

After a volley of firecrackers and the raising of the festival banner, signaling the start of the performance, the festival procession of the water puppets begins with a general *(tuong loa)* in red blowing a horn to announce the performance. This puppet is usually controlled by the leader of the troupe. The general is followed by four musicians. Then the palanquin appears, with a puppet attendant in red at the right of the palanquin, representing a civil official. This attendant carries the statue of Tu Dao Hanh to and from the palanquin. The puppet attendant in green, on the left, represents ordinary people. Because these puppets are manipulated by underwater wires from a

This actor from an opera troupe shares a laugh at a spring festival.

distance of several feet, only a highly skilled puppeteer can transfer Tu Dao Hanh's statue to the arms of the puppet attendant.

Although there are many water puppet troupes in the area around Chua Thay, the one at Binh Phu commune is considered the best, and it is the one that is invited to perform in the Thay Festival. This group has won renown for its effort to preserve their puppetry tradition. The troupe has performed in Hanoi and has also performed at an international puppetry festival in Taiwan.

A shaman with her three-stringed lute and fan becomes the commanding general of her spirit army during a Ky Yen ritual of the Tay people. To Hieu commune, Lang Son province, February 2001.

THE PERILOUS
JOURNEY OF THE
THEN SPIRIT ARMY:
A SHAMANIC RITUAL
OF THE TAY PEOPLE

La Cong Y

12

THE JOURNEY OF AN ENTRANCED SHAMAN who braves a perilous terrain and battles malevolent spirits and monsters has intrigued the imagination of readers of ethnography for decades, if not centuries.[1] Eliade and others built their scholarly understanding of shamans on ethnographic accounts of far northern cultures where, with some noteworthy exceptions, these heroic journeying shamans were almost invariably men.[2] The exploits of the shamans of the Tay ethnicity, in the north of Vietnam, match these other quests, but here the heroic shamans are usually women. Indeed, in the Ky Yen ritual that I shall be describing, a white-haired eighty-year-old-woman becomes the commanding general of a spirit army on the march.

Most of the shamanic journeys described in ethnographic texts have come to us from the songs that shamans or their attendants chant while the shaman is traveling in trance. This is also the dynamic of the Ky Yen ritual, but because this is a living tradition, it is possible to understand this journey not only as a folkloric text but also as an integral part of a ritual process involving music, ritual acts, dramatic gestures, entranced dancing, and a colorful array of paper votive offerings.

■ The Ky Yen Ritual

THE KY YEN RITUAL is an important part of the ritual life of the Tay; indeed, it is central to Tay culture and is performed wherever Tay people are found. The particular Ky Yen ritual described below took place in Binh Gia district, Lang Son province, in the spring of 2001, where I was conducting fieldwork. I am also familiar with Tay rituals from my own community in Thai Nguyen province.

There are 1.5 million ethnic Tay living in Vietnam, making them the country's largest ethnic minority population. They live in the northeastern provinces of Cao Bang, Bac Kan, Lang Son, Tuyen Quang, Ha Giang, Thai Nguyen, Yen Bai, and Lao Cai. Most Tay practice a highly developed form of wet-rice agriculture.

Ky Yen rituals are usually sponsored by families, who hold them in the spring between the period after the lunar new year and the third lunar month. There are several different reasons for holding a Ky Yen ritual. One is to prolong the longevity of a family member. A person's life span, whether long or short, depends on a predestined fate as assigned by King Nam Tao, the god of birth and death. It is often said that every day about "3,000 people are born and 500 die." When a person falls ill and treatments are to no avail, his or her relatives usually consult a fortune-teller to learn whether the patient's predestined end is near. Then they hold a Ky Yen ritual and petition King Nam Tao to prolong the sick person's life, in part by restoring a soul that has been spirited away to other realms. Like many other Asian peoples, the Tay describe a living person as having several souls and vitalities, some of which may be lost or captured by malevolent spirits, causing weakness, illness, or in extreme cases, death.

A run of bad luck may also occasion a Ky Yen ritual. According to a person's individual horoscope, he or she is likely to suffer a year of bad luck every third year of his or her life. The ages of seven, nineteen, thirty-one, forty-three, fifty-five, sixty-seven, and seventy-nine are considered particularly inauspicious, a time when one is particularly prone to illness, disease, and accidents. At these ages, a person might sponsor a ritual and pray to the star to which his or her destiny is linked at the time of birth to mitigate misfortune. On a more auspicious occasion, the children of a parent who passes the age of sixty may hold a birthday anniversary feast to "pray for peace and happiness" *(hat khoan)* in old age.

If one's parents die at the age of thirty-six, forty-five, fifty-four, sixty-three, seventy-two, or eighty-one or in an unlucky hour, one's own life may become turbulent or unlucky. Many people also consider nightmares or unusual natural phenomena, such as having snakes or wild animals enter their house, as bad omens. In such cases they must hold a religious ritual to exorcise malevolent spirits and drive disasters away. This type of Ky Yen is called "cleaning up one's house" *(het giai, an ruon an lang)*.

In addition to these major objectives, Ky Yen rituals also bring good health, peace, prosperity, and good luck for the sponsors' family. Some families organize Ky Yen rituals whenever the host is at an inauspicious age. Others hold Ky Yen every year because it is an opportunity to relieve all worries among family and friends.

■ **The *Then***

A (USUALLY) FEMALE SHAMAN, called the *then*, presides over the Ky Yen. A *then* is someone who is said to have "bright eyes," someone who can see what others cannot—the past, present, and future. A *then* has the ability to communicate with the gods and the responsibility to save human beings from suffering.

Some women become *then* by inheriting this ability from a family member. Others are told by a fortune-teller that they have this destiny, or—like shamans in many other societies—they become mysteriously ill as a sign of their calling. The *then*'s students may eventually become *then* themselves, keeping their own shrines in their own homes and officiating at rituals for

A shaman *(then)* performs the Ky Yen ritual with her assistants, who chant together with their master, shake bell rattles, and dance. To Hieu commune, Lang Son province, February 2001.

their own clients, but when they return to the shrine of the *then* who instructed them to assist in her rituals, they must once again perform the role of assistants. Usually only one or possibly two women in each generation become *then* in a line of succession from *then* to student, having been designated by their teacher and mastered the requisite skills. Other women are drawn to performing Ky Yen and assist the *then* by shaking the bells, dancing, preparing offerings, and ministering to the *then*'s needs by bringing her water and helping her with her shoes. Sickly children might become the "adopted" children of the *then* and are sometimes trained to assist her in rituals.

Mrs. Mo Thi Kit, a respected *then* in Binh Gia district, Lang Son province, was an apprentice of her mother-in-law. Mrs. Kit's own daughter-in-law is now her apprentice. The daughter-in-law is a schoolteacher, but when she suffered from a chronic weakness, a fortune-teller divined that she must become a *then*.

Becoming an authentic *then* requires a long process of study and practice as an assistant. When the prospective *then* has mastered all of the incantations and procedures she must know to perform religious rituals, she will hold a great initiation ritual at which an experienced *then* bestows on her the authority to practice the profession. There are six different levels of *then*, which are distinguished by the quantity of ribbons on the hat they wear when performing rituals (all rituals except Ky Yen). The hat of every new *then* has five ribbons. When she is promoted to a higher level, her hat has two ribbons more. The highest-level *then* will wear a hat with fifteen ribbons; these are highly capable *then* with great prestige. A *then* also acquires additional battalions of spirit soldiers to command each time she advances a rank in her profession, as a measure of her growing power and experience.

At present in Binh Gia district there are about twenty *then* of different lines of succession. Seventy-year-old Mrs. Mo Thi Kit, also known as Phap Quan, "The Law's Illumination," is one of the best-known and most respected *then*. She became a *then* at the age of twenty-four and is now the head of a great line of *then*, having seven followers (*luc so*) and hundreds of "adopted children" (*luc huong*). She wears a nine-ribbon hat and is invited to perform religious rituals all over the Binh Gia district and in the surrounding areas. The following is a typical "praying for peace and happiness" ritual as conducted by Mrs. Kit.

▪ Preparations

A KY YEN RITUAL OFTEN STARTS in the evening and ends at noon the next day. Before leaving her own shrine for her client's home, the *then* burns some incense sticks at the altar of the founder of her *then* line of succession, informing her teachers of the work she would like to undertake and asking their permission to mobilize the *then* spirit army. She recites the formulas that will expel pollutions from her own body and turn her ritual instruments into tools and weapons capable of repelling evil influences. During the ritual, even mundane things like a tray for betel chews, a mat, or an ashtray can be mobilized to act as barriers, which are potentially as formidable as an electrically charged fence. Upon arriving at the house where the ritual is to be held, the *then* informs the householder's ancestors of the ritual's aim and invites them to supervise her work.

In the ritual, the *then*, on behalf of the householder, carries offerings to the spirit realm and makes petitions to the gods and lesser spirits on her way to retrieve the missing soul. In the client's house, elaborate offerings and paper votive goods have been prepared. The *then* tray *(bom then)* or the commandant tray *(bom tuong)*, dedicated to the spirit army and lined with red paper, is put in front of the ancestors' altar. On the tray there are two rice bowls: the first one holds a small paper cutout of a human figure covered with a parasol, whose task it is to find the wandering souls, and a chicken egg to contain the souls once they have been retrieved; the other bowl contains twelve paper figures, serving as scapegoats for the sponsor, which are offered to the twelve mandarins who control misfortunes and unhappiness. In addition, five seals are arranged on the tray as symbols of the four supreme deities of the Taoist pantheon and Buddha, along with five red paper–covered cups of rice liquor, five cups of tea, and five incense sticks. When the *then* offers feasts to her troops, the number of incense sticks is increased to nine.

Additional offering trays are prepared for the time when the *then* and her army pass through the gates of each of nine magistrates' courts, where they make petitions on behalf of the sponsor and his or her family and to the gods of the mountain and the land and to the village tutelary spirits. The trays hold rice bowls, chopsticks, incense sticks, cones of rice cake, cups, a bottle of alcohol, and for some spirits, specially prepared meats. If someone in the host's family died away from home, a tray needs to be put in a corner of the house for him. A tray of offerings for demons and wandering spirits *(bom giai)*, containing some meat and boiled rice, is set in the corner as well.

Sparkling Bridge (Cau Hao Quang) or Destiny Bridge (Cau So Cau Sang), which the *then* army must cross on the final stage of its journey, is represented by a ladder of seven or nine rungs made of an entire bamboo tree with its roots. It is balanced against the summer beams of the outer room, opposite the ancestor altar, and covered with five colored cloths: black (indigo), white, blue, yellow, and red. The bridge-pier tray *(bom coc cau)* is put at the base of the Destiny Bridge to welcome the host's retrieved souls when they return home with the *then* army at the end of the ritual. On this tray are placed six segments of banana stalk, on which are fixed one

In a Ky Yen ritual, the shaman carries offerings to spirits and makes petitions to them to retrieve the sponsor's missing souls. Inside the two big cakes there is a hard-boiled egg or a rooster's head to receive the returning souls. To Hieu commune, Lang Son province, February 2001.

votive paper golden tree and one or two votive paper flowering trees made from bamboo sticks; another banana segment holding a parasol; four bags of money; a rice bowl holding five incense sticks, and some fruits, sweets, and cakes. Besides this tray, there may be another tray of cake plates contributed by the householder's married daughters. Each plate contains two big round sticky rice cakes and ten smaller ones. All cakes are decorated with red paper or dye. Inside the two large cakes is a boiled egg or a rooster's head to receive the returning souls of the sponsor. After the ceremony, all of the spectators and participants surround the tray and break open the cake. The person the rooster's head faces will have good fortune. Also arranged beside the pier of the Destiny Bridge is a bag of vital spirits (*thong ton khoan*) made of indigo-dyed cloth; it contains the used shirts or scarves of all members of the host's family to welcome their missing souls and vital spirits back.

The Bridge of Gold and Silver (Cau Kim Ngan) is put near the Destiny Bridge as well. It is woven from bamboo and its seven or nine steps are made of paper. If the host couple are still strong, a large bridge will be made with seven steps on one end and nine steps on the other. After the ceremony, it will be put on the roof, above the sleeping place of the householder.

The Bridge of Souls and Vital Spirits (Cau Lac) is a ladder with seven steps for a man and nine steps for a woman. It is raised facing the ancestral altar.

A two-story house is offered on behalf of people over sixty years old and four one-story houses on behalf of adults (big size) and children (small size). The houses contain paper servants, plates, bowls, tea sets, clothes, and wildflowers or rice ears. Ngoc Quyen village, Lang Son province, February 1997.

Tiny houses made of colored paper and banana stalks are arranged on the floor. These will be burned during the ritual as votive offerings. A two-story house with two four-sided roofs or a three-story house with three four-sided roofs *(long dinh)* is offered on behalf of people over sixty years old: the house contains a paper servant, a set of paper garments, and paper household wares including a tray, a plate, four bowls, a tea set, and some wildflowers or rice ears. Four tile-roofed one-story houses *(ruon ngoi)* are offered on behalf of adults (big size) and children (small size). These contain a paper servant, a set of paper clothes, and a cone-shaped rice cake. A colored paper replica of a bamboo-lattice rice silo *(xang)* is made of colored paper and put on a rice basket near the Destiny Bridge with a seven- or nine-wicked lamp beside it.

The Pine Tree of Prosperity or the De Thich Banana Tree (Co Thong Luc Minh) is erected near the entrance door. It is a banana tree decorated with cones made of split bamboo, each containing a small rice cake. Other votive goods include a hammock to carry back the souls of family members under twelve years old, three maidservants, an elephant, two horses, four swords, and four rifles, all made of wood or bamboo covered with colored paper, to symbolize the *then*'s troops and weapons. If the host is the descendant of a scholar, rather than a commander or Buddha, there must be a colored-paper "trunk of books" *(hom su hom sec)*, containing, in addition to votive paper books, seven or nine paper writing brushes. Votive paper offerings are burned at intervals during the ritual when offerings are made to various officials, gods, and goddesses in the spirit world.

If the sponsor of the ritual is believed to have "a weak vital spirit," he or she must pay additional tribute at the start of the ritual. A "raft" and a dam, both about one span long, are made of five segments of banana slender-stalk and put in a basin containing seven or nine fish to symbolize the fish pond of the Birth-Protecting Goddess. A length of cloth is also laid in an east-west direction. At the two ends of the cloth are two rice bowls with three incense sticks in each. Seven or nine bowls turned upside down are placed on the cloth. The *then* stands in the center of the cloth, pointing five incense sticks toward the sun and reciting an incantation. The host or the ill person sits behind her, holding a wine cup and a hen offered by his or her maternal relatives. If the hen drinks wine three times, all will be well. The fish basin will be poured down a pond or spring to return fish to the Birth-Protecting Goddess.

■ The Ritual as Performance

THE ITINERARY OF THE *then* army is recounted in a three-thousand-verse poem, which the shaman chants as her disembodied soul leads her assistants and spirit troops on their campaign. The poem is divided into fifty-six stanzas, each of which relates an incident in the story in appropriate and varied tones of voice—high- or low-pitched, quick or slow, depending on the action of the journey. The first eleven stanzas recount the preparation for the trip; the next forty-three stanzas describe the arduous and thrilling journey to Heaven; and in the final two stanzas, the *then* troops return. The *then* chants, accompanied by her assistants who sit beside her on the floor of the house. The cadence of her song is in some places very solemn and mysterious, in others loud and lively. The *then* strums her *dan tinh*, a three-string lute made of gourd, wood, and plastic fishing line; shakes her bundle of brass bells; and flourishes her paper fan. These objects are more than props and musical accompaniment; they are instruments of magic, a means of communicating with and traveling through the spirit world. When the *then* points forward with the neck of her lute, the *then* army enters or exits the great gate of an official's residence in the spirit world. When she holds the

The paper fans, when folded, become shamans' batons of command, and when the army travels by boat on the river and on the sea they become oars. When the shamans stand at the gate of a high official to make their petitions, they unfold the fans and cover their faces. To Hieu commune, Lang Son province, February 2001.

neck at an angle, the army crosses a plain or a river or ocean. Her bells, attached to the links of several metal chains, become the sound of horses' bells when the *then* army rides by. The folded paper fan becomes her baton of command. When the army travels by boat on the river and on the sea, the fan becomes an oar, and when the *then* stands at the gate of a high official to make her petition, she unfolds the fan and covers her face.

■ The Journey

AS THE CHANT RELATES, the way to the Inauspicious Gate is extremely dangerous, so the *then* must first dispatch her spirit aides to reconnoiter the terrain. She invites her teachers and the celestial generals to supervise her trip and asks for the help of the celestial army before she gathers and harnesses her horses and elephants. She opens her weapon store to equip her soldiers with armor, rifles, swords, cartridge belts, lacquered conical-shaped hats, and colorful flags embroidered with the sun, the moon, and the constellations. After listing and loading up all offerings and receiving the celestial army, the *then* uses her shamanic power to kill all demons, ghosts, monsters, and fierce beasts and drive bad omens away. She recites special incantations to make her escort and offerings clean and pure.

After having a feast, symbolized by lighting nine incense sticks on the offering tray, the *then* troops start on their trip to the Inauspicious Gate. First they come to the shrine of the local earth god, where they offer incense sticks and joss papers and ask the god to instruct them. They also give offerings to the tutelary deity of the sponsor's village at the communal house to obtain permission to pass through his territory and recruit more porters.

The *then* troops pass a nodding bamboo forest, a hillside thicket of rose myrtle, and a shady area and enter a thick forest rich in cicadas. According to the Tay people, these cicadas are the reincarnations of beautiful unmarried women. Their heart-rending wails about their destiny tire and exhaust the *then* troops. The *then* must use her shamanic arts to nullify the cicadas' cries. Then the troops stop in a jungle and hunt a number of prey to offer to the local mountain god.

Leaving the jungle, the *then* troops enter the area of monsters. The *then* must fiercely fight against Da Din, a loathsome demon with wonder-working powers. Eventually, she defeats the demon and grabs its magic stick, which can "resuscitate the dead with its top; kill the living with its foot." At a limpid spring, the *then* allows her troops to stop and fish. When the sun is burning hot, the *then* troops climb up Khac Khan Vai, a barren high mountain, and make offerings to Po Khuong Po Khac, the mountain god defending the area.

Passing a hamlet of widows and widowers and a cloudless sky zone, the troops come to the Moon's palace, where the Moon Goddess and many beautiful nymphs are dancing and singing. They stop and exchange love songs and ditties with the nymphs. Continuing their journey, they cross a high pass covered with trees to a guard station on the bank of the Milky Way. This is a large river with charming scenery. If the host must pay tribute to the water god, the *then* troops will recruit boatmen by force and take boats to cross the river.

The *then* dispatches her soldiers to inform the concerned gods and deities that her troops are going to pay offerings to them. Then she orders her troops to fell timber in the forest to repair the houses and bridges of Madame Sinh, the goddess who protects the sponsor from misfortunes and unhappiness. After that, they bring votive offerings and religious effigies to the Kitchen God (Khau tu Tao Quan), the host's ancestors *(khau tu dam)*, the *then* ancestress *(khau tu phap)*, heavenly generals *(khau tu tuong)*, and Buddha Avalokitesvara (Khau tu Phat Ba).

After crossing an immense field where a nine-hundred-branch banyan tree grows, coming to a small market that sells the polluting foods meat and fish, and crossing another immense, barren rice field, the *then* troops pass three strange hamlets, homes, successively, to the homeless, the handicapped, and hermaphrodites.

Finally the *then* troops come to the sea, which must be crossed in order to reach the highest level of heaven. They stop to recruit boatmen once again. In heavy seas, they see the white-bearded immortals playing chess and a duck bringing a cock on its back to call the sunrise. Going ashore, they pass a busy **T**-junction and come to Nam Tao's palace to pay tribute — here the *then* and her assistants burn effigies and pray for the host's happiness and prosperity.

At the next **T**-junction, the *then* informs the controller of Dinh Trung Market that her troops will enter his market to purchase supplies. She also orders him to provide her troops with tea and her horses with grass and to clear the road for her troops to proceed. Dinh Trung is a big crowded and bustling market in which there are plenty of goods. The *then* allows her troops to stop here. The sacred flags are planted in the four market corners to impose a curfew and prevent strangers from entering the garrison area.

After having this second feast, the *then* troops enter the territory of Madam Sinh. Most of the offerings are presented here. Two offering trays have been dedicated to Madam Sinh, the first containing a boiled chicken, the second a boiled pig's head. Votive paper tribute in the form of paper dragon-roofed houses, tile-roofed houses, bridges, a breeder pig in the form of a calabash, chickens in the form of banana flowers, and paper scapegoats are burned so that Madam Sinh can receive these offerings in the spirit world. The *then* puts some coins and rice into the paper silo as a gift for Madam Sinh. Following her, the host's children, grandchildren, relatives, and neighbors likewise place rice in the silo, each one repeating the gesture three times. When the silo is nearly full, packets of salt and tea are added. The *then* utters a prayer to make the host's soul and vital spirit enter an egg, which she places in the silo as well. She pours rice into the silo three times more, then covers it. The eldest son of the host now burns five joss sticks and places the silo on the ancestral altar. The rice in the silo is considered very sacred. It will be cooked and served to the host to improve his health and prolong his longevity.

The *then* invites Madam Sinh to enjoy her tribute and sends the troops to serve her by sweeping the yard to prepare the area for rice drying, making rice containers, and bringing rice into the storehouse. At the same time, the *then* has her troops plant "pine, yellow bamboo, apricot, and *loc menh* trees" and a nine-leaf *mon* tree in Madam Sinh's garden of flowers and ornamental plants, graze "the buffaloes of souls and vital spirits," drain muddy well water from, and channel clear water, into the well, and repair the beams on the bridge. As the *then* army crosses the new bridge, the *then*'s assistants and her enthusiastic followers dance ecstatically to the sound of shaking bells.

If someone in the host's family is still a child, the *then* army visits the area of the Birth-Protecting Goddess. Eventually they reach the area of the Officials of Misfortunes and Unhappiness. Here they also give offerings in the form of votive paper tile-roofed houses and paper servants, all of which are burned, and an offering tray of cooked sticky rice and boiled chicken. These gifts are made with a petition for the householder's happiness.

Thus, the *then* corps has passed a thirty-six-stage route via three heavenly layers to nine magistrates' courts to pay tribute and pray for the host's good fortune. After fulfilling the task, the *then* troops withdraw to return to the earthly world through a shortcut across immense fertile fields of "sugar and molasses" and pass once again by the major landmarks of their journey. At the Milky Way, they stop to bathe their souls and vital spirits. Finally, they pass Dinh Huong Market and arrive home. The *then* orders her troops to take off the harnesses and howdahs and release their horses and elephants.

After giving the sponsor all the souls just ransomed from Madam Sinh and the mandarins and reporting the results to her ancestors, the *then* gives her troops the third feast before taking them back to her headquarters. The entire journey began early one evening and now ends late in the morning of the following day.

The *then* shaman utters a prayer to make the sponsor's souls and vital spirits enter an egg and then places it in a miniature paper silo full of rice. The rice will be cooked and served to the sponsor to improve his health and ensure his longevity. Ngoc Quyen village, Lang Son province, February 1997.

As many as thirty-six spirits have the potential to descend on and enter the body of a medium during a Len Dong ritual. Once present in the medium, a spirit is dressed in its own special costume. The spirit admires itself and expresses its own unique character through a brief performance, as in this ritual, held near Danang in November 1972.

LEN DONG:

SPIRITS' JOURNEYS

Ngo Duc Thinh

In the south appears the Tenth Prince,
The wonderful figure,
Talented, courageous, intelligent,
Good at literature and martial arts.
He deliberately wanders everywhere
With a bag of poems and Buddhist sutras,
Sometimes erotic, sometimes benevolent,
Sometimes he admires a blooming flower,
sometimes he waits for moonrise. . . .

—SONG TO THE TENTH PRINCE

WHILE THE SHAMANIC ACTIVITIES found among many of Vietnam's minority peoples involve soul journeys—like that of the Tay *then* who leads her spirit army on a campaign to recover her client's soul—in the Len Dong (Going into Trance) ritual of the Kinh (Viet) people, the spirits are invoked into the ritual space and incarnated in the body of the medium.[1] Many of the songs performed during Len Dong rites describe spirits descending into the ritual space or journeying through the landscape.

Len Dong rituals, also called *hau bong* (service to the spirits) or *hau dong* (medium's service), are performed throughout Vietnam as an intrinsic part of the Religion of Mother Goddesses (Dao Mau), honored by the

Kinh.[2] In this ritual, the mediums are only the "skeletons" or the empty bodies or "seats" in which the souls or shades of the spirits are incarnated. Many spirits are figures who served the country in the past and were subsequently deified and worshipped by the common people. Nearly seventy spirits are worshipped in the temples of the Religion of Mother Goddesses. However, depending on the characteristics of the occasion and the medium's destiny, only a few spirits will descend and be incarnated during a particular performance of Len Dong, and some spirits seldom or never descend.

The spirits' journey into this world via the medium's body is expressed through a number of ritual actions: dancing, giving advice, distributing favors, curing diseases, and driving away evil ghosts or demons. In contrast to many other religious expressions and the activities of other spirit mediums among the Kinh, the Religion of Mother Goddesses does not orient people toward the world of the dead but toward an earthly existing world of good health and prosperity, which they believe they will achieve through the agency of the spirits they encounter as a consequence of the Len Dong ritual. Mother Goddess worship is thus very popular among business people in the new market economy.

To make the spirits enter the medium's body, the medium relies on a range of techniques, exploited before and during the rituals, to achieve a trance state. Techniques for achieving the trance state vary, but it is enhanced by the sensory elements of the Len Dong ritual: the strong colors of the costumes and offerings (green, red, yellow), music and invocation songs, dances, and even such stimuli as alcohol, cigarettes, betel and areca nut, tea, incense sticks, and flowers. Today, however, many of the mediums' performances seem contrived and their trances shallow.

Nobody can voluntarily become a medium; the spirits must select the medium, and if the medium does not accept the calling, he or she will experience frequent misfortunes (co day).[3] Similarly, because the spirits descend at will into the medium, the medium is supposed to have no control over the spirits who appear during a particular performance of Len Dong. In practice, however, many mediums clearly determine in advance which spirits they will incarnate, in accord with their destined relationship to those spirits or their specific intentions in the ritual.

Although Len Dong is a religious ritual of the Religion of Mother Goddesses, it incorporates many artistic elements, including music, singing, dancing, and costuming. The invocation songs (*hat van*) and music are a particularly noteworthy expression of the performing art of the Kinh people. Recent research has demonstrated the close relationship between the *hat van* and other categories of folk songs. However, *hat van* could have originated only in the environment of the Religion of Mother Goddesses and the rituals of Len Dong. Today, some tunes of the *hat van* have been adapted from the ritual of Len Dong and become secular folk songs in their own right, but it is only in the rituals of Len Dong that the full performative power of this music can be truly appreciated.

▪ The Pantheon of the Religion of Mother Goddesses

DISTINCT FROM OTHER FOLK BELIEFS, the Religion of Mother Goddesses has its own complete and well-articulated hierarchy. The supreme divinity is the Mother Goddess (Thanh Mau). Sometimes the Mother is supervised by the Jade Emperor (Ngoc Hoang) or Lady Buddha Kwan-yin (Phat Ba Quan Am). Despite the nominal supremacy of these figures, however, Taoist or Buddhist elements of belief and practice enter into the Religion of Mother Goddesses only loosely.

Carved lintel pieces, inscribed "The Mother's virtue is an example for the whole world," are hung in temples honoring the Mother Goddesses. Wood and gold lacquer, late nineteenth or early twentieth century.

The Mother can be embodied in three or four Mother Goddesses who govern the different realms, or "palaces," that make up the universe: Thien Phu (Realm of Heaven), Dia Phu (Realm of Earth), Thoai Phu (Realm of Water), and Nhac Phu (Realm of Mountains and Forests). Each realm has a characteristic color—red for heaven, yellow for earth, white for water, and green for mountains and forests. All of the spirits appearing in Len Dong wear colored costumes that link them with one of these realms as a follower of one of the Mother Goddesses. Under these Mother Goddesses other spirits are classified in a hierarchical order:

- Great Mandarins (Quan Lon): There are ten spirits in this category, but only the first five (ngu vi quan lon) are worshipped often and incarnated through the medium.

- Dames (Chau Ba): There are twelve Dames. In this category, the first four Dames govern the four realms and are the reincarnations of the four Mother Goddesses. They are the most important and most often incarnated.

- Princes (Ong Hoang): There are ten Princes, hierarchically enumerated. The three most frequently incarnated are the Third (Hoang Ba), the Seventh (Hoang Bay), and the Tenth (Hoang Muoi).

- Damsels (Co): Attendants of the Mother Goddesses and the Dames, the Damsels are hierarchically listed from the First to the Twelfth but often have local names as well that link them to the places of their worship. For example, the Twelfth Damsel is often called the Little Damsel of Bac Le (Lang Son province), or one may hear the Second Damsel referred to more specifically as the Second Damsel of Cam Duong (Lao Cai province), the Ninth Damsel as the Ninth Damsel of Chin Gieng (Thanh Hoa province), and so on.

- Boy Attendants (Cau): There are ten Cau, who are mischievous attendants of the Princes. The Third (Cau Bo) and the Youngest (Cau Be) are often incarnated.

In addition to these spirits, which make up the pantheon of the Religion of Mother Goddesses, the Sir Lot (Snake) and the Five Great Tiger Man-

The Mother Goddess of the Realm of Mountains and Forests is associated with the ethnic minorities who inhabit mountainous terrain. Her jewelry resembles the silver jewelry of the costumes of northern ethnic minorities. Her principal temples are located in Bac Giang and Lang Son provinces.

darins (Quan Lon Ngu Ho) are worshipped under the altar and some-times incarnated.

In addition to the four palaces or realms associated with the Mother Goddesses, folk belief also recognizes a Palace of the Tran dynasty (Phu Tran Trieu), associated with the worship of General Tran Hung Dao (1226–1300), who vanquished the Mongols in the thirteenth century. Some Mother Goddess temples include Tran Hung Dao, and some honor him as the highest spirit, equating him with the Jade Emperor. When he and his attendants are incarnated, they punish evil ghosts and demons and cure diseases.

Other spirits have been similarly associated with historical figures. For example, the Mother Goddess of Heaven (Mau Thuong Thien) is identified with Princess Lieu Hanh, a daughter of the Jade Emperor transfigured as a girl in the earthly world. The Mother Goddess of Mountains and Forests (Mau Thuong Ngan) is Princess La Binh, a daughter of Genie Son Tinh and Princess My Nuong, and a granddaughter of Hung King. The First Prince (Ong Hoang De Nhat) embodies the brilliant general Le Loi, who won national independence from the Chinese Ming dynasty in the fifteenth century. The Tenth Prince (Ong Hoang Muoi) was a mandarin of the Le dynasty (fifteenth century) who helped expand the territory of the nation. The historicization of the spirits of the Religion of Mother Goddesses makes a link between daily life, expressed through the needs and desires of worshippers, and national history. Mother Goddess worship is thus at once an evocation of the nation's history and a deification of patriotism.

The spirits of the Religion of Mother Goddesses are worshipped in a number of temples or shrines, wherever the Kinh people have settled, from the north to the south, from the plains to the mountains. In general, each spirit has his or her principal temple and many subordinate ones. Although the principal temple of the Mother Goddess Lieu Hanh is situated in Phu Giay (Nam Dinh province), and that of the Mother of Mountains and Forests is at Bac Le in Lang Son province, they are also worshipped in many other localities. At temples or shrines associated with a particular spirit, their followers often leave their own incense pots to secure the protection of these spirits. These are also places where Len Dong rituals are conducted.

Manikins are offered to spirits as their assistants in the other world during the *hinh nhan the mang* (manikins as sacrifices for humans) rite during a Len Dong ritual. Each manikin holds a petition to the spirits *(so)* that contains the name, age, and request of an adherent. This set, made for a Len Dong ritual in Hanoi in the early 1950s, reflects the fashions of the day.

■ Len Dong, or the Journeys of the Spirits of the Religion of Mother Goddesses

LEN DONG RITUALS are organized at temples or shrines on different occasions throughout the year. A temple guardian-medium *(chu den)* must hold the rituals of *hau xong den* (temple first-footing, after the ritual of passage to the new year), *hau thuong nguyen* (the fifteenth day of the first lunar month), *hau nhap ha* (beginning of summer, in the fourth lunar month), *tan ha* (end of summer, in the seventh lunar month), *hau tat nien* (end of the year, in the twelfth lunar month), and *hap an* (seal washing, the twenty-fifth day of the twelfth lunar month). A medium must also organize the ritual on the death day anniversaries of his or her patron spirit. For example, if her patron spirit is the Third Damsel, she must hold a Len Dong to honor her on the twelfth day of the sixth lunar month. Most Len Dong rituals

Each spirit's realm is associated with a particular color that is matched with offerings of the same color. Red cans of Coca-Cola are appropriate offerings for spirits from the Heavenly Realm. Hanoi, February 2001.

occur in the third lunar month, the death anniversary of the Mother Goddess, and the eighth lunar month, the death of the Father God, identified with the Jade Emperor, King Bat Hai, and Saint Tran.

Before a Len Dong ritual, a medium must make meticulous preparations. Preparations include choosing an auspicious day that matches the medium's horoscope, selecting a temple or shrine, inviting a religious master *(thay cung)*, four assistants *(hau dang)*, singers *(cung van)*, disciples, close friends, and family members.

The preparation of garments and votive offerings also requires much time and labor. Each spirit has a specific costume, which a medium puts on when the spirit is incarnated. Before initiation into the service to the spirits (ra dong), therefore, the medium must purchase suitable costumes, especially those of his or her patron spirits.

The votive offerings should match the special character of the occasion on which the medium conducts the ritual. They may include cakes, sweets, flowers, fruits, alcohol, cigarettes, toys, and jewelry. On the anniversaries of the Dames, there may be dishes such as crabs, snails, and fish. The medium pays special attention to the color of the votive offerings, so that each spirit receives offerings that are the same color as the realm with which she or he is associated. For example, red cans of Coca-Cola are appropriate for spirits from the celestial sky palace, while green areca used to make betel chews are appropriate for spirits associated with the realm of the mountains and forests.

The following is a typical Len Dong ritual for the Thuong Nguyen Festival (fifteenth day of the first lunar month) held by a female medium, whom I shall call "H," at the Dau Temple in Hanoi.

■ Preparation and Ritual

FOR SEVERAL DAYS BEFORE THE RITUAL, H must abstain from sexual intercourse, eat vegetarian food, and sometimes fast completely to put her body into an unusual state of purity. According to mediums, this act of purification is necessary before they can use their bodies as a vehicle for the spirits. Before the Len Dong can begin, a religious master (thay cung) conducts rites to petition the Buddha and the deities (thinh thanh thinh Phat) for permission to carry out the ritual. Then he conducts the rite of wandering ghosts (co hon) by the temple door, offering gruel, dried rice, popcorn, and fresh water to these unfortunate entities.

After these preparatory rituals, the medium emerges from her private room in white garments. She greets all participants and leisurely walks onto the mat, taking her place in the middle of four assistants (hau dang).[4] These assistants, female or male, must be individuals who have undertaken service to the spirits. As trainees or close associates of medium H, they help

Votive offerings of gold and money are burned as a means of transmitting them to the spirits after a religious master makes petitions. Vicinity of Hanoi, 2000.

her burn incense sticks, offer alcohol, cover her face with fans, and change costumes during the ritual.

The singers sit on the right side of the mat. They play music and sing invocation songs (*chau van*) accompanied by traditional musical instruments (a moon-shaped zither, drums, tom-toms, bamboo flutes, and cymbals), of which the zither (*dan nguyet*) is the most typical. Sometimes the singer is also the *dan nguyet* player. In general, each temple, particularly the big ones, has its own band of singers, who remain closely related to the temple

A red veil is placed over the medium's head and face whenever a spirit enters or leaves the medium, signaling its arrival and departure. To village, Thanh Tri district, Hanoi, 2000.

and the guardian-medium throughout their lives. The bands practice regularly so that they can perform in perfect synchronization with the medium's actions. They are often rewarded with money for their good performance or punished by the medium for unsatisfactory work. The bands usually have some well-known singers who are much loved by the mediums.

Generally, the mediums and participants cannot predict which spirits are going to descend *(giang)* and which are going to be incarnated *(nhap)*. Divine descents and incarnations *(gia)*[5] are a consequence of both the spirit's own desire and the medium's invitation. When a spirit descends, the medium signals with her left fingers for male spirits or right ones for female spirits. If the spirit is incarnated, the assistants rush to find the appropriate robe and head cloth, and carefully dress and groom the medium.

When medium H sits down, four assistants put a rectangular red veil, called the *khan phu dien* (face-covering veil), on her head. This is the most important element of the entire ritual, repeated many times whenever a spirit enters *(nhap)* or leaves *(thang)* the medium. The red veil signals the journey of spirits into and out of the incarnating medium.

The descents of the Mother Goddess always occur at the beginning of the ritual. Medium H, her face covered with the red veil, puts her hands on her thighs and sways slightly. The singers now perform songs devoted to the Mother Goddess: "We respectfully request the First Mother Goddess of the Realm of Heaven." Medium H's fingers will indicate the descent of the Mother Goddess (one, two, or three fingers for the First, Second, or Third Mother Goddess), and the singers then perform the invocation song of that goddess. When the medium crosses her hands on her forehead, she is signaling the spirit's ascent *(thang)*, and the singers play the appropriate air: "The spirit goes back to her realm."

In general, because the First, Second, and Third Mother Goddesses descend *(giang)*[6] but are not incarnated, the medium does not take the red veil from her face. This step in the ritual is called *hau trum khan* (alternatively, *hau trang bong* or *hau trang man*) to distinguish it from *hau mo khan*, when the spirit descends and is incarnated, in which case the cloth must be removed. Medium H's horoscope is not compatible with Saint Tran, so she can conduct only *hau trum khan* services for Saint Tran and for the First and Second Loyal Damsels, who are his daughters. Saint Tran's mediums are known for such remarkable feats as running skewers through their faces or nearly strangling themselves with a long cloth when they incarnate this fearless general.

The incarnations of the Great Mandarins follow those of the Mother Goddesses. Among the ten Great Mandarins, only the First, Second, Third, and Fifth are incarnated in medium H. The spirits are military commanders, so their costumes and gestures are stately and imposing. They usually carry bows, swords, and their flags of command. These four mandarins belong to various realms. The First Mandarin (Quan De Nhat) is from the Realm of Heaven and wears red garments. He descends to offer votive incense sticks to the Mother Goddess and returns to his realm in his chariot *(xe gia hoi cung)*. The Second Mandarin (Quan De Nhi) and the Fifth Mandarin (Quan De Ngu) are from the Realm of Mountains and Forests and wear green costumes. After paying tribute to the Mother Goddess, they are incarnated, perform dances with sword and spears, and show appreciation of the songs praising their deeds and merits. The Second Great Mandarin is the keeper of the Book of Death and Birth:

> *The Book on Death and Birth written by the Mandarin;*
> *Everyone's destiny is decided by the Mandarin.*
> *Whoever is dutiful and benevolent,*
> *The Mandarin will bless him.*

—SONG TO THE SECOND GREAT MANDARIN

When incarnated in mediums, spirits give advice, listen to requests, distribute favors, and then, as their songs describe it, "go back to their realms in their chariots." Here a medium incarnates the Seventh Prince at a ritual in Hanoi in the early 1950s.

Together, the two mountain and forest mandarin spirits give advice, listen to requests, distribute favors, and then "go back to their realms in their chariots." Finally, the Third Great Mandarin (Quan De Tam), of the Realm of Water, wears costumes of white, the color associated with this realm. After being incarnated, he gives offerings, performs a dance with a sword, receives wine and cigarettes presented by participants, listens to the invocation song, distributes favors, and, ultimately, "ascends" back to his realm. The Fourth Great Mandarin (Quan De Tu) does "descend on" the medium—who wears the red veil over her face—but only for a short moment, and then leaves immediately, without being incarnated.

Among the twelve Dames, only five are incarnated in medium H: the Second Dame of Mountains and Forests (Chau De Nhi), the Dame of Thac Bo (Chau Thac Bo), the Sixth Dame (Chau Luc), the Tenth Dame of Dong Mo (Chau Muoi Dong Mo), and the Little Dame of Bac Le (Chau

The Second Dame dances with torches in her hands. All twelve Dames are regarded as incarnations of the Mother Goddesses and have their origins in minority groups who live in mountainous areas.

Be Bac Le). The First and Fourth Dames (Chau De Nhat and Chau De Tu) descend, but are not incarnated. All the spirits of this category are goddesses of human origin, representing and assisting the Mother Goddesses of the four realms. Several of them are identified with ethnic minorities: the First Dame is associated with the Yao, the Sixth Dame with the Nung, the Tenth Dame with the Tay, and the Dame of Thac Bo with the Muong. Thus their garments and the music and dances dedicated to them are loosely inspired by those of the minorities.

In all incarnations, after a spirit leaves and the next spirit arrives, the assistants must hurriedly dress the medium in the costume corresponding to the new spirit. The costumes and accessories of the Dames are particularly beautiful and resemble the garments of the ethnic minorities with whom they are associated. After giving votive offerings, the Dames—as incarnated in the medium—often perform dances with a small torch (*mua moi*), an oar (*mua cheo do*), a fan (*mua quat*), or a sword (*mua kiem*). The dance with torches can be particularly lively, as the dancer holds the *moi*, a roll of crude paper soaked with a flammable substance, between her fingers. When medium H is dancing, the followers and attendants surround her, praising her beauty and her skill. During the dances, the Dames throw money to reward the singers and participants. The invocation songs to the Dames are very evocative and sometimes borrow songs from the ethnic minorities.

After these incarnations are those of the Princes. According to folk thinking, Princes are civil officials, not military commanders. All ten of them were originally humans who rendered good services to the common people and their country. During medium H's Len Dong, only three Princes are incarnated. They have refined and elegant gestures, manners, and bearing, and in their presence the participants become even more attentive.

The Third Prince of the Palace of Water (Ong Hoang Ba Thoai Phu) wears a white costume: a white brocade tunic, a white turban, white flower pins above his ears, a white robe encrusted with sparkling white beads, and a yellow belt. He is described thus in the Song to the Third Prince:

> As *bright as a mirror without any dust,*
> *Carrying a sacred wine gourd and a bag of poems,*
> *Wearing the royal white robe and yellow belt rewarded by the King,*
> *With a pair of military shoes under his feet and two* heo *on*
>   *his shoulders.*[7]

The Seventh Prince of Bao Ha (Ong Hoang Bay Bao Ha), who hails from the Realm of Mountains and Forests and so is dressed in green, is a mandarin who once defended the Lao Cai/Yen Bai region on the northern border.

The Princes, carrying two *heo* on their shoulders, often recruit servant-soldiers (*cham linh* or *bat dong*) for the Mother Goddess. From among the followers of the Religion of Mother Goddesses they will select those possessing the destiny of a medium (*can dong*) and force them to undertake service to the spirits (*cham dong*).[8]

The Seventh Prince often tries to recruit some servant-soldiers for the Mother Goddess. Today, all of the participants are visibly anxious for fear that they will be chosen as prospective mediums. After offering incense sticks, the Prince dances with his *heo*; suddenly, he throws it to a woman who is a trader at Dong Xuan Market in Hanoi. The woman picks up the *heo*, fixes a note of 10,000 dong (about U.S. $0.70) to one end, and returns it to the Prince. This action implies that she accepts his invitation to become a servant of the Mother Goddess, but requests a delay in her initiation ritual.

The Tenth Prince distributes money to musicians and participants at a ritual honoring the Mother Goddess of Mountains and Forests at a temple on Thanh Nien Road, Hanoi, in October 1999. Of the ten Princes, the Third, Seventh, and Tenth are often incarnated in mediums.

The Tenth Prince (Ong Hoang Muoi), of the Realm of Earth, wears yellow garments. According to legend, he was the defender-mandarin of Nghe An region who performed great deeds for his country. Nghe An continues to be the center of his cult, where a temple is dedicated to him. He is known as an elegant and cheerful prince.

The Tenth Prince is reputed to be a literary connoisseur. Manifesting this prince, medium H sits down to listen attentively to his invocation song sung in the tune of *phu co* (the declamatory style for ancient poems). The Prince expresses his pleasure by tapping on his thighs and shouting for joy; then he rewards the singers with money. The Prince is always open-handed in distributing favors *(loc)* in the form of money, cakes, sweets, and jewelry, particularly to women.[9] Everybody receives his favors with deep respect, and some participants give him votive offerings, asking for his protection; he returns some of these offerings to contributors, accompanied by good advice and good wishes.

Today a participant gives the Prince offerings and prays for his assistance in advancing her son's educational prospects. The Prince accepts. He then signals that he is "going back to his palace," and the assistants quickly cover

The Tenth Prince is incarnated in a medium during a Len Dong ritual, Dau Temple, Hang Quat Street, Hanoi, 2000. The Prince is about to prostrate himself before the altar dedicated to the Mother Goddesses. During his incarnation the spirit behaves like a prince, but, far from imperious, he is jolly and entertains the audience.

medium H's head with the veil. All participants regret the departure of this cheerful incarnation.

Following the incarnations of the Princes are those of the twelve Damsels. This time, six Damsels descend and are incarnated in medium H—the Second (Co Doi or Co De Nhi), the Third (Co Bo), the Sixth (Co Luc), the Ninth (Co Chin), and the Little Damsels of Bac Le and Dong Cuong (Co Be Bac Le and Co Be Dong Cuong). The Damsels are young and unmarried, so their incarnations are always cheerful, with colorful costumes and fluttering dances.

Like the Dames, the Damsels are usually of ethnic origin, and their costumes bear some characteristics of the ethnic minorities. Their turbans and tunics are made of brocade cloth. The Third Damsel is dressed in the style of a Muong girl, but her costume is white, the color of the Realm of Water.

During the incarnations of the Damsels, the assistants must continually prepare their costumes. In the incarnations of the Great Mandarins and the Princes, the medium puts on whatever garments the assistants give her. In the incarnations of the Dames and Damsels, however, the medium carefully preens and sometimes embarrasses the assistants by rejecting their choice of garment. During the incarnations of the Damsels, there are performances of songs and dances, invocations, distribution of favors, and the "ascent" of the spirit. The invocation songs have little to say about the stories of the Damsels, but rather praise their beauty, as in the Song to the Second Damsel:

> On the green hills, there are butterflies and flowers,
> In the forest, the Damsel descends to flirt with passers-by.
> Her garments and shoes are so elegant,
> Her two lamps are bright in the sky,
> As a halo.
> In her belt tuck the comb and flowers.
> Her lamps shine everywhere.

The Ninth Goddess's magic highlights the powers of her fan:

> The Ninth Damsel fans to create winds
> To make everybody, male and female, old and young, happy,
> To make flowers bloom in the hills,
> To refresh the hearts of the common people.

A Damsel amuses participants with her colorful costume and fluttering dance at a ritual in Dau Temple, Hang Quat Street, Hanoi, 2000. Damsels are the maiden attendants of Mother Goddesses, and several of them are identified with ethnic minorities.

In the incarnations of the Damsels, there are always dances with fans (*mua quat*), oars (*mua cheo do*), small torches (*mua moi*), scarves (*mua khan*), flower baskets (*mua ganh hoa*), and small bells (*mua lac chuong*). In contrast to the animated *then* ritual dances of the Tay people or of powerful shamans elsewhere, the dances of the Damsels are lithe, gentle, and cheerful. Today all the participants are clapping, and some shout out their praise: "You, the Damsel, dance so beautifully, so skillfully." In the *mua ganh hoa*, the Damsel, carrying two baskets of flowers, executes a series of elegant steps. When somebody shouts, "You, the Damsel, please rain down your favors," the spirit throws money, fruit, and flowers to participants. Everyone rushes and tries to catch some of the favors; the atmosphere of the ritual becomes very playful.

Because the Ninth Damsel is good at curing diseases, participants often pay tribute to her abilities and ask for remedies. Today, a couple prays for a cure. Medium H, as the Ninth Damsel, puts a cup of water onto a plate and then takes three burning incense sticks from the altar. While murmuring some magic words, she drops some incense ashes into the cup, holds the stick of incense in her mouth, and inhales the incense smoke, breathing it into the cup three times. At that point, the singers shift mood, glorifying the Damsel's ability:

> Bright heart, she points to the sky, it gets blue.
> She points to the earth, it's damaged.
> She points to blood, it melts.
> She points to demons, they must run away.
> She points to diseases, they disappear.

Medium H gives the cup to the couple. They take it and drink immediately, then prostrate themselves before the Damsel in gratitude.

The final incarnations conducted by medium H are those of the Boy Attendants, of whom there are ten, ranging from one to nine years in age. Today, only the Third Boy Attendant (Cau Bo) descends and is incarnated. His costumes, gestures, and words are childlike, reflecting his playful nature. In addition to the requisite rituals, today the little Boy Attendant also performs unicorn and lion dances, shaking his *heo*.

At the end of the ritual, medium H takes off the veil and costumes. She stands up and expresses her gratitude to all participants. A cycle of reciprocity has been going on throughout the ritual, with medium H providing offerings to her spirits, with additional offerings coming from her attendants and other visitors, and the spirits, in the person of medium H, redistributing these offerings to the attendants and visitors. In a grand final gesture she invites the participants to a banquet that is a favor from the spirits.

NOTES

INTRODUCTION

1. Arnold Van Gennep, *The Rites of Passage* (Chicago: University of Chicago Press, [1908] 1960); and Victor W. Turner, *The Drums of Affliction: A Study of Religious Processes among the Ndembu of Zambia* (Ithaca: Cornell University Press, [1968] 1974) and *Dramas, Fields, and Metaphors: Symbolic Action in Human Society* (Ithaca: Cornell University Press, 1974).

2. Eric Hobsbawm and Terence Ranger, *The Invention of Tradition* (Cambridge: Cambridge University Press, 1983).

3. Shaun Malarney, "The Limits of 'State Functionalism' and the Reconstruction of Funerary Ritual in Contemporary Northern Vietnam," *American Ethnologist* 23, no. 3 (1996): 540–560; and John Kleinen, *Facing the Future, Reviving the Past: A Study of Social Change in a Northern Vietnamese Village* (Singapore: Institute of Southeast Asian Studies, 1999).

4. D. B. Freeman, "Doi Moi Policy and the Small-Enterprise Boom in Ho Chi Minh City, Vietnam," *Geographical Review* 86, no. 2 (1994): 178–197; and T. O. Sikor and D. O. O'Rourke, "Economic and Environmental Dynamics of Reform in Vietnam," *Asian Survey* 36, no. 6 (1996): 601–617.

5. Anthropological exhibitions developed by the American Museum of Natural History—*Chiefly Feasts: The Art of the Potlatch*; *African Reflections: Art from Northeastern Zaire*; *Drawing Shadows to Stone: Photographing North Pacific Peoples, 1897–1902*; *Spirits in Steel: The Art of the Kalabari Masquerade*; and *Body Art: Marks of Identity*—have won acclaim not only for their substantive and visually exciting content but also for conveying a sense of their subjects as producers of and commentators on culture, both in the past and in the present. In the case of *Body Art*, New York–based exemplars of tattooing and body-piercing were part of a broad human portrait.

CHAPTER 1

1. George Coedès, *Les états hindouisés d'Indochine et d'Indonésie* (Paris: E. de Boccard, 1948); translated into English as *The Making of Southeast Asia* (London: Routledge and Kegan Paul, 1966).

2. Alexander Woodside, *Vietnam and the Chinese Model: A Comparative Study of Nguyên and Ching Civil Government in the First Half of the Nineteenth Century* (Cambridge, Mass.: Harvard University Press, 1971).

3. Gerald C. Hickey, *Ethnohistory of the Vietnamese Central Highlands*, vol. 1: *To 1954: Sons of the Mountains* and vol. 2: *1954–1976: Free in the Forest* (New Haven: Yale University Press, 1982).

4. For the situation in Cochin China, see Pierre Brocheux, ed., *Histoire de l'Asie du Sud-Est: Révoltes, réformes, révolutions* (Lille: Presses Universitaires de Lille, 1981); and Tran Tu Binh, *The Red Earth: A Vietnamese Memoir of Life on a Colonial Rubber Plantation* (Athens, Ohio: Ohio University, Center for Southeast Asian Studies, 1985). For the Central Highlands, see Hickey, *Sons of the Mountains* and *Free in the Forest*; and Oscar Salemink, "*Moïs* and *Maquis*: The Invention and Appropriation of Vietnam's Montagnards from Sabatier to the CIA," in *Colonial Situations: Essays on the Contextualization of Ethnographic Knowledge*, ed. George W. Stocking (Madison: University of Wisconsin Press, 1991), 243–284. And for Tonkin, see Ta Thi Thuy, "Les concessions agricoles françaises au Tonkin de 1884 à 1914," 2 vols. (doctoral diss., EHESS, Paris, 1993).

5. Martin Grossheim, *Nordvietnamesische Dorfgemeinschaften: Kontinuität und Wandel. Vom Beginn der Kolonialzeit bis zum Ende der Vietnamkriege* (Hamburg: Institut für Asienkunde, 1997).

6. Jan Breman, *The Shattered Image: Construction and Deconstruction of the Village in Colonial Asia*, Comparative Asian Studies Series, no. 2 (Amsterdam: Centre for Asian Studies in Amsterdam, 1987); and John Kleinen, "The Village as Pretext: Ethnographic Praxis and the Colonial State in Vietnam," in *The Village in Asia Revisited*, ed. Jan Breman, Peter Kloos, and Ahwani Saith (New Delhi: Oxford University Press, 1997), 353–393. See also Paul Mus, "The Role of the Village in Vietnamese Affairs," *Pacific Affairs* 22, no. 9 (1948): 265–272; idem, *Viêt-Nam, sociologie d'une guerre* (Paris: Editions du Seuil, 1952); and James C. Scott, *The Moral Economy of the Peasant: Rebellion and Subsistence in Southeast Asia* (New Haven: Yale University Press, 1976).

7. One could interpret Vietnam's most famous ethnic minority tale, the canonical Ede epic *Dam San*, in similar terms. See Léopold Sabatier, *La chanson de Damsan* (Paris: Leblanc et Trautmann, 1927); and Georges Condominas, "Observations sociologiques sur deux chants épiques Rhadés," *Bulletin de l'École française d'Extrême-Orient* 47 (1955): 555–568.

8. This phenomenon is described in Hue-Tam Ho Tai, "Monumental Ambiguity: The State Commemoration of Ho Chi Minh," in *Essays into Vietnamese Pasts*, ed. K. W. Taylor and John K. Whitmore (Ithaca: Southeast Asia Program, Cornell University, 1995), 272–288; and Kleinen, *Facing the Future, Reviving the Past.*

9. Evangelical Protestantism was introduced much later and represents a much smaller segment of the overall population, although it is currently winning many converts among Vietnam's ethnic minorities.

10. Keith Taylor, "Surface Orientations in Vietnam: Beyond Histories of Nation," *Journal of Asian Studies* 57, no. 4 (1998): 949–978.

11. Chapter 2 in this volume, "Vietnam's Ethnic Mosaic" by Frank Proschan, deals with the diversity among Vietnam's ethnic groups in much more detail. In what follows I concentrate on the Kinh ethnic group.

12. Twenty-five percent of students drop out of primary school, according to UNICEF, "Paving the Way for Children's Future by Keeping Them in School," 2001 http://www.unicef.org/vietnam/.

13. Tine Gammeltoft, "Second Trimester Abortion in Contemporary Vietnam: Social Vulnerability and Moral Responsibility" (paper presented at the AAS annual meeting, Washington, D.C., March 2002).

14. National Committee for the Advancement of Women, "Situation Analysis and Policy Recommendation to Promote the Advancement of Women and Gender Equality in Viet Nam" (draft report, Hanoi, 2000).

15. Le Thi Quy, "Domestic Violence in Vietnam and Efforts to Curb It," in *Vietnam's Women in Transition*, ed. Kathleen Barry (New York: St. Martin's Press, 1996), 263–274.

16. UNICEF, *Children on the Edge: Protecting Children from Sexual Exploitation and Trafficking in East Asia and the Pacific* (Bangkok, 2001).

CHAPTER 2

1. The principles underlying this process of classification are outlined in Dang Nghiem Van, *Ethnological and Religious Problems in Vietnam/Problèmes ethnologiques et religieux du Viet Nam* (Hanoi: Social Sciences Publishing House, 1998). When it was adopted for administrative purposes by the General Department of Statistics in 1979, the list was provisional; in the meantime it has accumulated greater authority and permanence than was perhaps intended. Several ethnologists have recently advocated revising the list to better represent communities' own self-identifications and aspirations.

2. Electronic versions of the Vietnamese texts of the 1946 and 1992 constitutions may be found on the web page of the Communist Party of Vietnam at http://www.cpv.org.vn/vietnam/hp46.html and http://www.cpv.org.vn/vietnam/hp92.html, respectively; the latter may also be found on the web page of the National Assembly, http://www.na.gov.vn/vietnam/hienphap.html. English versions may be found at http://www.cpv.org.vn/vietnam_en/constitution/1946/index.htm (1946) and http://www.cpv.org.vn/vietnam_en/constitution/1992/index.htm or http://www.na.gov.vn/english/legal.html (1992). The English texts here are my own translation.

3. Bui Quang Tung, Nguyen Huong, and Nguyen The Anh *Le Dai-Viet et ses voisins: D'après le Dai-Viet su ky toan thu (Mémoires historiques du Dai-Viet au complet)* (Paris: L'Harmattan, 1990), 68, 70–71.

4. Nghiem Tham, "Seeking to Understand the Highland Comrades: Two Tributary Kingdoms of the Vietnamese Court in the Past" (originally published as "Tim hieu Dong bao Thuong: Hai phien Vuong cua Trieu Dinh Viet Nam hoi truoc, Thuy Xa va Hoa Xa"), trans. Donald E. Voth, *Southeast Asia* 1, no. 4 (1971): 335–65 (quotation p. 339).

5. "Dai Nam liet truyen so tap 931," *Thu tich co Viet Nam viet ve Dong Nam A, Phan Chiem Thanh, Thuy Xa, Hoa Xa, Mien Dien, Cha Va* (Hanoi: Uy ban Khoa hoc Xa hoi Viet Nam, Ban Dong Nam A, 1977), 122. Nghiem Tham offers a different translation: the Giarai chief of Thuy Xa should "know his close, subordinate relationship to us and increasingly adopt [our] good and beautiful customs and culture" (Nghiem Tham, "Seeking to Understand," 355). The phrase of Minh Mang's decree is echoed in an important recent policy statement, Resolution 5, which refers to "the nation's fine traditions and customs," although in 1998 the phrase encompasses both the majority culture and the diversity of minority cultures (Resolution of the Fifth Plenum of the Central Committee [Eighth Tenure], "Ve xay dung va phat trien nen van hoa Viet Nam tien tien, dam da ban sac dan toc" [On building and developing an advanced Vietnamese culture deeply imbued with national identity], Nghi quyet 03/NQ-TW [Decision 3 of the Central Committee], 16/7/1998).

6. A number of ethnicities have well-developed codes of customary law that have recently been the focus of scholarly attention (see Ngo Duc Thinh, ed., *Luat tuc va Phat trien Nong thon Hien nay o Viet Nam* [Hanoi: Chinh tri Quoc gia Publishing House, 2000). Recently, too, initiatives have been proposed in some localities to integrate customary law with state law, giving the former precedence in certain civil matters such as marriage, inheritance, and property disputes and recognizing the latter as authoritative in criminal matters.

7. "Political Report of the Central Committee [Seventh Tenure] to the VIIIth National Congress," in *VIIIth National Congress Documents* (Hanoi: The Gioi, 1996), 69.

CHAPTER 4

1. Nguyen Van Huyen, "La mi-automne (15e jour du 8e mois: 24 septembre 1942): Fête du dragon et de la lune," *Indochine* 108 (1942).

2. Ibid.

3. This project was supported by a grant from Ford Foundation Vietnam and resulted in a temporary exhibition at the Vietnam Museum of Ethnology.

4. As seen in old photographs, star lanterns for the Mid-Autumn Festival had six points before 1945.

5. Nguyen Van Huyen, "La mi-automne."

CHAPTER 5

1. Other holidays set by the lunisolar calendar are Nguyen Tieu (the fifteenth day of the first month), Han Thuc (Cold Food Day, the third day of the third month), Doan Ngo (Double Five, the fifth day of the fifth month), and the New Crop Rice Holiday (the tenth day of the tenth month).

2. Traditionally, two rice crops were harvested in Vietnam, the winter crop (*chiem*), planted in the first month and harvested in the fifth month, and the summer crop (*mua*), planted in the sixth month and harvested in the tenth month. In the period between the tenth and twelfth months, short-term crops were planted and harvested.

3. Every Vietnamese dynasty had its own calendar office. The Ly dynasty (1010–1225) had the Lau Chinh Duong, the Tran dynasty (1225–1400) had the Thai Su Cuc, the Le dynasty (1428–1527) had the Thai Su Vien, the Restored Le dynasty (1533–1788) had the Tu Thien Giam, and the Nguyen dynasty (1802–1945) had the Kham Thien Giam. History records the famous calendarmen Dang Lo (Tran dynasty), Tran Nguyen Dan (1325–1390), Nguyen Huu Than (1754–1831), and Nguyen Huy Ho (1783–1844).

CHAPTER 6

1. For a capsule history, see Regina Krahl, "Vietnamese Blue-and-White and Related Wares," in *Vietnamese Ceramics: A Separate Tradition*, ed. J. Stevenson and J. Guy (Chicago: Arts Media, 1998), 147–157.

2. John Guy, "Vietnamese Ceramics: New Discoveries," in *Treasures from the Hoi An Hoard: Important Vietnamese Ceramics from a Late 15th/Early 16th Century Cargo* (Butterfields Auctioneers Corp., 2000), xvi–xvii.

3. For a general history of the Bat Trang ceramic industry, see Vu Quy Vy, "The Bat Trang Ceramics Works," *Vietnamese Studies* 62 (1980): 111–123.

4. Hy Van Luong, "Engendered Entrepreneurship: Ideologies and Political-Economic Transformation in a Northern Vietnamese Center of Ceramics Production," in *Marketing Cultures: Society and Morality in the New Asian Capitalism*, ed. R. Hefner (Boulder, Colo.: Westview Press, 1998), 293.

CHAPTER 8

1. Le Sy Giao, "Dao Certificate of Participation in the Qua Tang Ceremony: Custom and Its Educational Meaning," in *The Scientific Report at the 7th International Seminar on the Dao Held in Thai Nguyen Province, Vietnam, December 1995* (1995); Be Viet Dang, Nguyen Khac Tong, Nong Trung, and Nguyen Nam Tien, *The Dao in Vietnam* (Hanoi: Social Sciences Publishing House, 1971); Nguyen Quoc Loi, "Dao Certificate of Participation in the Qua Tang Ceremony Custom" (1966), reserved reference in Library of the History Department of Social Science and Human Civilization University, Hanoi, ref. no. L.V.1159; Le Hong Ly, "A Cultural Festival of

the Dao Ho in Lao Cai Province," *Folk Culture Review* 1 (1997): 31–36; Nguyen Duc Loi, "Yao Quan Chet Certificate of Participation in the Qua Tang Ceremony Custom in Bac Thai," in dissertation of Do Duc Loi (typescript, Hanoi, 1997); and Xuan Mai, "Dancing Ritual Ceremony of the Dao Ho People, Lao Cai Province," in *Scientific Report at the 7th International Seminar on the Dao*; and A. Bonifacy, *Monographie des Mans Quan Coc, Revue Indochinoise*, nos. 10–11 (1904).

2. Be et al., *The Dao in Vietnam*; and Nguyen Khac Tung, "The Dao," in *Ethnic Minorities in Vietnam* (Hanoi: Social Sciences Publishing House, 1978), 312–335.

3. Population figures are from the 1989 national census (Hanoi: Hanoi Statistical Office) and the 1994 *Statistical Yearbook* (Hanoi: General Statistical Office), respectively.

4. Khong Dien, *Population and Ethnic Population in Vietnam* (Hanoi: Social Sciences Publishing House, 1995).

5. Based on cultural practices, the Yao (Dao) in Vietnam are classified by ethnologists within the following groups: Yao Do, Yao Tien, Yao Quan Chet, Yao Thanh Phan, Yao Quan Trang, Yao Thanh Y, and Yao Ao Dai. Based on their language, the Yao can be divided also into Kim Mien (the first four of the above groups) and Kim Mun (the final three groups). See Nguyen Khac Tung, "Back to Yao Classification in Vietnam," *Ethnology Review*, no. 3 (1997): 30–37.

6. These participants are called by the following names in the Yao Tien language: the first leading ritual master is *khoi giao sai*, the second is *chong sai*, the dancer is *co nhung*, the three young men singers are *biao ton* or *dang ton*, the three young women singers are *biao xia* or *dang xia*, the three poem-reading ritual masters are *bien chi*, and the three servants are *nang con mien*.

7. Ly Hanh Son, "Taking Notes on the Dancing of the Dao Tien and Dao Do," *Folk Culture Review*, no. 4 (1994): 26–35.

8. Be et al., *The Dao in Vietnam*; and Le Sy Giao, "Some Popular Customs in the Yao's Lives," in *The Scientific Report at Frontier Conference Held in Hanoi, 1979* (1979); and Nguyen Quoc Loi, "Dao Certificate of Participation in the Qua Tang Ceremony Custom" (see note on previous page).

9. Phan Ngoc Khue, "Yao Worship Pictures in the Southern [sic] of Vietnam," in *Scientific Report at the 7th International Seminar on the Dao*.

10. Examples of these songs include "One Day," "The Moon Rises," "Girlhood," "Loving Season," and "The Apricot Blossom," all of which have been translated into Vietnamese. See also "Certificate of Participation in the Qua Tang Ceremony Custom in Bac Thai," in Ph.D. dissertation of Do Duc Loi, Hanoi University, 1997.

CHAPTER 9

1. Toan Anh, *Nep cu: Lang xom Viet Nam* (Old Ways: The Vietnamese Village) (Saigon: Nam Chi Tung Thu, 1968).

CHAPTER 10

1. The Muong are Austroasiatic speakers, living in the narrow valleys between the high mountains of Hoa Binh and Thanh Hoa Provinces in northern Vietnam. Muong practice intensive wet-rice agriculture as well as cattle and poultry raising, hunting, fishing, gathering forest products, and producing handicraft. There are about 1.1 million Muong in Vietnam today (1999 census).

The Thai are divided into two main groups, Black Thai and White Thai, with Thai communities spread from the northwest through Hoa Binh Province to the western part of Thanh Hoa and Nghe An Provinces. The Thai practice a highly developed form of wet-rice agriculture and produce sophisticated textiles. There are 1.3 million Thai in Vietnam (1999 census).

The Hmong are a subgroup of the Chinese Miao ethnicity who migrated from China into northern the border regions of Vietnam, Laos, Thailand, and Burma in the late eighteenth century. Although Hmong communities are concentrated along the northern border, they can also be found scattered along the western border as far south as central Vietnam. The 1999 census counted 787,600 Hmong in Vietnam. Hmong live on steep, high mountains where they produce maize, rice, vegetables, hemp, and cotton in the sparse soil. Until recently, the cultivation of opium poppies was also a significant part of the Hmong economy. In Vietnam the Hmong are divided into the following subgroups: Hmong Du (Black Hmong), Hmong Do (White), Hmong Sua (Green), Hmong Lenh (Flower), Hmong Su (Red), and Na Mieo (although recent research indicates that this local group is not Hmong but Hmu, another branch of Miao from China).

The Giarai are Austronesian speakers living in the Central Highlands of Vietnam, mostly in Gia Lai Province. In common with many other Austronesian peoples in Southeast Asia, the Giarai reckon kinship through the mother's line. Traditionally, the Giarai practiced swidden agriculture and hunted, although in some areas they now practice wet rice agriculture. Today, many Giarai are engaged in farming cash crops, particularly coffee. According to the 1999 census, nearly 320,000 Giarai live in Vietnam today and a smaller number in Cambodia.

According to the 1999 census, more than 1 million Khmer live in the Mekong Delta of Vietnam, cultivating wet rice. Khmer culture has been influenced by the Brahmanic worldview of early Southeast Asian kingdoms and Theravada Buddhism.

CHAPTER 11

1. Nguyen Van Huyen, "Contribution à l'étude d'un génie tutélaire annamite Lí-Phuc-Man," *Bulletin de l'École française d'Extrême-Orient* 38, fasc. 1 (1938).

CHAPTER 12

1. Piers Vitebsky, *The Shaman* (London: Duncan Baird, 1995).

2. See, generally, Mircea Eliade, *Shamanism: Archaic Techniques of Ecstasy* (New

York: Pantheon, 1964). For exceptions to the male-only rule in shamanism, see Marjorie Balzar, "Introduction," in *Shamanic Worlds: Ritual Lore of Siberia and Central Asia* (Armonk, N.Y.: M. E. Sharpe, 1997), xiii; Caroline Humphrey, with Urgunge Onon, *Shamans and Elders: Experience, Knowledge, and Power among the Daur Mongols* (Oxford: Clarendon Press, 1996), 183–184; and Margaret Nowak and Stephen Durrant, *The Tale of the Nishan Shamaness* (Seattle: University of Washington Press, 1977). On the tradition of men as shamans, see especially I. M. Lewis, *Ecstatic Religion: An Anthropological Study of Spirit Possession and Shamanism* (Harmondsworth, England: Penguin Books, 1969); and Vitebsky, *Shaman*.

CHAPTER 13

1. For more information on the Religion of Mother Goddesses, see Ngo Duc Thinh, ed., *Dao Mau o Viet Nam* (The Religion of Mother Goddesses in Vietnam) (Hanoi: Nha Xuat ban Van hoa, 1996); and idem, *Hat van* (The Invocation Songs) (Hanoi: Nha Xuat ban Van hoa Dan toc, 1992).

2. Dao Mau (the Religion of Mother Goddess) here is understood as the Religion of the Mother Goddesses of the Three (Four) Palaces, to distinguish it from Mother Goddess worship in general.

3. *Co day* is suffering (illness, disease, madness, etc.) imposed by spirits on somebody with *can dong* (the destiny to be a medium) who has not yet taken the initiative to sponsor the ritual to become a medium.

4. In practice, the number of *hau dang* needed for each ritual varies from two to four people.

5. *Gia* is a period of incarnation of a spirit in the medium. Thus, in a ritual of Len Dong the number of *gia* is the same as that of spirits who are incarnated. *Gia* also means "seat" of the spirits.

6. *Giang* is a spirit that descends on the body of a medium, and *nhap* (entering) is a spirit that descends and is incarnated in the medium. In the ritual of Len Dong, it is not true that every spirit can be incarnated; some descend but do not enter the body of the medium.

7. The *heo* is a 50–60 cm stick with two or three bells at its end. It symbolizes the horse and whip used by princes.

8. According to folk thinking, a person with *can dong* is one who has the destiny to become a medium of the Religion of Mother Goddesses. She or he must serve the spirits; if not, they will mete out punishment.

9. *Loc* means all favors distributed by a spirit, both in the ritual of Len Dong and in some other religious rituals. These favors therefore are very sacred and valuable: "A single piece of spirit favors is more precious than a load of mundane favors."

LIST OF CONTRIBUTORS

A BAO is a retired member of the staff of the Institute of Education Studies, Ministry of Education, in Vietnam.

CLAIRE BURKERT has coordinated several projects in Vietnam devoted to the preservation and promotion of traditional crafts and is currently advising on the development of a handicraft master plan for Vietnam. With Vo Mai Phuong, she is the author of *A Yao Community in Sapa, Vietnam* (Hanoi: Vietnam Museum of Ethnology, 2001).

CAM TRONG is Researcher Emeritus of Vietnam Museum of Ethnology (VME) and a widely respected scholar of the Thai people. His publications include *Les Thaï du Nord-Ouest du Vietnam* (Hanoi: Social Sciences Press, 1978) and, with Phan Huu Dat, *La Culture des Thaï du Vietnam* (Hanoi: Ethnic Culture Press, 1995).

CHU VAN KHANH is a researcher at the Vietnamese State Bureau of the Calendar, Center for Information and Archives, National Center for Natural Sciences and Technology, Hanoi.

LAUREL KENDALL is Curator in Charge of Asian Ethnographic Collections at the American Museum of Natural History (AMNH). As an anthropologist who specializes in Korea, she has written extensively on shamanism, issues of gender, and, more recently, the cultural construction of "tradition" and "modernity."

LA CONG Y is Director of Northern Minorities Research at VME. A member of the Tay minority, he is a specialist on that community and has published books on economic and cultural changes in the highland provinces of North Vietnam and languages in Vietnam.

LUU HUNG is Director of Central Highlands Research at VME. He is coeditor of *Ethnic Minorities in Vietnam* (Hanoi: The Gioi, 2000).

LY HANH SON is a researcher at the Vietnam Institute of Ethnology. He has done extensive work on the ritual life of the Yao people.

SHAUN KINGSLEY MALARNEY, Associate Professor of Cultural Anthropology at International Christian University in Tokyo, has written on a variety of topics including transformations of wedding and funeral practices, local politics, and the cultural ideas associated with commerce and entrepreneurship. He is author of the monograph *Culture, Ritual, and Revolution in Vietnam* (Richmond, Surrey: Curzon Press, 2003).

NGO DUC THINH is a director of the Folklore Institute at the Vietnam National Center for Social Sciences and Humanities in Hanoi and an adjunct professor in the History Department at Vietnam National University. He has conducted fieldwork in Vietnam, Laos, Cambodia, and South China, investigating the cultural diversity of ethnic groups, indigenous folk beliefs, and vernacular knowledge such as customary laws and village regulations.

NGUYEN ANH NGOC, Director of Kinh (Viet) Research at VME, has directed major projects on coastal fishing and the city of Hanoi and its environs, including the Bat Trang ceramic works.

NGUYEN HUY HONG is President of the Vietnam branch of the Union International des Marionettes and of the Traditional Puppetry Club. He is an internationally recognized authority on Vietnamese puppetry traditions and the author of *Les Marionnettes sur eau traditionnelles du Vietnam* (Hanoi: The Gioi, 1996).

NGUYEN TRUNG DUNG is Director of Education at VME. He has published on the Doi Temple in the south and on education in museums.

NGUYEN VAN HUY, Director of the Vietnam Museum of Ethnology, has written extensively on Vietnam's diverse ethnic populations, including *Cultural Mosaic of Ethnic Groups in Vietnam* (Hanoi: Education Publishing House, 2001). In 2000 Dr. Huy was the recipient of the Asian Cultural Council's John D. Rockefeller III award for promoting cultural understanding between East and West.

FRANK PROSCHAN, an anthropologist and folkorist specializing in the highland minorities of Vietnam and neighboring countries, is project director at the Smithsonian Center for Folklife and Cultural Heritage. He edited the compact disk *Bamboo on the Mountains: Kmhmu Highlanders from Southeast Asia and the United States* (Smithsonian Folkways SFW CD 40456).

OSCAR SALEMINK lectures on social and cultural anthropology at the Vrije Universiteit in Amsterdam and from 1996 to 2001 served as program officer for the Ford Foundation's Vietnam office. His publications include *Colonial Subjects: Essays on the Practical History of Anthropology*, coedited with Peter Pels (University of Michigan Press, 1999), and *The Ethnography of Vietnam's Central Highlanders: A Historical Contextualization, 1850–1990* (London: Routledge Curzon/Honolulu: University of Hawaii Press, in press).

TRAN THI THU THUY, an ethnologist and member of the Education Department at VME, is a specialist on the Hmong minority. She has published several articles on ethnic groups in Vietnam.

VI VAN AN, a specialist on the Thai minority and a member of this community, is Vice Director of Northern Minorities Research at VME. He has researched and published on the Thai minority.

VO THI THUONG is a researcher at VME and a specialist on the Thai and Muong peoples. She has conducted research and published on ethnobotany and folk medicine in Vietnam.

PHOTO CREDITS

INDEX

Note: Page references in italics indicate illustrations.